CONFRONTING
THE CLASSICS

ALSO BY MARY BEARD

Pompeii: The Life of a Roman Town
The Parthenon
All in a Don's Day
It's a Don's Life
The Roman Triumph

CONFRONTING THE CLASSICS

Traditions, Adventures and Innovations

MARY BEARD

LIVERIGHT PUBLISHING CORPORATION
A Division of W. W. Norton & Company
New York   London

For information about permission to reproduce selections from this book,
write to Permissions, Liveright Publishing Corporation,
a division of W. W. Norton & Company, Inc.
500 Fifth Avenue, New York, NY 10110

For information about special discounts for bulk purchases, please contact
W. W. Norton Special Sales at specialsales@wwnorton.com or 800-233-4830

Manufacturing by RR Donnelley, Harrisonburg
Production manager: Devon Zahn

Library of Congress Cataloging-in-Publication Data

Beard, Mary, 1955–
Confronting the classics : traditions, adventures, and innovations / Mary Beard.
— First American edition.
pages cm
Includes bibliographical references and index.
ISBN 978-0-87140-716-0 (hardcover)
1. Civilization, Classical. 2. Classical antiquities. I. Title.
DE59.B43 2013
930—dc23
                                    2013016133

Liveright Publishing Corporation
500 Fifth Avenue, New York, N.Y. 10110
www.wwnorton.com

W. W. Norton & Company Ltd.
Castle House, 75/76 Wells Street, London W1T 3QT

1 2 3 4 5 6 7 8 9 0

This book is for Peter Carson

Contents

Contents

PREFACE

This book is a guided tour of the classical world, from the prehistoric palace at Knossos in Crete to that fictional village in Gaul,
where Astérix and his friends are still holding out against the Romans.
In between we encounter some of the most famous, or infamous,
characters in ancient history: Sappho, Alexander the Great, Hannibal,
Julius Caesar, Cleopatra, Caligula, Nero, Boudicca and Tacitus (and
that's just a selection). But we also get a glimpse of the lives of the
vast majority of ordinary people in Greece and Rome – the slaves, the
squaddies in the army, the millions of people across the Roman empire
living under military occupation (not to mention my own particular
favourite, from Chapter 19, Eurysaces the Roman baker). What made
these people laugh? Did they clean their teeth? Where did they go
if they needed help or advice – if their marriage was in trouble, or if
they were broke? I hope that *Confronting the Classics* will introduce,
or re-introduce, readers to some of the most compelling chapters
of ancient history, and some of its most memorable characters from
many walks of life; and I hope it will answer some of those intriguing
questions.

But my aim is more ambitious than that. *Confronting the Classics*
means what it says. This book is also about how we can *engage* with
or *challenge* the classical tradition, and why even in the twenty-first
century there is so much in Classics still to *argue* about; in short, it's
about why the subject is still 'work in progress' not 'done and dusted'
(or, in the words of my sub-title, why it's an 'adventure' and an 'innovation' as well as a 'tradition'). I hope that this comes across loud and
clear in the sections that follow. There should be some surprises in
store, as well as a taste of fierce controversies old and new. Classicists

are still struggling to work out what exactly the horribly difficult Greek of Thucydides means (we're doing better, but we're not there yet), and we are still disagreeing about how important Cleopatra really was in the history of Rome, or whether the Emperor Caligula can be written off as simply bonkers. At the same time, modern eyes always find ways to open up new questions and sometimes to find new answers. My hope is that *Confronting the Classics* will bring to life, for a much wider audience, some of our current debates – from what the Persian sources might add to our understanding of Alexander the Great to how on earth the Romans managed to acquire enough slaves to satisfy their demand.

Debate is the key word. As I shall stress again in the Introduction, studying Classics is to enter a conversation – not only with the literature and material remains of antiquity itself, but also with those over the centuries before us who have tried to make sense of the Greeks and Romans, who have quoted them or recreated them. It is partly for this reason – because they're in the conversation too – that the scholars and archaeologists of earlier generations, the travellers, artists and antiquarians, get a fair share of attention in this book. And that's why the indomitable Astérix gets a look in as well, because – let's be honest – very many of us first learned how to think about the conflicts of Roman imperialism through his band of plucky Gauls.

It is fitting that all the chapters of this book are adapted and updated from reviews and essays that have appeared over the last couple of decades in the *London Review of Books*, the *New York Review of Books* or the *Times Literary Supplement*. I shall have more to say about the craft of reviewing in the Afterword. For now let me simply insist that reviews have long been one of the most important places where classical debates take place. I hope that those that follow give a flavour of why Classics is a subject still worth talking about with all the seriousness – not to mention the *fun* and good humour – that we can muster.

****

But *Confronting the Classics* kicks off with a version of the Robert B. Silvers lecture I was more than a little honoured to give at the New York Public Library in December 2011. The title 'Do Classics have a Future?' hits the nail on the head. It is, if you like, my manifesto.

Introduction

DO CLASSICS
HAVE A FUTURE?

The year 2011 was an unusually good one for the late Terence Rattigan: Frank Langella starred on Broadway in his play *Man and Boy* (a topical tale of the collapse of a financier), its first production in New York since the 1960s; and a movie of *The Deep Blue Sea*, featuring Rachel Weisz as the wife of a judge who goes off with a pilot, premiered at the end of November in the UK and opened in the US in December. It was the centenary of Rattigan's birth (he died in 1977), and it brought the kind of re-evaluation that centenaries often do. For years – in the eyes of critics, although not of London West End audiences – his elegant stories of the repressed anguish of the privileged classes were no match for the working-class realism of John Osborne and the other angry young dramatists. But we have been learning to look again.

I have been looking again at another Rattigan play, *The Browning Version*, first performed in 1948. It is the story of Andrew Crocker-Harris, a forty-something schoolteacher at an English public school – an old-fashioned disciplinarian who is being forced into early retirement because of a serious heart condition. The Crock's other misfortune (and 'the Crock' is what the children call him) is that he is married to a truly venomous woman called Millie, who divides her time between an on-off affair with the science teacher and devising various bits of domestic sadism to destroy her husband.

But the title of the play takes us back to the classical world. The Crock, as you will already have guessed, teaches Classics (what else could he teach with a name like Crocker-Harris?), and the 'Browning Version' of the title refers to the famous 1877 translation by Robert Browning of Aeschylus' play *Agamemnon*. Written in the 450s BC, the Greek original told of the tragic return from the Trojan War of King Agamemnon, who was murdered on his arrival home by his wife Clytemnestra and by the lover she had taken while Agamemnon had been away.

This classic is, in a sense, the real star of Rattigan's play. It is given to the Crock as a retirement present by John Taplow, a pupil who has been taking extra Greek lessons, and who has gradually come to feel some affection for the crabby old schoolmaster. The giving of the gift is the key moment, almost the moment of redemption, in the plot. It is the first time that Crocker-Harris's mask slips: when he opens the 'Browning Version', he cries. Why does he cry? First, because it forces him to face how he himself is being destroyed, as Agamemnon was, within an adulterous marriage (this is not exactly a feminist play). But he cries also because of what young Taplow has written on the title page. It's a line from the play, carefully inscribed in Greek, which the Crock translates as 'God from afar looks graciously upon a gentle master.' He interprets this as a comment on his own career: he has made sure not to be a *gentle* schoolmaster, and God has *not* looked graciously upon him.

Rattigan is doing more here than exploring the tortured psyches of the British upper-middle class (and it's not just another 'school story', that quirky fixation of some British writers). Well-trained in the Classics himself, he is also raising central questions about Classics, the classical tradition, and our modern engagement with it. How far can the ancient world help us to understand our own? What limits should we place on our re-interpretation and re-appropriation of it? When Aeschylus wrote 'God from afar looks graciously upon a gentle master', he certainly did not have a schoolmaster in mind, but a military conqueror; in fact, the phrase – and this too, I guess, was part of Rattigan's point – was one of the last spoken by Agamemnon to Clytemnestra before she took him inside to kill him.

To put it another way, how do we make the ancient world make sense to us? How do we translate it? Young Taplow does not actually rate Browning's translation very highly, and indeed – to our tastes – it is written in awful nineteenth-century poetry-speak ('Who conquers mildly, God, from afar, benignantly regardeth,' as Browning puts the key line, is hardly going to send most of us rushing to the rest of the play). But when, in his lessons, Taplow himself gets excited by Aeschylus' Greek and comes out with a wonderfully spirited but slightly inaccurate version of one of the murderous bits, the Crock reprimands him – 'you are supposed to be *construing Greek*' – that is, translating the language literally, word for word – 'not *collaborating with Aeschylus.*'

Most of us now, I suspect, are on the side of the collaborators, with their conviction that the classical tradition is something to be engaged with, and sparred against, not merely replicated and mouthed. In this context, I can't resist reminding you of the flagrantly modern versions of Homer's *Iliad* by the English poet Christopher Logue, who died in December 2011 – *Kings, War Music*, and others – 'the best *translation* of Homer since [Alexander] Pope's,' as Garry Wills once called them. This was, I think, both a heartfelt and a slightly ironic comment. For the joke is that Logue, our leading collaborator with Homer, knew not a word of Greek.

Many of the questions raised by Rattigan underlie the points I have to make here. I am not trying to convince anyone that classical literature, culture, or art is worth taking seriously; I suspect that would, in most cases, be preaching to the converted. I want instead to suggest that the cultural language of Classics and classical literature continues to be an essential and ineradicable dialect of 'Western culture', embedded in the drama of Rattigan, as much as in the poetry of Ted Hughes or the novels of Margaret Atwood or Donna Tartt – *The Secret History* could not, after all, have been written about a department of Geography. But I also want to examine a bit more closely our fixation on the decline of classical learning. And here too Rattigan's *The Browning Version*, or its sequels, offers an intriguing perspective.

The play has always been popular with impoverished theatre and TV companies, partly for the simple reason that Rattigan set the whole thing in Crocker-Harris's sitting room, which makes it extremely cheap to stage. But there have also been two movie versions of *The Browning Version*, which did venture outside Crocker-Harris's apartment to exploit the cinematic potential of the English public school, from its quaint wood-panelled classrooms to its rolling green cricket pitches. Rattigan himself wrote the screenplay for the first one, starring

Michael Redgrave, in 1951. He used the longer format of the film to expand on the philosophy of education, pitting the teaching of science (as represented by Millie's lover) against the teaching of Classics (as represented by the Crock). And he gave the Crock's successor as the Classics teacher, Mr Gilbert, a bigger part – making it clear that he was going to move away from the hard-line Latin and Greek grammar grind, to what we would now call a more 'pupil-centred' approach.

In 1994 another movie version was made, this time starring Albert Finney. It had been modernised: Millie was renamed Laura, and her science-master lover was now a decidedly preppy American. There was still some sense of the old story: Finney held his class spellbound when he read them some lines of Aeschylus and he cried at the gift of the 'Browning Version' even more movingly than Redgrave had. But in a striking twist, a new narrative of decline was introduced. In this version, the Crock's successor is in fact going to stop teaching Classics entirely. 'My remit,' he says in the film, 'is to organise a new languages department: modern languages, German, French, Spanish. It is after all a multicultural society.' The Crock is now to be seen as the very last of his species.

But if this movie predicts the death of classical learning, it inadvertently appears to confirm it too. In one scene, the Crock is apparently going through with his class a passage of Aeschylus in Greek, which the pupils are finding very hard to read. Any sharp-eyed classicist will easily spot why they might have been having trouble: for each boy has on his desk only a copy of the Penguin translation of Aeschylus (with its instantly recognisable front cover); they haven't got a Greek text at all. Presumably some bloke in the props department had been sent off to find twenty copies of the *Agamemnon* and knew no better than to bring it in English.

That spectre of the end of classical learning is one that is probably familiar to most readers. With some trepidation, I want to try to get a new angle on the question, to go beyond the usual gloomy clichés, and (with the help in part of Terence Rattigan) to take a fresh look at what we think we mean by 'Classics'. But let us first remember what recent discussion of the current state of Classics, never mind their future, tends to stress.

The basic message is a gloomy one. Literally hundreds of books, articles, reviews, and op-ed pieces have appeared over the last ten years or so, with titles like 'The Classics in Crisis', 'Can the Classics

Survive?', 'Who Killed Homer?', 'Why America Needs the Classical Tradition', and 'Saving the Classics from Conservatives'. All of these in their different ways lament the death of Classics, conduct an autopsy upon them, or recommend some rather belated life-saving procedures. The litany of gloomy facts and figures paraded in these contributions, and their tone, are in broad terms familiar. Often headlined is the decline of Latin and Greek languages in schools (in recent years fewer than three hundred young people in England and Wales have taken classical Greek as one of their A' levels, and those overwhelmingly from independent schools) or the closure of university departments of Classics all over the world.

In fact, in November 2011 an international petition was formally launched to ask UNESCO – in the light of the increasing marginalisation of the classical languages – to declare Latin and Greek a specially protected 'intangible heritage of humanity'. I am not sure what I think about treating classical languages as if they were an endangered species or a precious ruin, but I am fairly confident that it was not great politics, at this moment, to suggest (as the petition does) that their preservation should be made the particular responsibility of the Italian government (as if it did not have rather too much on its plate already).

What has caused this decline attracts a variety of answers. Some argue that the supporters of Classics have only themselves to blame. It's a 'Dead White European Male' sort of subject that has far too often acted as a convenient alibi for a whole range of cultural and political sins, from imperialism and Eurocentrism to social snobbery and the most mind-numbing form of pedagogy. The British dominated their Empire with Cicero in hand; Goebbels chose Greek tragedy for his bedside reading (and, if you believe Martin Bernal, he would have found confirmation for his crazed views of Aryan supremacy in the traditions of classical scholarship itself). Chickens have come home to roost, it is sometimes said, for Classics in the new multicultural world. Not to mention the fact that, in England at least, the learning of the Latin language was for generations the gatekeeper of rigid class privilege and social exclusivity – albeit at a terrible cost to its apparent beneficiaries. It gave you access to a narrow elite, that's for sure, but committed your childhood years to the narrowest educational curriculum imaginable: nothing much else but translation into and out of Latin (and when you got a little older, Greek). In the movie of The

5

Browning Version we find Crocker-Harris making his pupils translate into Latin the first four stanzas of Tennyson's 'The Lady of Shalott': an exercise as pointless as it was prestigious.

Others claim that Classics have failed within the politics of the modern academy. If you were to follow Victor Davis Hanson and his colleagues, you would in fact lay the blame for the general demise of the subject firmly at the door of careerist Ivy League, and no doubt Oxbridge, academics who (in the pursuit of large salaries and long sabbaticals) have wandered down some self-regarding postmodern cul-de-sac, when ordinary students and the 'folks out there' really want to hear about Homer and the other great paragons of Greece and Rome. To which the retort is: maybe it is precisely because professors of Classics have refused to engage with modern theory and persisted in viewing the ancient world through rose-tinted spectacles (as if it was a culture to be admired) that the subject is in imminent danger of turning into an antiquarian backwater.

The voices insisting that we should be facing up to the squalor, the slavery, the misogyny, the irrationality of antiquity go back through Moses Finley and the Irish poet and classicist Louis MacNeice to my own illustrious nineteenth-century predecessor in Cambridge, Jane Ellen Harrison. When I should be remembering the glories of Greece, wrote MacNeice memorably in his *Autumn Journal*,

> I think instead
> Of the crooks, the adventurers, the opportunists,
> The careless athletes and the fancy boys ...
> ... the noise
> Of the demagogues and the quacks; and the women pouring
> Libations over graves
> And the trimmers at Delphi and the dummies at Sparta and lastly
> I think of the slaves.

Of course, not everything written on the current state of Classics is irredeemably gloomy. Some breezy optimists point, for example, to a new interest among the public in the ancient world. Witness the success of movies like *Gladiator* or Stacy Schiff's biography of Cleopatra or the continuing stream of literary tributes to, or engagements with, Classics (including at least three major fictional or poetic re-workings of Homer in 2011 alone). And against the baleful examples of

Goebbels and British imperialism, you can parade a repertoire of more radical heroes of the classical tradition – as varied as Sigmund Freud, Karl Marx (whose Ph.D. thesis was on classical philosophy), and the American Founding Fathers.

As for Latin itself, a range of different stories is told in the post-Crocker-Harris world. Where the teaching of the language has not been abolished altogether, you are now likely to read of how Latin, freed of the old-fashioned grammar grind, can make a huge impact on intellectual and linguistic development: whether that's based on the studies from schools in the Bronx that claim to show that learning Latin increases children's IQ scores or on those common assertions that knowing Latin is a tremendous help if you want to learn French, Italian, Spanish, or any other Indo-European language you care to name.

But there's a problem here. Some of the optimists' objections do hit home. The classical past has never been co-opted by only one political tendency: Classics have probably legitimated as many revolutions as they have legitimated conservative dictatorships (and Aeschylus has over the years been performed both as Nazi propaganda and to support liberation movements in sub-Saharan Africa). Some of the counterclaims, though, are plain misleading. The success of *Gladiator* was absolutely nothing new; think of *Ben-Hur*, *Spartacus*, *The Sign of the Cross*, and any number of versions of *The Last Days of Pompeii* right back almost to the very beginning of cinema. Nor is the success of popular classical biography; countless people of my generation were introduced to antiquity through the biographies by Michael Grant, now largely forgotten.

And I am afraid that many of the arguments now used to justify the learning of Latin are perilous too. Latin certainly teaches you about language and how language works, and the fact that it is 'dead' can be quite liberating: I am forever grateful that you don't have to learn how to ask for a pizza in it, or the directions to the cathedral. But honestly, if you want to learn French, you would frankly be better off doing that, not starting with some other language first. There is really only one good reason for learning Latin, and that is that you want to read what is written in it.

That is not quite what I mean, though. My bigger question is: what drives us so insistently to examine the 'state' of Classics, and to buy books that lament their decline? Reading through opinion after opinion it can sometimes feel that you are entering a strange form of hospital drama, a sort of academic ER, with an apparently sick patient ('Classics') surrounded by different doctors who cannot quite agree on either the diagnosis or prognosis. Is the patient merely malingering and really fighting fit? Is a gradual improvement likely, but perhaps never back to the peak of good health? Or is the illness terminal and palliative care or covert euthanasia the only options?

But, perhaps even more to the point, why are we so interested in what's going to happen to Classics, and why discuss it in this way, and fill so many pages with the competing answers? There is something a bit paradoxical about the 'decline of Classics debate' and the mini publishing industry that appears to depend on a large number of key supporters of Classics buying books that chart their demise. I mean, if you don't give a toss about Latin and Greek and the classical tradition, you don't choose to read a book on why no one is interested in them any more.

Of course, all kinds of different assumptions about what we think 'Classics' are underlie the various arguments about their state of health: from something that comes down more or less to the academic study of Latin and Greek to – at the other end of the spectrum – a wider sense of popular interest in the ancient world in all its forms. Part of the reason why people disagree about how 'Classics' are doing is that when they talk about 'Classics' or (more often in America) 'the classics' they are not talking about the same thing. I do not plan here to offer a straightforward redefinition. But I am going to pick up some of the themes that emerged in Terence Rattigan's play to suggest that Classics are embedded in the way we think about ourselves, and our own history, in a more complex way than we usually allow. They are not just from or about the distant past. They are also a cultural language that we have learned to speak, in dialogue with the idea of antiquity. And to state the obvious, in a way, if they are about anybody, Classics are, of course, about us as much as about the Greeks and Romans.

But first the rhetoric of decline, and let me offer you another piece of gloom:

On many sides we hear confident assertions ... that the work of Greek and Latin is done – that their day is past. If the extinction of these languages as potent instruments of education is a sacrifice inexorably demanded by the advancement of civilization, regrets are idle, and we must bow to necessity. But we know from history that not the least of the causes of the fall of great supremacies has been the supine-ness and short-sightedness of their defenders. It is therefore the duty of those who believe ... that Greek and Latin may continue to confer in the future, as they have done in the past, priceless benefits upon all higher human education, to inquire whether these causes exist, and how they may be at once removed. For if these studies fall, they fall like Lucifer. We can assuredly hope for no second Renaissance.

As you will have guessed from the rhetorical style, that was not written yesterday (although you could have heard much the same points made yesterday). It is, in fact, by the Cambridge Latinist J. P. Postgate, lamenting the decline of Latin and Greek in 1902 – a famous lament, published in an influential London magazine (*The Fortnightly Review*) and powerful enough to lead directly, over one hundred years ago, to the establishment in the UK of the Classical Association, whose aim was to bring like-minded parties together explicitly to save Classics.

The point is that you can find such lamentations or anxieties almost anywhere you look in the history of the classical tradition. As is well known, Thomas Jefferson, in 1782, justified the prominence of the classics in his own educational curriculum partly because of what was happening in Europe: 'The learning of Greek and Latin, I am told, is going into disuse in Europe. I know not what their manners and occupations may call for: but it would be very ill-judged in us to follow their example in this instance.'

All this seems almost preposterous to us; for, in our terms, these are voices from the Golden Age of classical study and understanding, the age that we have lost. But they are a powerful reminder of one of the most important aspects of the symbolic register of Classics: that sense of imminent loss, the terrifying fragility of our connections with distant antiquity (always in danger of rupture), the fear of the barbarians at the gates and that we are simply not up to the preservation of what we value. That is to say, tracts on the decline of Classics are not commentaries upon it, they are debates within it: they are in part the expressions of the loss and longing and the nostalgia that have always tinged classical studies. As so often, creative writers capture this sense rather more acutely than professional classicists. The sense of fading, absence, past glories, and the end of an era is a very clear message of *The Browning Version*.

But another side of the fragility is a major theme of Tony Harrison's extraordinary play *The Trackers of Oxyrhynchus*, first performed in 1988 – featuring (in one part of a complex plot that mixes ancient and modern) a pair of British classicists who are excavating in the rubbish dumps of the town of Oxyrhynchus in Egypt for the scraps of papyrus, with all the 'new' bits of classical literature that they may contain, or the precious glimpses they might give of the mundane and messy real life of the ancient world. But as Harrison insists, all you ever get are the fragments from the wastepaper baskets – and the frustration and disappointments of the process send one of the excavators mad.

The truth is that Classics are by definition in decline; even in what we now call the 'Renaissance', the humanists were not celebrating the 'rebirth' of Classics; rather like Harrison's 'trackers', they were for the most part engaged in a desperate last-ditch attempt to save the fleeting and fragile traces of Classics from oblivion. There has been no generation since at least the second century AD that has imagined that it was fostering the classical tradition *better* than its predecessors. But there is of course an upside here. The sense of imminent loss, the perennial fear that we might just be on the verge of losing Classics entirely, is one very important thing that gives them – whether in professional study or creative re-engagement – the energy and edginess that I think they still have.

I am not sure that this helps us very much in predicting the future of Classics, but my guess is that in 2111 people will still be engaging with Classics, edgily and creatively, that they will still be lamenting their decline – and probably looking back to us as a Golden Age of classical studies.

But the question still remains: what do we mean by 'Classics'? I am conscious that I have been almost as inconsistent as those I have criticised. Sometimes I have been referring to Latin and Greek, sometimes to a subject studied by people who self-describe as classicists, sometimes to a much more general cultural property (the stuff of movies, novels and poetry). Now definitions are often false friends. The smartest and most appealing tend to exclude too much; the most judicious and broadest are so judicious as to be unhelpfully dull. (One recent attempt to define Classics runs: 'the study of the culture, in the widest sense, of any population using Greek and Latin, from the beginning to (say) the Islamic invasions of the seventh century AD.' True, *but ...*)

I am not going to construct an alternative. But I do want to reflect on what the coordinates of a definition might be – on a template that might be more helpful in thinking about what 'Classics' are, and how their future might lie. At its simplest, I think that we have to go beyond the superficially plausible idea (embedded in the definition I've just quoted) that Classics are – or are about – the literature, art, culture, history, philosophy and language of the ancient world. Of course they are partly that. The sense of loss and longing that I described is, to some extent, for the culture of the distant past, the fragments of papyrus from the wastepaper baskets of Oxyrhynchus. But not solely. As the nostalgic rhetoric makes absolutely clear, the sense of loss and longing is also for our predecessors whose connections to the ancient world we often believe to have been so much closer than our own.

To put this as crisply as I can, the study of Classics is the study of what happens in the gap between antiquity and ourselves. It is not only the dialogue that we have with the culture of the classical world; it is also the dialogue that we have with those who have gone before us who were themselves in dialogue with the classical world (whether Dante, Raphael, William Shakespeare, Edward Gibbon, Pablo Picasso, Eugene O'Neill or Terence Rattigan). Classics (as writers of the second century AD had already spotted) are a series of 'Dialogues with the Dead'. But the dead do not include only those who went to their graves two thousand years ago. This is an idea nicely captured in another article in *The Fortnightly Review*, this time a skit that appeared in 1888, a sketch set in the underworld, in which a trio of notable classical scholars (the long-dead Bentley and Porson, plus their recently deceased Danish colleague Madvig) have a free and frank discussion with Euripides and Shakespeare. This little satire also reminds us that the only actual speakers in this dialogue are us; it is we who ventriloquise, who animate what the ancients have to say: in fact, here the classical scholars complain what a terrible time they are having in Hades, because they are constantly being told off by the ancient shades who complain that the classicists have got them wrong.

Two quite simple things follow from this. The first is that we should be much more alert than we often are to the claims we make about the classical world – or, at least, we should be more strategically aware of whose claims they are. Take, for example, the common statement 'The ancient Athenians invented democracy'. Put like that, it is simply not true. As far as we know, no ancient Greek ever said so; and anyway democracy isn't something that is 'invented' like a piston engine. Our word 'democracy' derives from the Greek, that is correct. Beyond that, the fact is that we have chosen to invest the fifth-century Athenians with the status of 'inventors of democracy'; we have projected our desire for an origin onto them. (And it's a projection that would have amazed our predecessors two hundred years ago – for most of whom fifth-century-BC Athenian politics was the archetype of a disastrous form of mob rule.)

The second point is the inextricable embeddedness of the classical tradition within Western culture. I don't mean that Classics are synonymous with Western culture; there are of course many other multicultural strands and traditions that demand our attention, define who we are, and without which the contemporary world would be immeasurably poorer. But the fact is that Dante read Virgil's *Aeneid*, not the epic of Gilgamesh. What I have stressed so far is our engagement with our predecessors through their engagement with Classics. The slightly different spin on that would be to say that it would be impossible now to understand Dante without Virgil, John Stuart Mill without Plato, Donna Tartt without Euripides, Rattigan without Aeschylus. I'm not sure if this amounts to a prediction about the future; but I would say that if we were to amputate Classics from the modern world, it would mean more than closing down some university departments and consigning Latin grammar to the scrap heap. It would mean bleeding wounds in the body of Western culture – and a dark future of misunderstanding. I doubt we'll go that way.

I would like to close with two final points, one a slightly austere observation about knowledge and expertise; the other something rather more celebratory.

First, knowledge: I have referred several times to the way that we ourselves have to ventriloquise the ancient Greeks and Romans, and to animate their writings and the material traces they have left; the dialogue that we have with them is not an equal one; we're in the driver's seat. But if it is going to be a useful and constructive dialogue, not an incoherent and ultimately pointless Babel, it needs to be founded on expertise in the ancient world and in ancient languages. Now I do not mean by this that everyone should learn Latin and Greek (any more than I mean that no one can get anything out of Dante unless they personally have read Virgil). Luckily, cultural understanding is a collaborative, social operation.

The important cultural point is that *some* people should have read Virgil and Dante. To put it another way, the overall strength of Classics is not to be measured by exactly how many young people know Latin and Greek from school or university. It is better measured by asking how many believe that there should be people in the world who do know Latin and Greek, how many people think that there is an expertise in that worth taking seriously – and ultimately paying for.

My one concern, I suppose, is that while there is still a huge and widespread enthusiasm for Classics, expertise in the sense I have just mentioned is more fragile. Christopher Logue knew no Greek when he embarked on the *Iliad*; but he knew a man who did know it, very well – Donald Carne-Ross, who went on to become professor of Classics at Boston University. Compare that collaboration to the way, even in significant publications in academic disciplines bordering on Classics (in art history, for example, or English), you repeatedly find misprinted, garbled, wrongly translated Latin and Greek. I don't mind the authors not knowing the languages; that's fine. But I do mind that they do not bother to call on someone else's expertise to help them get it right. Most ironically of all, perhaps, in my own recent copy of Rattigan's *Browning Version*, the bits of Greek that are central to the play are so misprinted that they make little sense. The Crock would be turning in his grave. Or to put it my way, you cannot have a dialogue with nonsense.

But I would like to end with a less curmudgeonly thought. Looking over what I had written, I noticed that there was one important thing about Classics that I had left out: a due sense of wonderment. Professional classicists are not good in this respect. You will most often hear them complaining about all the things we don't know about the ancient world, bemoaning that we have lost so many books of Livy, or that Tacitus does not tell us about the Roman poor. But that is to miss the point. What is truly amazing is what we have, not what we don't have, from the ancient world. If you did not already know, and someone were to say that material written by people who lived two millennia ago or more still survived in such quantities that most people would not be able to get through it all in a lifetime – you wouldn't believe them. It is astonishing. But it is the case; and it offers the possibility of a most wondrous shared voyage of exploration.

At this point it is worth going back to Browning's translation of the *Agamemnon* and looking more carefully at how he introduced it. 'May I be permitted,' he writes, 'to chat a little, by way of recreation, at the end of a somewhat toilsome and perhaps fruitless adventure?' Toilsome? Probably. Fruitless? I don't think so, despite the very old-fashioned ring of Browning's language. Adventure? Yes certainly – and adventures in Classics are something we can all share.

Robert B. Silvers lecture, New York Public Library, December 2011

ANCIENT GREECE

What can we know about the distant prehistoric past of ancient Greece? How do we get back to those earliest civilisations in the Mediterranean that flourished hundreds of years before Pericles sponsored the building of the Parthenon, or Socrates drank the hemlock? Sir Arthur Evans is one of the key figures in the rediscovery of Greek prehistory. In 1899 he bought a piece of land outside the Cretan city of Heraklion, excavated the remains of a vast palace, dating back to almost 2000 BC, and then proceeded to rebuild it in the form that we still visit today. It's sometimes jokingly said that this apparently 'prehistoric' palace is actually one of the first reinforced concrete buildings on the island of Crete.

The first chapter in this section takes a look at what Evans discovered at Knossos, and at 'Minoan civilisation' (as he was the first to call it) more generally; it asks how accurately, or imaginatively, he reconstructed the palace and its famous paintings, and how his aims, methods and motives continue to be argued over even now – stopping briefly, en route, to wonder why it is that disagreements among archaeologists so often turn into nasty personal vendettas.

That underlying theme of how we know what we think we know about ancient Greece continues through the rest of this section, in different ways. Chapter 2 asks how we can ever recapture the voice of Greek women, when so little writing by them survives. The truth is that we do have a little bit more than we often assume (not many people, for example, have heard of the poets Korinna, Nossis or Melinno, who wrote – probably in the second century BC – a 'Hymn to Rome', which we can still read). But, all the same, it doesn't amount to much. And when it does survive, what it means is often fiercely debated; never more fiercely than with the poetry of Sappho, who lived and wrote on the island of Lesbos in the early sixth century BC. She has always been by far the most famous of Greek women poets (in fact some Greeks dubbed her 'the tenth Muse'). But what her work is really 'about', and in particular how erotic her lines on other women were intended to be, is still controversial. She has given the modern world the sexual sense of the word 'lesbian', derived from the name of her home island. But whether she was a lesbian in our terms, or simply very emotionally invested in female friends and pupils (as many buttoned-up nineteenth-century critics wanted to believe), is another matter.

Different issues of interpretation come into play when we look at the fifth-century Greek historian Thucydides, or at the life story of Alexander the Great. Thucydides' account of the great 'Peloponnesian War' between Athens and Sparta is usually thought of as a landmark in careful, rigorous history writing – and its sometimes chilling analysis of ancient power relations has made it a favourite of modern foreign policy analysts. Here, as Chapter 3 shows, the question is not merely whether Thucydides' explanation of why Athens lost the war is correct (did they really, as Thucydides suggests, overstretch themselves by going off to invade Sicily? Were they wrong to reject the cautious policies of their great general Pericles, after his death early in the war?). Even more to the point is quite how we make any sense at all of Thucydides' extraordinary difficult Greek. It turns out that some of his most famous bons mots are woeful, or at least very over-optimistic, mistranslations and that we're still trying to work out what quite a lot of his Greek actually meant. True, we're getting closer, but it's one nice example of how even the basic groundwork of classical scholarship is far from finished.

In the case of Alexander the Great, the problem is that we have plenty of vivid ancient accounts of his campaigns and occasionally extravagant lifestyle – but none of the many histories and memoirs that were written by his fourth century BC contemporaries has come down to us. Instead we have accounts written hundreds of years later, all of them composed against the background of Roman imperialism. Chapter 4 chances its arm a little (and a bit provocatively, I suppose I should warn you) to suggest that we should see Alexander the Great not as a Greek hero/thug at all, but as a Roman literary creation.

The final chapter in this section takes one of those subjects that everyone knows they can't really answer: what made people laugh in the past? It tries to bring back to life some ancient jokes from the one surviving ancient joke book (though whether we have understood them right, who knows – 'Monty Pythonesque' as some of them seem to be). And it wonders quite why the city of Abdera (in north Greece) was so closely associated with people laughing and being laughed at. How many Abderites did it take to change a light bulb … ?

1

BUILDER OF RUINS

Evelyn Waugh was characteristically unimpressed by the remains of the prehistoric Minoan palace at Knossos and its famous decoration. His 1930 travelogue, *Labels*, contains a memorable account of his disappointment, not so much at the excavation site itself ('where,' he writes archly, 'Sir Arthur Evans … is rebuilding the palace') but at its collection of prize paintings and sculpture, which had been removed to the museum in Heraklion. In the sculpture, he 'saw nothing to suggest any genuine aesthetic feeling at all'. The frescoes were much more difficult to judge, 'since only a few square inches of the vast area exposed to our consideration are earlier than the last twenty years, and it is impossible to disregard the suspicion that their painters have tempered their zeal for accurate reconstructions with a somewhat inappropriate predilection for covers of *Vogue*.'

It seems to have been relatively easy for Waugh, visiting soon after the paintings' restoration, to spot quite how little of these masterpieces of Minoan art was actually Minoan. Almost a century on, and after a good deal of fading, most visitors to the Heraklion museum today are happily unaware that the icons of prehistoric Cretan culture that feature on thousands of postcards, posters and museum souvenirs (the 'Dolphin' fresco, the 'Ladies in Blue' or the 'Prince of the Lilies') have only an indirect connection with the second millennium BC, being largely recreations of the early twentieth century AD. Nor do most of them realise that those distinctively primitive, stumpy red columns, which are the trademark of the site of Knossos, are built wholly of modern concrete and are part of the 'rebuilding' by Evans.

1. Prehistoric art or *Vogue* cover? The 'Prince of the Lilies'
was one of Arthur Evans's favourite Minoan paintings –
but it is a hotch-potch of misleading restoration.

Arthur Evans directed the excavation and restoration of the palace at Knossos over the first twenty-five years of the last century, though most of the best-known discoveries were made in the earliest campaigns, between 1900 and 1905. Born in 1851, the son of a well-known antiquarian (who had made a fortune from paper manufacture), Evans read Modern History at Oxford. When he failed to win a college fellowship despite a first-class degree, he turned to travelling in Eastern Europe, combining his interest in archaeology with service as Balkan correspondent for the *Manchester Guardian*. Investigative journalism, then as now, had its risks, especially in the Balkans. Accused of spying in Herzegovina and unceremoniously banned from the entire Austro-Hungarian Empire, he returned to Oxford, where in 1884 he was appointed Keeper of the Ashmolean (beating his father to the job, or so the story goes).

It turned out to be a revolutionary appointment. In the face of all kinds of objections from Benjamin Jowett and the like, Evans set about raising money to develop the Ashmolean collection into a research resource for the whole of European archaeology, from prehistory onwards; and he orchestrated its move in 1894 into large new premises behind the University Galleries in Beaumont Street, where it remains. From the mid-1890s his interests increasingly focused on the island of Crete. To start with, he was on the trail of prehistoric writing systems, for Evans had become convinced that Crete would provide the evidence of early literacy that Heinrich Schliemann's excavations at Mycenae had so signally failed to turn up. As time went on, however, it became clear that a vision of Greek prehistory was at stake: he was searching for a site that could challenge the dominance of Mycenae and the macho, warrior version of early Greece that went with it.

Evans took advantage of the family money and by 1899 had succeeding in buying the site of Kephala outside Heraklion, which small-scale excavations had long suggested was the location of prehistoric Knossos, in legend the city of King Minos, Princess Ariadne and the murderous Minotaur in its labyrinth. Others had tried to get their hands on the place; Schliemann himself had made a half-hearted attempt to acquire it in the 1880s, boasting that with a hundred men he could excavate it in a week. But in the end, Evans's cash up front, and his persistence in dealing with the various local landowners, won out. Excavations began in 1900 and within weeks the famous 'throne' had been discovered in its 'throne room', complete with 'bathing pool' (or 'lustral basin' or 'fish pond', according to choice), as well as a whole series of enticingly fragmentary pieces of fresco that had once decorated the walls. Evans was instantly drawn into imaginative interpretation. No sooner had a few square inches of faded plaster come out of the ground than he was busy restoring it in his mind's eye (was it Ariadne herself? or perhaps a cup-bearer?); and at the same time, he was giving evocative names to the rooms he discovered: the 'Hall of the Double Axes', the 'Queen's Megaron' – tentative titles originally, maybe, but they have stuck. All this contributed to a powerful image of the civilisation he was excavating ('Minoan' was his name for it), which in due course was accorded material form by his team of artists and architects, who 'completed' the fragmentary paintings and rebuilt much of the palace to Evans's specification.

From the very beginning, this procedure was controversial. Waugh was not the only one to have doubts about what he saw in the Heraklion museum and its suspicious similarity, if not to the covers of *Vogue,* then at least to Art Deco; nor the only one to feel uneasy about Evans's role as a 'builder of ruins' (as one French newspaper called him) on the site itself. R. G. Collingwood (pp. 257–63) declared that 'the first impression on the mind of a visitor is that Knossian architecture consists of garages and public lavatories'. There were plenty of other comments along similar lines.

It was not only a question of 'modernising'. These elaborate restorations also included what have proved to be some notoriously embarrassing mistakes. Most notorious of all was the so-called 'Blue Monkey' fresco. Its few fragments were originally restored by Evans's artists as a delicate young boy gathering saffron flowers: a perfect emblem of the carefree folk, with their innocent love of nature, that were supposed to inhabit this Minoan world. It was only much later, when someone questioned the strange blue colour and spotted what appeared to be a tail, that the painting was re-restored as a blue monkey in a field of crocuses. A similar question mark still hangs over the 'Prince of the Lilies' (Fig. 1) – a powerful silhouette, with a loincloth, a necklace of lilies and an elaborate plumed headdress featuring more lilies. Despite some early doubts about how this figure was to be restored, Evans soon convinced himself that it was the representation of the 'priest-king' of the Minoan state, and he had the headdress expensively gold-embossed on the cover of each volume of his publication of the site. It now seems very unlikely that the three surviving fragments of the silhouette (headdress, torso and parts of a leg) originally belonged to the same figure at all; and much more likely that the headdress, far from being the royal crown of a Frazerian priest-king (p. 254), adorned the head of a neighbouring sphinx.

But neither controversy nor blatant error did much to dent the popularity of Evans's recreations. Celebrity visitors trooped to see Knossos (Isadora Duncan was said to have performed an 'impromptu' dance on the grand staircase). And tourists more generally found it a sufficient reason to visit Crete. The 1888 edition of the Baedeker Guide to Greece had no entry for Crete: by 1904 it included fifteen pages on Knossos and other attractions; today, a million people a year visit the site. Evans's images have also fed strikingly back into the culture out of which they came. The palace's aesthetic may well have derived directly from the artistic world of the earlier twentieth century (Evans compared a fragment of Minoan painting to a piece of William Morris wallpaper). But later in the century, artists, film-makers and novelists (notably Mary Renault) in their turn found inspiration in what he and his team had created. There are very few movies set in the heroic age of Greece that do not derive their backdrop, at least in part, from the 'Palace of Minos'.

This popularity is hardly surprising. It was not simply that Evans took some rather unexciting ruins and dull fragments of painted plaster and made them worth seeing; if he had left the site in the state in which he excavated it far fewer than a million visitors would be queuing up at Knossos today. More influential was the fact that he gave (or rather fed back to) the early twentieth century exactly the image of a primitive culture that it wanted. The Minoans were not the rather off-putting, violent heroes of Schliemann's Mycenae; nor were they the darkly sinister people that the Minotaur myth might have suggested. Instead, they were by and large peaceable, in tune with nature, keen on the appropriately lusty (and quasi-religious) sport of bull-leaping, and satisfyingly tinged with the fashionable current of matriarchy. In his biography of Evans, J. A. MacGillivray resorts to some crude pop psychology to explain this stress on the mother-goddess in Evans's vision of Minoan culture: namely, the 'vacuum' left in his life 'by the death of his mother when he was six years old'. I suspect that current trends in anthropology and the study of myth had rather more to do with it; just as James Frazer was a major influence in the whole idea of the Minoan 'priest-king'.

But what of the archaeology underneath these elaborate recon-structions? The paradox of Evans is that, while it is easy to ridicule the romantic version of Minoan culture that he reinvented in concrete and paint (and publicised with the ready pen of a journalist), the exca-vations on site were hard-headed and, by the standards of the time, extremely careful. Some of this care, perhaps the majority of it, may have been the achievement of his excavation assistant, Duncan Mackenzie. Evans might have had the wherewithal to buy a large parcel of Cretan land, but when he started work at Knossos in 1900 he was relatively inexperienced in practical archaeology. The advice of the director of the British School in Athens was to engage the help of someone who knew how to dig; so he employed Mackenzie, who had supervised excavations on the island of Melos. Mackenzie was, as Colin Renfrew has put it, 'one of the very first scientific workers in the Aegean', a zealot for accurate recording, who kept a whole series (twenty-six all told) of 'Day Books' which detailed discoveries at Knossos and often formed the basis of Evans's later published accounts. He also used his experience on Melos to help Evans fathom the stratigraphical layers of the site, and so ultimately to arrive at some idea of a dated sequence of occupation.

The relatively high quality of the work, however, cannot entirely be put down to Mackenzie. For all Evans's superficial enthusiasm for Minoan culture, his trailing of the names of the mythical Minos and Ariadne, the glamourising titles that he all too quickly applied to newly excavated rooms ('throne room' etc.), his excavation reports and multi-volume publication of the site have stood the test of time extraordinarily well. Even in terms of modern scholarly theory and debate, there are very few major errors of interpretation. As Michael Ventris and John Chadwick were to show half a century later, Evans was quite wrong to conclude that Linear B script, preserved on hundreds of clay tablets from Knossos, was not a form of Greek (though the credit for inventing the names we still use, 'Linear A' and 'Linear B', for the pre-alphabetic writing of early Greece goes to him). He was also wrong to cast his 'Minoan' civilisation as the primary culture of the prehis-toric Aegean, with the 'Mycenaean' palaces of the mainland demoted to a subsidiary phenomenon. Those errors apart, however, and despite a series of bitterly hostile attacks from other scholars in the field (pre-Hellenic archaeology is not a particularly friendly discipline), most of the rest of Evans's major arguments remain if not accepted, then at least arguable. And the problems he raised still, by and large, set the agenda for discussion: what was the function of the palace at Knossos, and the others like it? What social and political structure do the remains imply? What brought about the end of this culture? Contrast this with the fate of Schliemann, whose finds remain central, but almost none of whose questions or arguments (chronological or interpretative) have survived the hundred or so years since his excavations. Who cares very much, after all, whether he did, or did not, gaze upon the face of Agamemnon?

MacGillivray's biography, which is centred on Evans's work at Knossos, does not trade in any such subtleties or paradox – but in snide put-downs and innuendo. MacGillivray himself worked for several years at Knossos; and it is hard to resist the conclusion that this book is partly a settling of old scores with a ghost whose presence must still be felt heavily there. Evans is not, from the outside, a particularly plausible villain and the tactics that MacGillivray must adopt to paint him as such become increasingly desperate as the book progresses: never let a sentence pass without the insertion of a pejorative adjective; never suggest a decent motive on Evans's part if a bad one will do. So, for example, Evans is dubbed a 'mediocre' journalist, when all the evidence suggests that his reports from Bosnia-Herzegovina were perceptive and influential. His degree is dismissed as 'barely managing to get a "first"' and corruption on the part of the examiners is hinted at – flagrantly stretching a point made in one of the obituaries of Evans. His generosity to the young Mortimer Wheeler, whose meagre scholarship money of £50 he doubled out of his own pocket, is bizarrely written off as 'merely observing the third and ninth Scout laws' (whatever they may be, it cannot possibly be true). And his enthusiasm for Minoan civilisation is insistently tarred with the brush of racism, Aryanism and blindness to the influence of African and Semitic culture when, in fact, one of the criticisms of Evans has always been that he was far too eager to find Egyptian influence in Crete – no doubt for that reason, he was let off relatively lightly by Martin Bernal in Black Athena. One of the strangest claims in this litany of 'faults' is that Evans 'never grew much beyond four feet', an assertion which is glaringly contradicted by the photographs that illustrate the book (unless all his fellow archaeologists were similarly diminutive, or he insisted on some very deceptive camerawork).

Inevitably, sex plays a walk-on part. Evans was briefly married, his wife Margaret dying of tuberculosis in 1893; there were no children. In 1924, at the age of 73, he was fined 'for committing an act in violation of public decency in Hyde Park' with a young man. MacGillivray makes a good deal of this, devoting a few suspicious pages to an analysis of Evans's role in the Boy Scouts, and even suggesting that his most conspicuous act of generosity was intended precisely to cover up this conviction. For, on the same day as the court hearing, his gift of the site of Knossos to the British School at Athens was announced. No doubt, there was more than a convenient coincidence of timing here; but the idea that this gift came as 'startling news' or that its main motive was to deflect attention from the court hearing is simply false. As Joan Evans (the art historian and Arthur's half-sister, more than forty years his junior) makes clear in her family memoir *Time and Chance*, his plan to make the site over had been actively in preparation since at least 1922. MacGillivray has little time for the understated irony of this elegant account of the Evans family, published in 1943 shortly after Arthur's death; he accuses it of 'lacking depth' and of reading 'as flatly as Sir William Richmond's portrait' (the flamboyant, and far from 'flat', painting of Evans surrounded by his finds that now hangs in the Ashmolean). More often than not, however, Joan Evans's story seems a far better guide to her half-brother's life and motivation than the cheap and often unsubstantiated innuendo of MacGillivray.

Partly because of its faults and its transparent desire to assault Evans's reputation, the book prompts an important general question about the history of archaeology. Why is it that, more almost than any other academic discipline, archaeology (and prehistoric archaeology in particular) invests its own past with such venom? Why is it that distinguished practising archaeologists are bothered to debate, not just the archaeological record, but the moral failings of the likes of Schliemann and Evans, often with almost no attention paid to the different historical and social context within which those predecessors were working? The fact that, in the grand seigneurial style of late nineteenth-century archaeology, Evans bought up his site as a private fiefdom (something which MacGillivray holds against him) should be no more or less relevant to his archaeological 'achievements' than Newton's treatment of his servants is relevant to the theory of gravity. Why then is it looked on as if it were? Or why does it seem to matter that Schliemann wasn't a very nice man?

Part of the answer, no doubt, lies in the usual heroic image of these early excavators-cum-explorers; they are obvious targets for taking down a peg or two, and any trick in the book will do (even nasty and very politically uncorrect insinuations about their height). But it also has something to do with the nature of the archaeological material itself and the impossibly close relationship between the excavators and their data. It is a truism that traditional archaeological 'excavation' is a euphemism for archaeological 'destruction'. What this means is that we must rely on the probity of the archaeologists: we cannot check up on them after the event or replicate their procedures (as we can with most scientific experiments) because the material for that has been destroyed in the course of excavation. Almost inevitably, this throws us back onto a whole range of desperate strategies to test archaeological trustworthiness: if Schliemann was a liar about his private life, is that not a hint that he might have been equally unscrupulous about his finds and excavations?

It also means that the excavators of the past have a powerful hold over the future of the subject. The sneaking thought arises that if Evans's work still provides much of the agenda for modern discussion of Knossos, it is not so much because of his own acuity in spotting the central issues, but because (unlike Schliemann?) he presented the material in such a way that those are the only questions that can, even now, productively be asked. How far that is true is obviously a much bigger question in the development of the whole discipline. But it certainly suggests that the giants of late nineteenth- and early twentieth-century excavation are likely to remain central to live debates in contemporary scholarship for some time to come. Evans, Schliemann and their contentious data still matter too much to be dispatched to a quiet corner of the 'history' of the subject.

Review of J. A. MacGillivray, *Minotaur: Sir Arthur Evans and the Archaeology of the Minoan Myth* (Jonathan Cape, 2000)

2

SAPPHO SPEAKS

'It is against the nature of things that a woman who has given herself up to unnatural and inordinate practices ... should be able to write in perfect obedience to the laws of vocal harmony, imaginative portrayal, and arrangement of the details of thought.' For David Robinson, writing in the 1920s and reprinted in the 1960s, the 'perfection' of Sappho's verse was clear enough proof of her unblemished character. He was perhaps unusual in his unshakeable confidence that (at least in the case of female writers) fine poetry could be found only in association with fine morals: but in other respects he was merely part of the great scholarly tradition that has attempted to rescue the Greek poet Sappho from the implications of her own writing – from the implication, in particular, that she enjoyed the physical love of other women. So, for example, even some recent critics have sought to portray her as a primarily religious figure, the leader of a cult of young girls devoted to the goddess Aphrodite. Others, with a yet more extreme capacity for fantasy, have seen her as some kind of female professor or headmistress, instructing her young charges in poetry, in music, even perhaps in the techniques of sensual pleasure that they would need in their future life as wives.

It is easy to ridicule these attempts to deny the central place of (lesbian) sexuality in Sappho's poetry. Jane Snyder, in *The Woman and the Lyre*, runs through the main strands of traditional Sappho criticism, pointing out the anachronistic absurdity that underlies most of these reconstructions of her social background and literary context. The tough, warring world of sixth-century BC Lesbos was no place for some prototype of a liberal arts college for young ladies and, as Snyder rightly sees, it is sheer bowdlerising whimsy to suggest that it was. But, in distancing herself from such vain attempts to 'imbue Sappho with respectability', in asserting instead a simple wish to read the poems 'for what they actually say', Snyder loses sight of some of the important issues involved in those traditional responses to Sappho and her writing. What was at stake was not just the anxiety of conservative classical scholars at Sappho's apparent sexual preference for young women – though that was, no doubt, an aggravating factor in the most strident reactions. More important, as Jack Winkler suggests in his essay on Sappho in *The Constraints of Desire*, was the plain fact that the writer, the speaking subject of these poems, was a woman – a woman claiming the right to talk about her own sexuality. What was at stake was not so much lesbianism as the 'woman's voice', and how that could be heard and understood.

Any discussion of women writers in Greece and Rome – of Sappho and her less well-known followers – must focus on the nature of that 'woman's voice'. The dominant ideology of most of the ancient world offered women no place in public discourse. The exclusion of women from politics and power was simply one side of that much greater disability – their lack of any right to be heard. As Homer's Telemachus put it to his mother Penelope in the *Odyssey* (when she dared publicly to interrupt a bard's recitation), 'talking must be the concern of men'. How, then, within this insistent ideology of female silence, could women writers find any space for their own creativity? How did they interact with the overwhelmingly male literary and cultural heritage? Did they succeed in appropriating and subverting male language for a distinctively female form of writing?

Snyder barely touches on these central questions. Starting from Sappho, at the turn of the seventh and sixth centuries BC, and ending with Hypatia and Egeria writing a thousand years later, she pieces together an account of the major women writers of antiquity and provides translations of the surviving fragments of their work. There are some odd omissions. Surprisingly, she makes no mention of St Perpetua, whose autobiographical account of her imprisonment and trial during the Christian persecutions is one of the most extraordinary documents to have been preserved from antiquity. Nor does poor Melinno (author of a surviving 'Hymn to Rome': 'I welcome you, Roma, daughter of Ares,/ War-loving queen … etc') find a place. But, even so, for those used to the familiar (male) roll call of classical authors, the list of women writers that Snyder has assembled is itself impressive – Myrtis, Korinna, Praxilla, Anyte, Nossis, Erinna, Leontion, Sulpicia, Proba and many more.

Not so impressive, unfortunately, are the paltry surviving fragments of their work and Snyder's generally banal attempts at literary and historical analysis. Among the best-preserved is the poetry of Korinna: three excerpts from what were probably much longer poems and a few isolated couplets, amounting to about a hundred lines in all. Snyder's main concern is to assign Korinna to her 'appropriate niche in the history of Greek literature': she reviews the modern controversy about her date (fifth century BC or third century?) and she searches vainly for the literal truth, rather than the much more important symbolic truth, in the conflicting stories of Korinna's victories in poetic contests over her male rival, Pindar. She does, in the end, admit the impossibility of reaching any firm conclusions on these areas of Korinna's life history. But her underlying preoccupation with the poet's biography tends all the time to deflect her attention from serious analysis of the poetry itself – such as the opening, preserved on papyrus, to what may have been a collection of 'tales of old':

> Terpsichore summoned me to sing
> Beautiful tales of old
> To the Tanagrean girls in their white robes.
> And the city rejoiced greatly
> In my clear, plaintive voice ...

Snyder discusses Korinna's work in only the most general terms: she compliments its 'swiftly-paced narrative', its 'simple, direct language', its refreshing treatment of 'parallels between the mythological world and everyday human behavior', while suggesting at the same time that it was 'essentially conservative', 'interested only in transmitting received tradition, not challenging it', and largely lacking in 'philosophical profundity'. These judgements may be all very well as far as they go; there is certainly no need to see Korinna as a creative genius. But they fail to engage directly with the central problem of women's writing within a male tradition. Was Korinna simply submerged by that tradition? Or do her 'conservative' mythological narratives (including, interestingly, in one of the longer fragments, the story of the rape of the nine daughters of the river god Asopus) hint at a more pointed parallel between 'the mythological world and human behavior'?

In many cases the very fragmentary state of what is preserved makes discussion of the literary issues associated with women's writing in antiquity next to impossible. Even with extraordinary scholarly ingenuity, there is not much that can usefully be said about the fewer than twenty surviving words of Telesilla of Argos ('But Artemis, O maidens,/ fleeing from Alpheus ...' as by far the most substantial fragment runs). But Sappho, with several substantial extracts, and at least one complete poem preserved, comes into a very different category. It is here, where some close analysis of a woman's writing is for the first time possible, that Snyder's evasion of the important issue is most glaring.

In discussing Sappho's output, Snyder does seek to identify 'female language' in her poetry. She appeals, for example, to the poet's sense of description, her apparent fondness for the natural world and her tendency to introspection. What she misses, however, by concentrating on these stereotypical 'female' characteristics is Sappho's radical subversion of the male literary (epic) tradition. This is seen most clearly in the poem known as the 'Hymn to Aphrodite', in which Sappho calls on the goddess to come once more to her aid in pursuit of the girl she loves. It starts:

O immortal Aphrodite of the many-coloured throne,
Child of Zeus, weaver of wiles, I beseech you,
Do not overwhelm me in my heart
With anguish and pain, O Mistress.

But come hither, if ever at another time
Hearing my cries from afar
You heeded them, and leaving the home of your father
Came, yoking your golden

Chariot: beautiful, swift sparrows
Drew you above the black earth
Whirling their wings thick and fast,
From heaven's ether through mid-air.

Suddenly they had arrived; but you, O Blessed Lady,
With a smile on your immortal face,
Asked what I had suffered again and
Why I was calling again ...

This poem was certainly written 'in imitation of the standard form of a Greek prayer', adapted by Sappho 'to suit her own purposes'. But Snyder does not appear to recognise that Sappho is echoing, much more specifically, the words of the hero Diomedes in the midst of battle in the fifth book of Homer's *Iliad*, when he prays for help to the goddess Athena ('Hear me, child of Zeus who wears the aegis, unwearied one ...'). As Winkler demonstrates, that echo provides the key to our understanding of Sappho's 'voice' (or 'voices') in this poem. It focuses our attention on the distance between the male world of epic heroism and the private domain of female concerns; it shows the poet reading and reinterpreting Homeric epic to give it a new meaning in distinctively female terms; it effectively subverts the whole 'heroic order', by 'transferring the language for the experience of soldiers to the experience of women in love'. Sappho's writing here amounts to a tactical inversion of the dominant male language.

The ancient ideology of 'female silence' was, of course, challenged in other ways. Women found a 'voice' not just in writing, but also most obviously in religious ritual, prophecy and oracular utterance. Giulia Sissa's *Greek Virginity* takes as its starting point the virgin priestess of Apollo at Delphi, the Pythia. What was the connection, she asks, between her oracular function and her virginity? How far can the Pythia's 'right to speak' (or at least to act as a human mouthpiece for the god) be related to Greek ideas on the structure of the female body? How are we to understand her 'form of language that was at once divine and feminine'?

Sissa argues that the 'openness' of the Greek virgin was central to the Pythia's role. There is a striking contrast here with modern (and some Roman) ideas of the 'closure' of the virginal body. For us, the seal of the hymen acts as a physical token of a girl's intactness – until that moment of violent, wounding rupture at first penetration. For the Greeks, virginity did not entail a physical barrier: their idea of a human body had no place for a hymen. The body of the virgin was open and ready for penetration. Its moment of closure came only when it sealed around the growing foetus during pregnancy – which was the one sure sign that virginity had been lost. In the case of Pythia, her virginity ensured her openness to Apollo, and (like a perfect bride) to him alone. Christian writers poured scorn on the way she sat (as they claimed) astride a tripod, legs apart, taking up the vapours of his prophetic spirit into her vagina. But that was precisely the point: the body of the Pythia was open to the word of the god.

There is more at issue here than strange notions of female physiology. The role of the Pythia highlights an inextricable connection between the 'woman's voice' and sexuality, between 'the mouth that speaks and eats' and the 'mouth' of the vagina. Sissa's book is a subtle exploration of the woman's body as a vehicle not just of divine prophecy but also of human speech.

Review of Jane McIntosh Snyder, *The Woman and the Lyre: Women Writers in Classical Greece and Rome* (Bristol Classical Press, 1989); J. J. Winkler, *The Constraints of Desire: The Anthropology of Sex and Gender in Ancient Greece* (Routledge, 1990); Giulia Sissa, *Greek Virginity*, translated by Arthur Goldhammer (Harvard, 1990)

3

WHICH THUCYDIDES CAN YOU TRUST?

Thucydides wrote his *History of the Peloponnesian War* in almost impossibly difficult Greek. Maybe the contorted language has something to do with the novelty of his enterprise. Writing at the end of the fifth century BC, he was attempting something never done before: an aggressively rational, apparently impersonal analysis of the history of his own times, utterly free from religious modes of explanation. In Thucydides' view, the Peloponnesian War, fought on and off for thirty years between the two leading Greek cities of Sparta and Athens, had to be understood with respect to human politics and power struggles, not – as Homer had earlier seen the Trojan War, or as Herodotus had explained the Greek wars against the Persians – by referring to quarrels among the gods on Mount Olympus. This was revolutionary.

But however we choose to excuse Thucydides, the fact remains that his *History* is sometimes made almost incomprehensible by neologisms, awkward abstractions, and linguistic idiosyncrasies of all kinds. These are not only a problem for the modern reader. They infuriated some ancient readers too. In the first century BC, in a long essay devoted to Thucydides' work, Dionysius of Halicarnassus, a literary critic and historian himself, complained – with ample supporting quotations – of the 'forced expressions', 'non sequiturs', 'artificialities,' and 'riddling obscurity'. 'If people actually spoke like this,' he wrote, 'not even their mothers or their fathers would be able to tolerate the unpleasantness of it; in fact they would need translators, as if they were listening to a foreign language.'

In his *Thucydides: The Reinvention of History*, Donald Kagan is kinder, but even he concedes that 'his style is often very compressed and difficult to understand, so that any translation is necessarily an interpretation.' There are big implications here for our modern admiration of Thucydides as a historian. First, the 'good' translations of his *History* (those that are fluent and easy to read) give a very bad idea of the linguistic character of the original Greek. The 'better' they are, the less likely they are to reflect the flavour of what Thucydides wrote – rather like *Finnegans Wake* rewritten in the clear idiom of Jane Austen. Second, many of our favourite 'quotations' from Thucydides, those slogans that are taken to reveal his distinctive approach to history, bear a tenuous relationship to his original text. As a general rule, the catchier the slogans sound, the more likely they are to be largely the product of the translator rather than of Thucydides himself. He simply did not write many of the bons mots attributed to him.

Take, for example, perhaps the most favourite of all Thucydidean catchphrases, repeated in international relations courses the world over, and a founding text of 'realist' political analysis: 'The strong do what they can, the weak suffer what they must.' It is taken from the famous debate that Thucydides evokes between the Athenians and the people of the island of Melos. The Athenians had demanded that the neutral state of Melos come over to the Athenian side in the war between Athens and Sparta; when the Melians resisted, the two sides debated the issue. The representatives of imperial Athens put forward a terrifying version of 'might is right': justice only existed between equals, they asserted – otherwise, the strong rule the weak and so the power of Athens could always ride roughshod over the aspirations of a small island.

The Melians, honourably but naively, stuck by their own independence. The immediate result was that Athenian forces besieged and captured Melos, killing all the men that they could get their hands on, and enslaving the women and children. Significantly, in the design of Thucydides' *History*, the next major event turns out to be the disastrous Athenian expedition to Sicily – where the idea of 'might is right' rebounded on its Athenian exponents and effectively sealed Athens's defeat by Sparta.

The famous slogan about the strong and the weak comes,

obviously, from the Athenian side of the argument, and its current popularity owes much to the nice balance between the powerful doing 'what they can' and the weak suffering 'what they must' – as well as that iron law of inevitability (or realism, depending on your point of view) that is introduced by the phrase 'what they must'. But that is not what Thucydides wrote. As Simon Hornblower correctly acknowledges in the third and final volume of his monumental, line-by-line commentary on the whole of Thucydides' *History*, a more accurate translation is: 'The powerful exact what they can, and the weak have to comply.' Even that exaggerates the idea of compulsion on the weak: to be precise, what Thucydides claimed was only that 'the weak comply' – no necessity was introduced at all. And Hornblower's commentary also raises the question of exactly what the action of the strong was supposed to be; it could equally well be translated from the original Greek as 'do' or 'exact' or even (as one Renaissance scholar thought) 'extort'. 'Do what they can' and 'extort what they can' conjure up very different pictures of the operation of power.

Whatever the linguistic nuances, the truth is that the 'jingle' that we attribute to Thucydides was, in part at least, the work of Richard Crawley, a not very successful nineteenth-century Oxford classicist whose main claim to fame was a few satirical verses in the style of Alexander Pope – apart, that is, from his translation of Thucydides, which was adopted in the early twentieth century by the Everyman Library (for it appeared clear and fluent, as the requirements of that series demanded); now long out of copyright, it has become a favourite version to republish. It is in this guise that 'Thucydides' has regularly been plundered for courses in political theory and international relations, and for the slogans that have supported either a neoconservative or realist, or sometimes even left-wing, political agenda.

The obscurity of Thucydides' Greek amply justifies Hornblower's project, on which he has worked for more than twenty years, to produce another detailed historical and literary commentary on the whole of his *History* – to add to a series of such works, stretching back to the Renaissance. We often do not know exactly what Thucydides was trying to say, but as the centuries go by, we do get better at understanding him. And without scholarship such as this, the lies and misquotations perpetrated in the name of Thucydides would go entirely unchecked.

In fact, over his three volumes, Hornblower himself gets better and better at his task – the final part of his trilogy presents a far more sophisticated reading of the text than the scholarly, but more pedestrian, first volume, which appeared in 1991. But incremental as his work is, throughout his more than two thousand pages of commentary (outnumbering the pages of the original Greek text more than tenfold), one consistent element is that Hornblower repeatedly demonstrates that Thucydides did not say what we often imagine that he said.

One of the best examples is a quotation drawn from earlier in Thucydides' *History*, which Hornblower discusses in his first volume. This is a favourite of the liberal left, rather than of the realist right, and is often taken as an uncanny precursor of some of George Orwell's points in *1984*. In a reflection on the effects on language (as on so much else) of a brutal civil war in the city of Corcyra (on modern Corfu), Thucydides writes, again according to the much-quoted Crawley: 'Words had to change their ordinary meaning and to take that which was now given them.' As many classicists have proudly observed, this looks very like a Thucydidean version of Orwellian Newspeak, and is a nice example of an ancient writer anticipating what we take to be a modern idea by more than two millennia.

But it is not. The truth is that in translating the original Greek into those particular words, Crawley perhaps did anticipate Orwell, by almost a century; but Thucydides (as Hornblower underlines, following a number of recent studies) certainly did not. His extraordinarily lumpy Greek at this point in his *History* is hard to decode, but there is no expressing a proto-Orwellian idea. He is making a much less sophisticated point that, in the context of the civil war in Corcyra – between a pro-Athenian democratic faction and a pro-Spartan oligarchic faction – actions that had previously seemed bad were reinterpreted as good. Hornblower translates this passage correctly, and in tune with the style of the original, as: 'And they exchanged their usual verbal evaluations of actions for new ones, in the light of what they thought justified.' What this meant, as Thucydides goes on to explain, was that acts of 'irrational daring' came to be viewed as acts of 'courage and loyalty to one's party'. However exactly we interpret this, it is not a point about language, but about a change in moral values.

In a long and distinguished academic career (he was born in 1932), Donald Kagan has devoted even more years than Hornblower to the study of Thucydides and fifth-century history. The first volume of his four-part history of the Peloponnesian War appeared in 1969, the final volume almost twenty years later in 1987. This was followed in 2003 by a popular five- hundred-page abridgement of the whole: *The Peloponnesian War: Athens and Sparta in Savage Conflict, 431–404 BC*. Increasingly, over the last decade or so, his scholarly work has been interspersed with some decidedly conservative interventions into modern politics: most famously *While America Sleeps* (2000). Co-written with his son Frederick, this was a hawkish appeal for a substantial increase in military expenditure – and for the United States to assume 'the true burdens of world leadership'. At the same time, it was a tribute to Winston Churchill's analysis of British passivity in foreign policy in the 1920s and 1930s, *While England Slept* (later picked up by John F. Kennedy for his senior thesis at Harvard, *Why England Slept*).

In *Thucydides*, Kagan returns to the story of the Peloponnesian War, but now focusing specifically on the quality and reliability of Thucydides' account. Many of his well-known arguments about the war reappear here, occasionally with a new contemporary resonance. For Kagan, what is usually thought to be the disastrous Athenian attempt to invade distant Sicily was not as misguided as is assumed, or as Thucydides himself suggests. It was not an unwinnable war, in a country about which the Athenians had too little reliable intelligence. The problem lay with the military personnel: if they had replaced the elderly Nicias as commanding officer, then they might have had a chance of securing victory.

In general, Kagan's position runs against the standard view (derived directly or indirectly from Thucydides) that Athens was brought down by its increasing imperial ambitions and overweening aggression. In tune with his contributions to contemporary political debate, his argument is that Athens was not aggressive enough – and so, for that very reason, suffered its terrible defeat at the hands of the Spartan alliance. Much of this will be familiar to anyone who has read Kagan's other histories. What is new in this book is a direct attempt to evaluate Thucydides' *History* itself.

Kagan is full of praise for Thucydides' hard-headed analytical methods and for his accuracy. Even the lengthy speeches that throughout the work Thucydides puts into the mouths of the leading characters in the war (and that are often expressed in Greek that is peculiarly contorted even by Thucydides' standards) are given a relatively clean bill of health. This has been for decades one of the most controversial topics in assessing the reliability of Thucydides' work.

How could he possibly have recorded accurately words that were spoken maybe twenty years before he composed his *History*? Even if he was sometimes himself present and was presciently taking notes, he certainly includes some speeches that he could not possibly have heard – for he was exiled from Athens after less than ten years of the war (a punishment for his responsibility, as an Athenian commander, for a major military defeat). Did he have other, reliable sources; or does his absence mean that some, at least, of the speeches are effectively fictional creations of Thucydides himself?

Some modern readers of Thucydides have embraced the idea of fictional creation without too many qualms, stressing the role of the speeches in the literary construction of the *History*. Hornblower, who does not himself rule out the possibility that some speeches in Thucydides do roughly represent what was originally said, certainly sees how important they are in other ways. He emphasises, for example, how often the speeches as reported, however well argued they might seem, fail to convince their audience – as if to expose 'the limits to the power of rational debate' (much the same point as Euripides was making, at roughly the same time, in his tragedies).

Others see this question of authenticity as a major sticking point. As Kagan wrote more than thirty years ago (and he does not appear to have changed his mind): 'We cannot allow the possibility that a speech is invented in any important way without destroying the credibility of Thucydides.' Sure enough, he does not allow it, thus endorsing Thucydides' credibility. Writing of the leading Athenian politician in the early stages of the war, Kagan insists that 'all the speeches of Pericles are here taken to present reliably the ideas of the speaker, not the historian.' And the same goes, more or less, for the speeches that Thucydides puts into the mouths of many others of the leading participants in the conflict.

This whole debate has been clouded rather than clarified by Thucydides' own comments on the subject in the remarks he makes, at the very beginning of the *History*, about his own methods. He frankly admits that he did not hear all the speeches he includes in his work, and did not have perfect recall of others. So how did he proceed? Here again it is very hard to understand what Thucydides writes. In taking his optimistic line on the historical accuracy of the speeches, Kagan cites Crawley's translation of the key passage:

> My habit has been to make the speakers say what was in my
> opinion demanded of them by the various occasions, of course
> adhering as closely as possible to the general sense of what they
> really said.

Kagan relies particularly heavily on the last part of this sentence, whose 'clarity of ... intent', he writes, 'cannot be ignored'. But the Greek is much trickier and far less clear than Kagan admits. That 'of course' is a pure invention by Crawley. And others have argued that 'overall intention of what was actually said' would be a much better reflection of Thucydides' language than 'general sense' – and would convey a significantly different message about Thucydides' own claims for the 'accuracy' of the speeches.

Kagan is not, however, a slavish follower of Thucydides. In fact, although defending Thucydides' historical methods, he also wants to show that in many respects his interpretation of events was incorrect, or at least very partial. In Kagan's view, Thucydides was a revisionist historian who was writing to overturn the popular orthodox interpretation of the Peloponnesian War and its strategy. But brilliant though Thucydides was, for the most part, he argues, the popular interpretation was right and Thucydides' revisionist position wrong. In a sense, for Kagan, Thucydides' main claim to fame is that he was so scrupulous a historian that we can now use his own narrative against him, to reveal the fundamental weakness of his interpretations: as Kagan writes, 'the evidence ... for a divergent reading comes from his own account.'

One of the clearest cases where Thucydides takes a revisionist view is his judgement on the quality of the different Athenian war leaders. He was a tremendous admirer of Pericles, whom he saw as playing a clever waiting game at the start of the war, letting the Spartans invade Athenian territory for a month or so each year and wreak havoc on the countryside, but not engaging them in battle – merely retreating behind the city walls and staying put until the enemy left. It was an unprecedented plan in the history of Greek warfare (for, as Kagan rightly observes, in the Greek tradition 'willingness to fight, bravery, and steadfastness in battle were the essential characteristics of the free man and the citizen'). But Thucydides compares the strategy favourably with the rash military decisions of the successors of Pericles, who embarked on all kinds of incautious policies – such as the Sicilian expedition – that led to disaster. In Thucydides' view, Pericles was right.

But not in Kagan's. He calculates the financial cost of Pericles' wait-and-see policy against the total amount of Athens's monetary reserves, as we know them from Thucydides. His conclusion is that the Athenians could only have afforded to adopt that strategy for three years at the most – and that was certainly not long enough for the Spartans to have become demoralised (which was Pericles' aim) with their repeated, fruitless, annual invasions. Although it might have made sense on paper, 'the plan did not work'; far from being a stroke of cautious genius, as Thucydides thought, it was leading Athens to almost certain defeat.

It was hardly surprising then that before his death, from the great plague, the Athenians had turned against Pericles. In fact, toward the end of his *History*, Thucydides reports more explicitly than in his earlier books the popular view of the Periclean strategy: 'Some thought that Athens could hold out for a year, some for two, but no one for more than three years.' According to Kagan's economic calculations, popular opinion was right, and Pericles' apparently cautious policy – so admired by Thucydides and by many modern scholars – was dangerous in the extreme.

The most notorious successor to Pericles in the military leadership of Athens was a man named Cleon, vehemently attacked by Thucydides for his reckless, ill-informed, aggressive schemes, as well as his vulgar, nouveau riche image. Here too Kagan reverses Thucydides' judgement, showing repeatedly that Cleon's policy worked, despite Thucydides' opposition to it – and despite the fact that the only laugh to enter his rather humourless *History* is reported as a response (in apparent disbelief) to Cleon's bravado boast, not long after the death of Pericles, that he would capture a large party of Spartan soldiers, marooned on the island of Sphacteria off the western Peloponnese, within just twenty days.

In fact, Cleon did exactly that, as well as initiating a number of other policies either derided or left unmentioned by Thucydides (for example, a major reassessment – upward – of the financial contributions paid to the imperial fighting fund by Athens' allies). For Kagan, it was these initiatives of Cleon, rather than the cautious policies of Pericles, that nearly won the war for Athens.

It is perhaps a pity that Kagan found no time to reflect on the long history of these questions – especially the relative merits of Pericles and Cleon – in modern discussions of Thucydides and the Peloponnesian War. These issues erupted with particular intensity in 1850s Britain, when George Grote, an avowed democrat, historian, and banker, attempted to use the history of fifth-century Athens in his campaign for widening the democratic franchise in his own day. In the process, he was, like Kagan, drawn to rehabilitate Cleon – whom, following Thucydides' account, most classicists saw as a power-hungry demagogue, and clear proof of why democracy and universal franchise might be very dangerous to the political order. In one of the most virulent academic disputes of the nineteenth century, the brilliant but ultraconservative Cambridge classicist Richard Shilleto responded in 1851 to the sixth volume of Grote's *History of Greece* with a pamphlet entitled *Thucydides or Grote?* How could Grote, Shilleto asked, have impugned the impartiality of Thucydides by supporting the likes of Cleon? Is that what extending the franchise meant?

But it is not the shadow of the nineteenth century that hovers most threateningly over Kagan's *Thucydides*, but the shadow of very recent scholarship. This book is, for the most part, rooted in the work of the 1960s and 1970s, as is amply reflected in its footnotes (most of the 'keen readers' of Thucydides' text to whom Kagan refers are keen readers of a generation or two ago; most of his 'brilliant modern historians' were writing half a century ago). Occasionally he alludes darkly to up-to-the-minute 'literary' approaches to the *History*, those that treat Thucydides as a 'purely literary genius, free from the trammels of historical objectivity.' If these allusions refer to the dominant strand of research in Thucydides over the last thirty years or so – studies that stress above all the literary construction of his *History*, and its links to other genres, such as drama and poetry – then Kagan has hardly appreciated their point at all.

Many modern students of Thucydides have sought to understand better how he designed his story. Far from being unconcerned with questions of history, or treating Thucydides himself as a literary genius entirely outside a historical setting, they have tried to use modern theories of literary analysis to show (for example) how he constructed an image of historical objectivity within a late fifth-century setting. They have shown how the question of the function of the speeches in the *History* is more important, and more answerable, than the old problem about how authentic a record they were. And they have started to ask why – and with what effect – the language of the *History* is so impenetrable.

Emily Greenwood, for example, has stressed that part of the point of Thucydides' carefully scripted speeches (and his careful description of his method) is to raise questions about the very nature of 'truth' in the construction of history – whether that lies with the words spoken on the occasion or with the written words of the historian (however remote they might be from what was really said). She is suggesting that we need to see Thucydides' *History* as partly a work of theory, not simply a history of the war, but a reflection about how history is most truthfully told. And that is not far from the aims of Hornblower in the later part of his work. In fact one of the reasons why the two later volumes of his *Commentary* are more convincing than the first is the clear influence on them of modern theories of literary criticism and narrative.

Kagan is probably affected by these new literary trends more than he would like to admit. But for the most part, his *Thucydides* is an elegantly written, sometimes trenchant, summation of a long lifetime spent thinking about the Peloponnesian War and its historians. It goes back to many of the key Thucydidean issues of the last century, some of which continue to be relevant today. But it is not a Thucydides for tomorrow.

Review of Donald Kagan, *Thucydides: The Reinvention of History* (Viking, 2009); Simon Hornblower, *A Commentary on Thucydides, Volume III, Books 5.25–8.109* (Oxford University Press, 2008)

4

ALEXANDER: HOW GREAT?

In 51 BC, Marcus Tullius Cicero, who had reluctantly left his desk in Rome to become military governor of the province of Cilicia in southern Turkey, scored a minor victory against some local insurgents. As we know from his surviving letters, he was conscious that he was treading in the footsteps of a famous predecessor: 'For a few days,' he wrote to his friend Atticus, 'we were encamped in exactly the same place that Alexander occupied when he was fighting Darius at Issus' – hastily conceding that Alexander was in fact 'a rather better general than you or I.'

Whatever the irony in Cicero's remarks, almost any Roman, given the command of a brigade of troops and a glimpse of lands to the East, would soon dream of becoming Alexander the Great. In their fantasies at least, they stepped into the shoes of the young king of Macedon who, between 334 and 323 BC, had crossed into Asia, conquered the Persian Empire under King Darius III, and taken his army as far as the Punjab, some three thousand miles from home – before dying, on the return journey, in the city of Babylon, at the age of thirty-two, whether (as the official version had it) from a deadly fever or (as others insinuated) from poisoning or some alcohol-related condition.

Other Romans had a much better claim to be 'new Alexanders' than the normally desk-bound Cicero; and they made even more of the connection, with less sense of irony. Cicero's contemporary, Cnaeus Pompeius, has been eclipsed in the modern imagination by his rival

2. Pompey the Great, the Roman Alexander – with his quiff.

Julius Caesar, but as a young man he had achieved even more decisive victories over even more glamorous enemies than Caesar ever did. After conquests in Africa in the 80s BC, he returned to Rome to be hailed 'Magnus' (or 'Pompey the Great,' as he is still known), in direct imitation of Alexander. And as if to drive the point home, in his most famous surviving portrait statue (now in the Ny Carlsberg Glyptotek in Copenhagen), Pompeius is shown aping Alexander's distinctive hairstyle, with a rising 'quiff' (or *anastole* as the Greeks called it) brushed back from the centre of his forehead.

Julius Caesar was not to be entirely outdone. When he visited Alexandria, where Alexander's body had finally ended up (hijacked in its hearse on the way back from Babylon to Macedon and claimed for Egypt by one of Alexander's 'successors'), he made sure to make a pilgrimage to the tomb: one demented despot paying homage to another, as the Roman poet Lucan derided the stunt.

There were, nonetheless, divergent views on Alexander at Rome (as Lucan's sour account of the tomb visit hints). In one of the first known attempts at counterfactual history, Livy raised the question of who would have won if Alexander had decided to invade Italy. Predictably, Livy concluded that the Roman Empire would have proved as invincible against Alexander as it had against its other enemies. True, Alexander was a great general, but Rome at that period had many great generals and they were made of sterner stuff than the Persian king, with his 'women and eunuchs in tow,' who was by any reckoning 'an easy prey'.

Besides, from early on, Alexander showed signs of fatal weaknesses: witness the vanity, the obeisance he demanded from his followers, the vicious cruelty (he had a record of murdering erstwhile friends around his dinner table), and the infamous drinking. An invasion of Italy would have been a tougher test than the invasion of India, which 'he strolled through on a drunken revel with an intoxicated army.'

Even Cicero, in his more hard-headed moments, could see the problems in Alexander's career. In a now fragmentary passage of his treatise *On the State*, he seems to have quoted an anecdote that would turn up again, almost five hundred years later, in the pages of Saint Augustine. The story was that a petty pirate had been captured and brought before Alexander. What drove him, Alexander asked, to terrorise the seas with his pirate ship? 'The same thing as drives you to terrorise the whole world,' the man sharply replied. There were plenty of acts of terror he could have cited: the total massacres of the male population after the sieges at Tyre and Gaza; the mass killing of the local population in the Punjab; the razing of the royal palace at Persepolis, after (so it was said) one of Alexander's inebriated dinner parties.

The ambivalence of Alexander's Roman image is nicely captured in the well-known 'Alexander Mosaic,' a masterpiece composed of literally millions of tiny tesserae, which once decorated a floor in the 'House of the Faun', the grandest house in ancient Pompeii (and now in the Naples Archaeological Museum). Depicting a battle between an instantly recognisable Alexander (his hair is arranged with the characteristic quiff) and King Darius in his chariot, it has almost always been taken to be a Roman mosaic copy of an earlier Greek painting – on the basis of no good evidence, but on the old assumption that Roman artists tended to be derivative copyists rather than original creators.

It is a more puzzling composition than it might seem. Alexander is charging in on horseback from the left, and has just impaled an unfortunate Persian on his long spear (the famous Macedonian *sarissa*); Darius meanwhile, facing across from the right, is just about to flee

3. The face of the loser. In this detail from the Alexander Mosaic,
Darius looks across at his opponent, before turning in flight.

the scene, and indeed his charioteer has already wheeled the horses around, ready to gallop off. We can be in no doubt about who the victor is. But our attention is focused not so much on Alexander but on Darius, who towers above the battle, his arm outstretched in the direction of Alexander. Whoever was responsible for this composition wanted certainly to draw our attention to the victim in this famous struggle between the waning power of Persia and the rising power of Macedon – even to elicit sympathy for the losing side.

These debates have continued through the centuries. To be sure, new themes come and go. Recently there has been some highly charged political controversy focused on Alexander's 'Greekness'. Was he, as the government of the Former Yugoslav Republic Of Macedonia (FYROM) would have it, a Slav (and so an appropriate symbol of the Slavic FYROM, and a good name for Skopje airport)? Or was he a bona fide Greek (and so had nothing to do with the FYROM at all)?

The fruitlessness of this dispute is obvious: ancient national identity is a slippery concept; and the ethnic identity of the Macedonians is almost completely shrouded in myth. But that did not prevent several hundred academics, mostly classicists, from writing a letter to President Obama in 2009, in which they declared that Alexander was 'thoroughly and indisputably Greek' and asked him to intervene to 'clean up' the FYROM's historical errors. Obama's reply is not recorded. More recently, this controversy flared up once more when a huge kitschy thirty-ton statue, almost fifty feet tall, on top of a thirty-foot pedestal, was erected in the central square in Skopje. Judiciously called merely 'Warrior on Horseback', it is strikingly similar to the standard image of Alexander – with that quiff again.

And from time to time, some new evidence surfaces to stir the popular imagination. In the 1880s this came in the shape of the 'Alexander Sarcophagus' found in Lebanon, now in the Archaeology Museums in Istanbul. Dating to the end of the fourth century BC, and almost certainly the marble coffin of a junior monarch installed by Alexander himself, it depicts scenes of battles and hunting from Alexander's life – and it was made closer in date to his lifetime than any other detailed image of him that we now have. (All the surviving large-scale 'portraits' of him were made after his death, often long after, even if they were based on contemporary works, now lost.)

Still more impressive have been the discoveries since the 1970s at Vergina, near the royal palace of Macedon itself: in particular, the series of fourth-century-BC tombs, found largely undisturbed, and loaded with precious jewellery, gold and silver vessels, elaborate furniture, and wall paintings. Undermining any impression that the Macedonians were a 'barbarian' people in the popular sense of that word, they are very likely the tombs of members of the Macedonian royal house: not Alexander himself, of course, but perhaps of his father Phillip II (assassinated in 336 BC) and various other relatives who met equally nasty ends in the power struggles after his death. Even if he himself is missing, the objects these tombs contain take us about as close to Alexander as we are ever likely to get.

But, for the most part, the debates about Alexander, and the evidence on which they are based, have not changed very much over two millennia: the basic dilemma – for writers, film-makers, artists, and statesmen – is still whether Alexander is to be admired or deplored. For many, he has remained a positive example of a 'great general', heroically leading his army to victory in increasingly distant terrain. Napoleon was a famous admirer, and a striking relic of his admiration survives in a precious table he commissioned, which ended up in Buckingham Palace. Made of porcelain and gilded bronze, it features the head of Alexander at the centre of the tabletop, surrounded by a supporting cast of other military giants of the ancient world. For Alexander, the message was, read Napoleon.

Philip Freeman, to judge from his biography *Alexander the Great*, is another admirer, albeit a more guarded one. In his summing up, he concedes that we might not approve of 'Alexander's often brutal tactics,' but, he continues, 'every reasonable student of history must agree that he was one of the greatest military minds of all time.' The final sentence of the book insists that 'we can't help but admire a man who dared such great deeds.'

Others have not found it difficult to curb their admiration. Dante found a place for 'Alexander' (we assume he meant 'the Great') in the Seventh Circle of Hell, screaming in pain, up to his eyebrows in a river of boiling blood, spending eternity alongside such monsters as Attila the Hun and Dionysius the tyrant of Sicily. Many modern writers have followed him. A. B. Bosworth, for example, another doyen among historians of Alexander, once summarised Alexander's career bleakly: 'He spent much of his time killing and directing killing, and, arguably, killing was what he did best'. And I myself, more flippantly, once described him as a 'drunken juvenile thug' whom it was difficult to imagine chosen by any modern country as its national symbol.

These critiques are dismissed as anachronistic value judgements by Freeman and by Pierre Briant, in his *Alexander the Great and His Empire*: Bosworth's is 'a sweeping judgement in harmony with our current values but not with those of Alexander's time' observes Briant; my own quip is 'much too simplistic,' notes Freeman. 'He was a man of his own violent times, no better or worse in his actions than Caesar or Hannibal.' It is, of course, a general rule that historians accuse each other of making anachronistic value judgements only when they do not share the judgement concerned. But in this case, as we have seen, it is hardly anachronistic at all. Already in the time of Caesar, some Romans could paint Alexander as no better than a pirate on a grand scale.

Closely related to the basic issue of how far we can admire Alexander's career is the question of what he was attempting to do. If we feel uneasy about his methods, then what about his aims? Here again we find wildly diverging views. The old idea, fitting neatly with some of the slogans of British nineteenth-century imperialism, was that Alexander had a 'civilising mission,' a high-minded project to bring the lofty ideals of Hellenic culture to the benighted East. In fact, this was not so far from the underlying theme of Oliver Stone's disastrous 2004 movie *Alexander* (for which Oxford historian Robin Lane Fox was historical consultant and, notoriously, an 'extra' in the cavalry charge); Stone's Alexander was a dreamy, sexually troubled visionary – but a visionary nonetheless.

Others too have seen all kinds of psychological underpinnings. One strand of scholarship stresses his compulsive and unsatisfiable 'yearning' or 'desire' (or *pothos*, to use the Greek term of Arrian – a Roman senator of Greek extraction – writing a history of the *Campaigns of Alexander*, in the mid second century AD). Another strand suggests a rather more literary sense of identification with the heroes of Homer's *Iliad*. On this reconstruction, Alexander is said to have seen himself as the new Achilles and, along with his friend Hephaestion as the new Patroclus, to have been replaying the Trojan War (on one occasion cruelly reworking the scene in the *Iliad* in which Achilles drags the body of the dead Hector from his chariot around the walls of Troy – though in Alexander's case the victim was, for a little while at least, still alive).

A rather more down-to-earth view would see him starting out as simply a follower of his father, who at the time of his assassination had already launched a limited series of military operations in Asia Minor; success went to Alexander's head and he simply didn't know where to stop. Or, to follow Ian Worthington's theory in *Philip II of Macedonia*, after modest beginnings, Alexander was driven to continue in his campaign of conquest right up to the Punjab specifically to outdo his father in every possible way (more psychology here: Worthington writes that Alexander suffered from a 'paranoia that grew from his feelings of marginalisation in the later years of Philip's reign').

Modern historians of Alexander find plenty to disagree about; but their arguments appear more intense than they really are, because – underneath all the superficial divergence and the conflicting value judgements – they are mostly trying to answer the same traditional range of questions, on the basis of the same approach to the same evidence. This point was powerfully made more than a decade ago in the *London Review of Books* by James Davidson, reviewing a collection of essays on Alexander edited by Bosworth and E. J. Baynham. It is a review that has become famous among ancient historians for calling attention to the very sorry state of the professional 'Alexander industry.' While most fields of classical studies, Davidson noted, had engaged with the new theoretical developments of the second half of the twentieth century, from narratology to gender studies, 'in Alexanderland scholarship remains largely untouched by the influences which have transformed history and classics since 1945.'

Specialists in this tiny period of ancient history (the campaigns lasted just over ten years) were still committed to reconstructing 'what really happened', on the basis of the vivid but deeply unreliable literary sources that have survived (Arrian's seven books are usually considered the 'best' evidence, but there is plenty of material also in Plutarch's *Life of Alexander* and Diodorus Siculus' *Library of History*, to name just two). This project, Davidson argued, was even more flawed than other attempts to reconstruct 'how it really was' in the ancient world, because of the particular nature of the surviving evidence. All the narrative accounts of Alexander's conquests that we have were written hundreds of years after his death, and the historian's project has usually been to identify the passages within them that might derive from some reliable, but lost, contemporary account – whether the *Journals* of Alexander's secretary, which were supposed to have given an account of his final 'illness', or the history of the period written by Ptolemy, the man who was responsible for hijacking Alexander's corpse and installing it in the capital of his own realm, Alexandria.

The problem is, Davidson insisted, that – even if we could hope to identify which surviving sections came from which lost source – we cannot assume (as classicists like to do) that what is lost was necessarily reliable. Some of the writing was almost certainly forgery (the *Journals* are a good candidate for being at least a pastiche); some of it, so far as we can tell from critics in the ancient world itself, was simply very bad history. ('The lost histories ... weren't mislaid,' as Davidson rightly points out, 'they were consigned to oblivion.') The result is that the historical edifice we know as 'Alexander's career' is extremely flimsy and modern scholars have been attempting to squeeze it for answers to questions that it could never deliver – not only what motivated him, but did he really love his wife Roxane, or believe that he was the son of the god Amun? This is not a game of history, but of smoke and mirrors.

Briant, in an appendix on the state of scholarship on Alexander, generously acknowledges that some of Davidson's points 'have hit home'. But if so, these books show only a faint trace of it. Freeman's *Alexander the Great* is a workmanlike biography of the traditional type, sometimes enjoyable, sometimes a bit too breezy ('Events in the field were looking up for the Macedonians'). It is full of remarks on feelings, emotions and character that are guesswork at best ('Alexander could not believe his luck'; 'One might wonder why he suddenly decided to marry a Bactrian woman at this point in his life. The answer is probably a mixture of politics and passion'). And it reminds us, with its impenetrable battle strategies and complex cast of characters (there are too many people with the same name), just how messy and difficult the Alexander story is, even in its simplified semi-fictional version.

Sometimes modern historians think we can get further by taking a sideways look at the career of Alexander. Worthington focuses on Philip II, attempting to see how far the achievement of the more famous son was already presaged by that of his father. It is a learned account, but (perhaps inevitably) rather too full of armchair generalship to make an easy read. Like many scholars, Worthington stands in awe of Philip's invention of the *sarissa*, his supposedly devastating new piece of military hardware. But it was only an extra-long spear, so it is hard to see why Philip's enemies didn't just copy it. And you would never guess from his detailed description, complete with map, of Philip's battle tactics in 338 BC against a Greek coalition at Chaeronea ('Phase II: Philip retreats, his centre and left advancing; Athenians, Centre and Boeotians advance to left front,' etc.) that this was all based on just a few confusing, and not wholly, compatible lines in a handful of much later sources.

James Romm, in *Ghost on the Throne*, moves in the other chronological direction, to examine the aftermath of the death of Alexander, and the conflicts between his various generals that led to the carve-up of the Greek world and the creation of the different Hellenistic dynasties (the Ptolemies, Antigonids, Seleucids, etc.), which in turn fell to the Romans. Romm is certainly right to see this period as more crucial, in geopolitical effects, than the conquests of Alexander. But despite some nice turns of phrase, he struggles to make the story particularly engaging – with its complex power-brokering among the rival generals, the series of dynastic murders in the family of Alexander, and the fickle manoeuvring among the unappealing leaders of Athens's expiring democracy, who were looking for a chance to reclaim some influence.

Potentially the most significant book is Briant's *Alexander the Great*, because Briant is one of the world's leading authorities on the Persian (Achaemenid) Empire. The promise of this book is that we might be able to see Alexander differently if we included the Persian evidence. Insights there are, but less significant ones than you would hope. There are two main problems. First, Briant writes from the professorial pulpit, slightly hectoring in tone about what historians should or should not do, and telegraphic in style (there are only 144 small pages of large print, so it is 'a short introduction' as the subtitle says); and he makes few concessions to anyone who, for example, may not already know the duties of a 'satrap'. On several occasions he refers to documents that are supposed to be particularly 'important' or 'useful', but he rarely explains to the outsider what the documents are and what impact exactly their content has on the history of the period.

I was baffled by the 'extremely important' Aramaic documents from Bactria, for instance, and how exactly the '18 wooden sticks recording debts, all from year 3 of Darius' throw light on the transition from Achaemenid to Macedonian rule. But second, and more disappointing, when Briant does spell out more clearly the contribution of the Persian documents to our understanding, it often turns out to be surprisingly little. There are, as he concedes, no 'continuous accounts' from Persian writers; but even the cuneiform tablets deliver less than he promises. He refers, for example, to a 'well-known Babylonian tablet' that 'gives us a detailed image' of the period in 331 BC between the Battle of Arbela (or Gaugamela) and Alexander's entry into Babylon. Detailed image? So far as I can see, it is an astronomical diary that refers in passing to 'panic breaking out in the camp of Darius' and to 'the severe defeat of the Persian troops' and the 'king's troops deserting', followed by the entry into Babylon of 'the king of the world'. A precious glimpse into a Persian point of view maybe, but hardly enough to rewrite history.

So what should we do with the Alexander story? Davidson argued that the 'blind spot' among modern historians of Alexander was 'love', and he urged that we turn our attention to the homoeroticism of the Macedonian court and its cult of the body. I would suggest a more prosaic blind spot: namely, Rome. Roman writers did not merely debate the character of Alexander, they did not merely take him as model, they more or less invented the 'Alexander' that we now know – as Diana Spencer came close to arguing in her excellent book *The Roman Alexander* (2002). In fact, the first attested use of the title 'Alexander the Great' is in a Roman comedy by Plautus, in the early second century BC, about 150 years after Alexander's death. I very much doubt that Plautus himself dreamed up the term, but it may well have been a Roman coinage; there is certainly nothing whatever to suggest that Alexander's contemporaries or immediate successors in Greece ever called him 'Alexander ho Megas'. In a sense, 'Alexander the Great' is as much a Roman creation as 'Pompey the Great' was.

Even more significant is the character and the cultural background of the surviving ancient accounts of Alexander's life. It is repeatedly said that these accounts were all written much later than the events they described. True; but more to the point is the fact that they were all written under the Roman Empire against the background of Roman imperialism. Diodorus Siculus, whose account is the earliest to survive, was writing in the late first century BC. Arrian, now the most favoured source, was born in the 80s AD in the city of Nicomedia (in modern Turkey), and undertook a Roman political career, becoming consul in the 120s, and later serving as governor of Cappadocia. Of course these Roman authors did not create the story of Alexander; and of course they depended on the writings of Alexander's contemporaries, however good, or bad, they may have been. But they are bound to have seen this story through a Roman filter, to have interpreted and adjusted what they read in the light of the versions of conquest and imperial expansion that were characteristic of their own political age.

Re-reading Arrian's *Campaigns of Alexander*, I was repeatedly struck by its Roman resonances. Occasionally Arrian himself draws an explicit comparison between Roman and Macedonian systems. But more often the implied comparisons do not need spelling out. The anxieties about Alexander's claim to be a god (or at least son of a god) show obvious similarities with Roman anxieties about the divine or semi-divine status of their own emperors. The stress placed on Alexander's use of foreign troops and on the ethnic mix of his court recall many aspects of Roman imperial practice (such as the use of provincial auxiliaries in the Roman army or the incorporation of members of the conquered elites – such as Arrian himself – into the imperial administration).

Perhaps the most striking overlap comes with the reaction of Alexander to the death of his friend Hephaestion. 'Some say', writes Arrian, 'that for most of that day … Alexander mourned and wept and refused to leave until his Companions carried him off by force.' Soon after, he established a cult to Hephaestion as a 'hero'. This is almost exactly what the Roman Emperor Hadrian (under whom Arrian served) is said to have done at the death of his own favourite, Antinous. Maybe

Hadrian was aping Alexander. Much more likely Arrian was modelling his own picture of Alexander on the behaviour of the emperor under whom he served.

I suspect that the change Davidson wanted in 'Alexanderland' will come only when we are prepared to realise that it is as much a Roman country as a Greek one. Maybe at the same time, we will at last be able to think of the Alexander mosaic from Pompeii as a proud Roman creation, rather than (as a caption in Romm's new edition of Arrian's *Campaigns* has it) 'copied from a Greek painting done within a few decades of the battle, perhaps based on eyewitness accounts.'

Review of Philip Freeman, *Alexander the Great* (Simon and Schuster, 2011); James Romm (ed), translated from the Greek by Pamela Mensch, *The Landmark Arrian: The Campaigns of Alexander* (Pantheon, 2010); Pierre Briant, translated from French by Amélie Kuhrt, *Alexander the Great and his Empire: A Short Introduction* (Princeton University Press, 2010); Ian Worthington, *Philip II of Macedonia* (Yale University Press, 2008); James Romm, *Ghost on the Throne: The Death of Alexander the Great and the War for Crown and Empire* (Knopf, 2011)

5

WHAT MADE THE GREEKS LAUGH?

In the third century BC, when Roman ambassadors were negotiating with the Greek city of Tarentum, an ill-judged laugh put paid to any hope of peace. Ancient writers disagree about the exact cause of the mirth, but they agree that Greek laughter was the final straw in driving the Romans to war.

One account points the finger at the bad Greek of the leading Roman ambassador, Postumius. It was so ungrammatical and strangely accented that the Tarentines could not conceal their amusement. The historian Cassius Dio, by contrast, laid the blame on the Romans' national dress. 'So far from receiving them decently', he wrote, 'the Tarentines laughed at the Roman toga among other things. It was the city garb, which we use in the Forum. And the envoys had put this on, whether to make a suitably dignified impression or out of fear – thinking that it would make the Tarentines respect them. But in fact groups of revellers jeered at them.' One of these revellers, he goes on, even went so far as 'to bend down and shit' all over the offending garment. If true, this may also have contributed to the Roman outrage. Yet it is the laughter that Postumius emphasised in his menacing, and prophetic, reply. 'Laugh, laugh while you can. For you'll be weeping a long time when you wash this garment clean with your blood.'

Despite the menace, this story has an immediate appeal. It offers a rare glimpse of how the pompous, toga-clad Romans could appear to their fellow inhabitants of the ancient Mediterranean; and a rare confirmation that the billowing, cumbersome wrap-around toga could look as comic to the Greeks of South Italy as it does to us. But at the same time the story combines some of the key ingredients of ancient laughter: power, ethnicity and the nagging sense that those who mocked their enemies would soon find themselves laughed at. It was, in fact, a firm rule of ancient 'gelastics' – to borrow a term (from the Greek *gelan*, to laugh) from Stephen Halliwell's weighty study of Greek laughter – that the joker was never far from being the butt of his own jokes. The Latin adjective *ridiculus*, for example, referred both to something that was laughable ('ridiculous' in our sense) and to something or someone who actively made people laugh.

Laughter was always a favourite device of ancient monarchs and tyrants, as well as being a weapon used against them. The good king, of course, knew how to take a joke. The tolerance of the Emperor Augustus in the face of quips and banter of all sorts was still being celebrated four centuries after his death. One of the most famous one-liners of the ancient world, with an afterlife that stretches into the twentieth century (it gets retold, with a different cast of characters but the same punchline, both in Freud and in Iris Murdoch's *The Sea, The Sea*), was a joking insinuation about Augustus' paternity. Spotting, so the story goes, a man from the provinces who looked much like himself, the emperor asked if the man's mother had ever worked in the palace. 'No', came the reply, 'but my father did.' Augustus wisely did no more than grin and bear it.

Tyrants, by contrast, did not take kindly to jokes at their own expense, even if they enjoyed laughing at their subjects. Sulla, the murderous dictator of the first century BC, was a well-known *philogelos* ('laughter-lover'), while schoolboy practical jokes were among the techniques of humiliation employed by the despot Elagabalus. He is said to have had fun, for example, seating his dinner guests on inflatable cushions, and then seeing them disappear under the table as the air was gradually let out. But the defining mark of ancient autocrats (and a sign of power gone – hilariously – mad) was their attempt to control laughter. Some tried to ban it (as Caligula did, as part of the public mourning on the death of his sister). Others imposed it on their unfortunate subordinates at the most inappropriate moments. Caligula, again, had a knack for turning this into exquisite torture: he is said to have forced an old man to watch the execution of his son one morning and, that evening, to have invited the man to dinner and insisted that he laugh and joke. Why, asks the philosopher Seneca, did the victim go along with all this? Answer: he had another son.

Ethnicity, too, was good for a laugh, as the story of the Tarentines and the toga shows. Plenty more examples can be found in the only joke book to have survived from the ancient world. Known as the *Philogelos*, this is a composite collection of 260 or so gags in Greek probably put together in the fourth century AD but including – as such collections often do – some that go back many years earlier. It is a moot point whether the *Philogelos* offers a window on to the world of ancient popular laughter (the kind of book you took to the barber's shop, as one antiquarian Byzantine commentary has been taken to imply), or whether it is, more likely, an encyclopedic compilation by some late imperial academic. Either way, here we find jokes about doctors, men with bad breath, eunuchs, barbers, men with hernias, bald men, shady fortune-tellers, and more of the colourful (mostly male) characters of ancient life.

Pride of place in the *Philogelos* goes to the 'egg-heads', who are the subject of almost half the jokes for their literal-minded scholasticism ('An egg-head doctor was seeing a patient. "Doctor", he said, "when I get up in the morning I feel dizzy for 20 minutes." "Get up 20 minutes later, then."'). After the 'egg-heads', various ethnic jokes come a close second. In a series of gags reminiscent of modern Irish or Polish jokes, the residents of three Greek towns – Abdera, Kyme and Sidon – are ridiculed for their 'how many Abderites does it take to change a light bulb?' style of stupidity. Why these three places in particular, we have no idea. But their inhabitants are portrayed as being as literal-minded as the egg-heads, and even more obtuse. 'An Abderite saw a eunuch talking to a woman and asked if she was his wife. When he replied that eunuchs can't have wives, the Abderite asked, "So is she your daughter then?" And there are many others on predictably similar lines.

The most puzzling aspect of the jokes in the *Philogelos* is the fact that so many of them still seem vaguely funny. Across two millennia, their hit-rate for raising a smile is better than that of most modern joke books. And unlike the impenetrably obscure cartoons in nineteenth-century editions of *Punch*, these seem to speak our own comic language. In fact, a few years ago, the stand-up comedian Jim Bowen managed to get a good laugh out of twenty-first-century audiences with a show entirely based on jokes from the *Philogelos* (including one he claims – a little generously – to be a direct ancestor of Monty Python's 'Dead Parrot' sketch).

Why do they seem so modern? In the case of Jim Bowen's performance, careful translation and selection had something to do with it (I doubt that contemporary audiences would split their sides at the one about the crucified athlete who looked as if he was flying instead of running). There is also very little background knowledge required to see the point of these stories, in contrast to the precisely topical references that underlie so many *Punch* cartoons. Not to mention the fact that some of Bowen's audience were no doubt laughing at the sheer incongruity of listening to a modern comic telling 2,000-year-old gags, good or bad.

But there is more to it than that. It is not, I suspect, much to do with supposedly 'universal' topics of humour (though death and mistaken identity bulked large then as now). It is more a question of a direct legacy from the ancient world to our own, modern, traditions of laughter. Anyone who has been a parent, or has watched parents with their children, will know that human beings learn how to laugh, and what to laugh at (clowns OK, the disabled not). On a grander scale, it is – in large part at least – from the Renaissance tradition of joking that modern Western culture itself has learned how to laugh at 'jokes'; and that tradition looked straight back to antiquity. One of the favourite gags in Renaissance joke books was the 'No-but-my-father-did' quip about paternity, while the legendary Cambridge classicist Richard Porson is supposed to have claimed that most of the jokes in the famous eighteenth-century joke book *Joe Miller's Jests* could be traced back to the *Philogelos*. We can still laugh at these ancient jokes, in other words, because it is from them that we have learned what 'laughing at jokes' is.

This is not to say, of course, that all the coordinates of ancient laughter map directly on to our own. Far from it. Even in the *Philogelos* a few of the jokes remain totally baffling (though perhaps they are just bad jokes). But, more generally, Greeks and Romans could laugh at different things (the blind, for example – though rarely, unlike us, the deaf); and they could laugh, and provoke laughter, on different occasions to gain different ends. Ridicule was a standard weapon in the ancient courtroom, as it is only rarely in our own. Cicero, antiquity's greatest orator, was also by repute its greatest joker; far too funny for his own good, some sober citizens thought.

There are some particular puzzles, too, ancient comedy foremost among them. There may be little doubt that the Athenian audience laughed heartily at the plays of Aristophanes, as we can still. But very few modern readers have been able to find much to laugh at in the hugely successful comedies of the fourth-century dramatist Menander, formulaic and moralising as they were. Are we missing the joke? Or were they simply not funny in that laugh-out-loud sense? Discussing the plays in *Greek Laughter*, Stephen Halliwell offers a possible solution. Conceding that 'Menandrian humour, in the broadest sense of the term, is resistant to confident diagnosis' (that is, we don't know if, or how, it is funny), he neatly turns the problem on its head. They are not intended to raise laughs; rather 'they are actually in part *about* laughter'. Their complicated 'comic' plots, and the contrasts set up within them between characters we might want to laugh at and those we want to laugh with, must prompt the audience or reader to reflect on the very conditions that make laughter possible or impossible, socially acceptable or unacceptable. For Halliwell, in other words, Menander's 'comedy' functions as a dramatic essay on the fundamental principles of Greek gelastics.

On other occasions, it is not always immediately clear how or why the ancients ranked things as they did, on the scale between faintly amusing and very funny indeed. Halliwell mentions in passing a series of anecdotes that tell of famous characters from antiquity who laughed so much that they died. Zeuxis, the famous fourth-century Greek painter, is one. He collapsed, it is said, after looking at his own painting of an elderly woman. The philosopher Chrysippus and the dramatist Philemon, a contemporary of Menander, are others. Both of these were finished off, as a similar story in each case relates, after they had seen an ass eating some figs that had been prepared for their own meal. They told their servants to give the animal some wine as well – and died laughing at the sight.

The conceit of death by laughter is a curious one and not restricted to the ancient world. Anthony Trollope, for example, is reputed to have 'corpsed' during a reading of F. Anstey's comic novel *Vice Versa*. But what was it about these particular sights (or *Vice Versa*, for that matter) that proved so devastatingly funny? In the case of Zeuxis, it is not hard to detect a well-known strain of ancient misogyny. In the other cases, it is presumably the confusion of categories between animal and human that produces the laughter – as we can see in other such stories from antiquity.

For a similar confusion underlies the story of one determined Roman 'agelast' ('non-laugher'), the elder Marcus Crassus, who is reputed to have cracked up just once in his lifetime. It was after he had seen a donkey eating thistles. 'Thistles are like lettuce to the lips of a donkey', he mused (quoting a well-known ancient proverb) – and laughed. There is something reminiscent here of the laughter provoked by the old-fashioned chimpanzees' tea parties, once hosted by traditional zoos (and enjoyed for generations, until they fell victim to modern squeamishness about animal performance and display). Ancient laughter, too, it seems, operated on the boundaries between human and other species. Highlighting the attempts at boundary crossing, it both challenged and reaffirmed the division between man and animal.

Halliwell insists that one distinguishing feature of ancient gelastic culture is the central role of laughter in a wide range of ancient philo-sophical, cultural and literary theory. In the ancient academy, unlike the modern, philosophers and theorists were expected to have a view about laughter, its function and meaning. This is Halliwell's primary interest.

His book offers a wide survey of Greek laughter from Homer to the early Christians (an increasingly gloomy crowd, capable of seeing laughter as the work of the Devil), and the introduction is quite the best brief overview of the role of laughter in any historical period that I have ever read. But *Greek Laughter* is not really intended for those who want to discover what the Greeks found funny or laughed at. There is, significantly, no discussion of the *Philogelos* and no entry for 'jokes' in the index. The main focus is on laughter as it appears within, and is explored by, Greek literary and philosophical texts.

In those terms, some of his discussions are brilliant. He gives a clear and cautious account of the views of Aristotle – a useful antidote to some of the wilder attempts to fill the gap caused by the notorious loss of Aristotle's treatise on comedy. But the highlight is his discus-sion of Democritus, the fifth-century philosopher and atomist, renowned as antiquity's most inveterate laugher, and the subject of a marvellous late seventeenth-century painting by Antoine Coypel, which decorates the cover of the book. Here the 'laughing philosopher' adopts a wide grin, while pointing his bony finger at the viewer. It is a slightly unnerving combination of jollity and threat.

The most revealing ancient discussion of Democritus' laughing

4. Antoine Coypel's image of Democritus 'the laughing
philosopher' – in seventeenth-century guise.

habit is found in an epistolary novel of Roman date, included among the
so-called *Letters of Hippocrates* – a collection ascribed to the legendary
founding father of Greek medicine, but in fact written centuries
after his death. The fictional exchanges in this novel tell the story of
Hippocrates' encounter with Democritus. In the philosopher's home
city, his compatriots had become concerned at the way he laughed
at everything he came across (from funerals to political success) and
concluded that he must be mad. So they summoned the most famous
doctor in the world to cure him. When Hippocrates arrived, however,
he soon discovered that Democritus was saner than his fellow citizens.
For he alone had recognised the absurdity of human existence, and
was therefore entirely justified in laughing at it.

Under Halliwell's detailed scrutiny, this epistolary novel turns
out to be much more than a stereotypical tale of misapprehension
righted, or of a madman revealed to be sane. How far, he asks, should
we see the story of Democritus as a Greek equivalent of the kind of
'existential absurdity' now more familiar from Samuel Beckett or

Albert Camus? Again, as with his analysis of Menander, he argues that the text raises fundamental questions about laughter. The debates staged between Hippocrates and Democritus amount to a series of reflections on just how far a completely absurdist position is possible to sustain. Democritus' fellow citizens take him to be laughing at literally everything; and, more philosophically, Hippocrates wonders at one point whether his patient has glimpsed (as Halliwell puts it) 'a cosmic absurdity at the heart of infinity'. Yet, in the end, that is not the position that Democritus adopts. For he regards as 'exempt from mockery' the position of the sage, who is able to perceive the general absurdity of the world. Democritus does not, in other words, laugh at himself, or at his own theorising.

What Halliwell does not stress, however, is that Democritus' home city is none other than Abdera – the town in Thrace whose people were the butt of so many jokes in the *Philogelos*. Indeed, in a footnote, he briefly dismisses the idea 'that Democritean laughter itself spawned the proverbial stupidity of the Abderites'. But those interested in the practice as much as the theory of ancient laughter will surely not dismiss the connection so quickly. For it was not just a question of a 'laughing philosopher' or of dumb citizens who didn't know what a eunuch was. Cicero, too, could use the name of the town as shorthand for a topsy-turvy mess: 'It's all Abdera here', he writes of Rome. Whatever the original reason, by the first century BC, 'Abdera' (like modern Tunbridge Wells, perhaps, though with rather different associations) had become one of those names that could be guaranteed to get the ancients laughing.

Review of Stephen Halliwell, *Greek Laughter: A study of cultural psychology from Homer to early Christianity* (Cambridge University Press, 2008)

Section Two

HEROES & VILLAINS OF EARLY ROME

According to legend Rome was founded in (what we call) 753 BC. We don't have any contemporary Roman literature, in large quantities, until the second century BC – although there are plenty of later Roman accounts looking back to the city's origins, elaborating the stories of Romulus and Remus, the Rape of the Sabine Women, and all kinds of (frankly unbelievable) deeds of heroism by self-sacrificing noble Romans.

One big question about early Roman history is how far those stories are founded on fact. And if many of them are more myth than history (as most people now believe), then how can we now tell the story of the early centuries of Roman history, before the city became the vast marble metropolis, and cosmopolitan capital of the empire? What was Rome really like, in other words, when it was still 'on the way up'?

This section starts (Chapter 6) by going right back to Romulus and Remus, and the puzzling question of why Rome had not just one but two founders; and, more than that, why one of them (Romulus) was supposed to have murdered the other (Remus). When was that story first told? Who invented the tale of fratricidal struggle, and why? This brings us face to face with a whole series of deductions and speculations (some inspired, some decidedly dodgy) about the culture of early Rome, and in particular about its lost traditions of public drama, in which the story of the unfortunate Remus may have taken shape. For Rome was almost certainly just as 'theatrical' a society as ancient Athens – and it used the stage to present shared myths, and to debate shared problems and concerns. But, in the Roman case, very few of the key plays actually survive, and they have to be reconstructed, almost wholesale, out of a few snatches of text, the occasional quotation in later authors, and maybe an early illustration or two. This is an adventurous business and it can open our eyes to a side of ancient Rome that we don't often see. But it's a risky business too (the classical equivalent of the virtuoso trapeze act) and it may not be all that far from the kind of imaginative reconstruction that we saw at Arthur Evans's 'prehistoric' Palace at Knossos (Chapter 1).

The final chapter in this section wonders how we might fill another gap in our surviving evidence for early Rome: that is, the point of view of the ordinary Roman. Almost all the Roman writing that we have comes from the pen of the wealthy and privileged, which leaves us wondering about what the other Romans made of the city's history and politics. What did the poor think of Rome's victories and massacres? How did they react when a cabal of the rich assassinated Julius Caesar in the name of (their own) 'Liberty'? Chapter 10 shows how clever detective work can help to unearth some of the views, heroes and political slogans of the Roman underclass.

I am not meaning by this that the more traditional characters of Roman Republican history have lost their allure. Far from it. Chapter 7 explores the leading figures in the great war between Rome and Hannibal (and finds the origin of the British 'Fabian Society' way back in ancient Rome). It reflects too on how the Roman historian Livy made a story out of this conflict – raising the question of quite how good an historian Livy was, and delivering a dose of scepticism on that famous boy-scoutish tale of Hannibal blasting a way through the Alps by pouring vinegar onto the frozen rocks.

Chapters 8 and 9 turn to one of the larger-than-life characters of the first century BC, Marcus Tullius Cicero: Rome's most famous orator, a self-advertising politician and an extraordinarily prolific writer (many volumes of his private letters, philosophical treatises, speeches, and a bit of dreadful doggerel poetry still survive). We probably know more about Cicero than about any other ancient Roman who ever lived (though, even so, as Chapter 8 insists, it proves very hard now to write a straight 'biography' of him); and we still find his words and the issues he raised all around us – in some unexpected places. His catchphrases have been quoted by modern political activists from John F. Kennedy to radical Hungarian demonstrators in 2012; and his presence lurks (or it ought to) behind our own discussions on all kinds of topics from art theft to the prevention of terrorism. Cicero was at one point driven into exile, precisely because – in the interests, he claimed, of homeland security – he executed a group of presumed Roman terrorists, without trial or due process. One of classical history's best warning lessons.

6

WHO WANTED REMUS DEAD?

Just next door to the imperial palace in Rome stood a small wooden hut, said by the Romans to be the house of Romulus, the sole surviving trace of Rome's very first settlement, built (if you follow the traditional dating) somewhere in the eighth century BC. Who really made this hut (some pious antiquarian, a Roman entrepreneur with an eye on the ancient tourist trade, or Romulus himself), we do not know. But it was lovingly (or cynically) cared for until the fourth century AD at least, as a memorial of the city's founder. For all who passed by, it would have prompted thoughts of Rome's origins, of the primitive village that had become the capital of the world, and of the baby Romulus, son of the god Mars by a disinherited princess, cast out by his wicked uncle, found and suckled by a wolf, then raised by herdsmen until he was old enough to overthrow his uncle and found his own city, Rome.

At the same time, Romulus must have prompted thoughts of his twin brother Remus. According to the familiar story (as told, with slight variations, by Livy and others), Remus was Romulus' partner until the very moment that the new city was to be established; the brothers at that point each took up different positions to watch for heavenly signs that would authorise their foundation; Romulus claimed his signs the stronger (he saw twelve vultures, Remus only six) and started to build fortifications; in jealousy, Remus jumped over Romulus' ditch and was immediately killed either by Romulus himself or by one of his men; 'so perish all who cross my walls', as Livy puts into the mouth of Romulus, a slogan that was no doubt used to justify many of the appalling acts of fratricide that were to mark Roman history over the next thousand years. Other versions, though, seem to have given different stories of this partnership: that, for a time, the twins ruled the new city together, until Romulus became tyrannical and murdered his brother; or even that Remus outlived Romulus.

One of the aims of T. P. Wiseman's *Remus: A Roman myth* is to focus attention back on to the murdered twin as a central element in Rome's foundation story (for Romans, in fact, who regularly spoke of 'Remus et Romulus', in that order, he was the prior element). Wiseman has three main questions. Why did this particular foundation legend involve twins at all? Why was Remus called Remus? And why, in the canonical tale, did he get murdered? Why, in other words, did the Romans invent the story of a twin founder only to kill him off before the foundation was done? What kind of community was it that made its founder's first act in power the callous destruction of his brother and helpmate?

Many modern historians have refused to be interested in Remus' story, its oddities, or what those oddities meant for Rome's view of its own past. This is not merely a question of the standard index entry 'Remus, see Romulus'. It is more a question of an almost wilful lack of concern for the implications of the myth. Even Arnaldo Momigliano could write (with an uncharacteristic lapse of curiosity) that 'the Romans took in their stride the idea that they ... had a fratricide in the foundation ritual of their city'. But Wiseman reserves his sharpest attacks for those of his predecessors who have actually tried to make sense of Remus and his death. Much of the first half of the book is concerned with a demolition, first of the theories of comparative Indo-Europeanists (for whom Remus is the cosmic primal twin, character-istic of creation myths in most early Indo-European cultures), followed by an elegant exposure of the inadequacies of almost every other expla-nation ever ventured. Hermann Strasburger's ingenious notion, for example, that the story of Remus and Romulus is so unflattering to the Romans (the rape of the Sabine women is the next problematic episode in the tale) that it can only have been invented by Rome's enemies, fails to explain why the Romans themselves took it up so enthusi-astically. Theodor Mommsen's idea that the twin founders in some way represent the institution of the Roman consulship (always a dual magistracy) hardly accommodates the murder of one of the twins; the

5. The so-called 'Bolsena Mirror'. Engraved on the reverse is
what appears to be an early image of the wolf and twins.

point of the consulship, after all, was that both consuls ruled together,
not that one speedily disposed of the other, to govern Rome alone.

Wiseman insists that you cannot possibly understand the myth
without understanding how, when and why it was first invented. And
so starts his own elaborate reconstruction. He first reviews every
surviving reference to the legend, visual and literary, and concludes
that (unlike Romulus) Remus did not emerge until the third century
BC, hundreds of years after the foundation of the city: our familiar
double act of 'Romulus 'n' Remus' was originally just 'Romulus'. This
argument alone is not without its difficulties. It involves, for example,
dismissing the evidence of a famous fourth-century engraved mirror
from Bolsena: this mirror depicts a scene that to any casual observer
would be instantly recognisable as the infants Romulus and Remus
suckled by the wolf, but which Wiseman (to preserve the idea of
Remus' late appearance) has to make into an illustration of the obscure
deities 'Lares Praestites'.

But more difficulties are to come. Wiseman returns to Mommsen's
idea of political duality, focusing not on the duality of the consulship itself, but on the sharing of the consulship between patricians
and plebeians (the late fourth century saw the end of the so-called

'struggle of the orders' and the full opening of magistracies, previously restricted to aristocratic patricians, to the rest of the citizens – the plebeians – as well). Remus, then, was invented to represent the plebeian principle in Roman politics. His name, deriving from the Latin for 'delay', indicates that the plebeians were long delayed in achieving their share of power. His story was developed in a series of plays (now lost, but whose existence Wiseman zealously reconstructs) presented in the late fourth and early third centuries. The idea of his murder was somehow (I am afraid I have failed to understand exactly how) connected to a human sacrifice in the early third century that accompanied the building of the new Roman temple of Victory.

This is all immensely enjoyable, often seductive, argument. Wiseman is well known for his influential work reasserting the importance of Roman myth and culture (against its better-known Greek counterpart); and in *Remus* he succeeds in communicating his own excitement in that enterprise. It is one of the best-written, most engaging and provoking books on ancient history to have appeared in the last fifty years; in many respects, quite simply brilliant. At the same time, much of it is closer to fantasy than history. A whole series of lost Roman plays are concocted out of next to no evidence at all, and then made into major agents in the transmission of the myth. (I see nothing, for example, to make his 'two-act performance at the far end of the Circus Maximus in front of the temple of Mercury, with the god coming out of his own temple and escorting Lara to the underworld via the nearby grove of the Bona Dea' anything more than a complete Wiseman figment.) Human sacrifice in the early third century is deduced from some literary references to a religious crisis, plus an unexplained (possibly quite innocent) grave under the foundations of the Victory temple. The list could go on and on.

So what has gone wrong? Wiseman knows a good argument when he sees one; and he repeatedly admits how perilous his own reconstructions are ('It will be obvious by now that my argument in this section is even more tenuous and conjectural than usual'). Why then does he do it? A large part of the answer lies in his understanding of the nature of myth. He does not see myth (as surely you must, particularly in Rome) as a process, a complex set of culturally specific ways of thinking about the world and its history; he sees it as a story (or stories), with an identifiable moment of invention, locked into the occasion of its first telling.

This leads him back relentlessly on a search for origins; and it enables him to conceal from himself, no doubt, as much as from his readers, that the one time when we can clearly see the myth of Remus and Romulus being important at Rome is not the murky third century BC at all, but the quite different, and much better-documented, period of the early Empire, three centuries later. The story of Romulus was a particularly live issue under the first emperor Augustus: when it came to choosing an imperial title, he apparently considered taking the name Romulus, but rejected it because of its fratricidal connotations; while the poet Horace writes of Roman civil war as an inevitable legacy of Rome's founding twins. Tacitus, too, more than a century later, reflects a similar attitude when he records public reaction to Nero's murder of his young brother Britannicus: brothers, so it was said, were traditional enemies; two kings wouldn't fit into one palace. Remus and Romulus, in other words, were paraded as a paradigm of imperial monarchy and its dynastic tensions.

A number of other books have chosen to examine in detail the specifically Augustan debates on Romulus and Rome's other early kings. None has the verve or the learning of Wiseman's *Remus*; but they all prise apart, with varying degrees of success, the complexities of these early imperial mythic tales. Matthew Fox's *Roman Historical Myths* takes each major Augustan writer individually, attempting to show in each case that the period of the early Roman kings was not (as some modern studies have come close to suggesting) simply a useful political metaphor through which writers could comment on the imperial regime – criticism of Romulus being altogether a safer option than criticism of Augustus himself. Fox argues cogently (though occasionally over-elaborately) that we should think more carefully about what it was the Romans thought they were doing when they retold the myth/history of their own city, and where they placed the boundary between mythic and historical truth, or between myth and contemporary history.

Gary Miles, by contrast, in his *Livy: Reconstructing early Rome*, concentrates on just one historical account of Rome's origins – a promising enough target and even now a text that does not always get its due attention. In fact, Miles offers a routinely fashionable set of observations about how Romans questioned their own cultural identity, intermingled with some (not always necessary) tabulations which look like a parody of structural anthropology (illustrating, for example, how the 'rusticity', 'marginality' and 'egalitarianism' that in Livy characterised the cooperation of Romulus and Remus are to be contrasted with the 'urbanism', 'centrality' and 'authoritarianism' of the rule of Romulus on his own).

A far more interesting study of an individual text is Carole Newlands' *Playing with Time*, focusing on Ovid's *Fasti*, an extraordinary poem on the Roman calendar, which retells many of the myths of regal Rome to explain the origin of the city's many religious festivals. Only once in the *Fasti* does Romulus seem to appear in a noticeably positive light, when the murder of Remus is ascribed not to the new king himself, but to one of his thuggish henchmen. But, as Newlands sharply points out, the narrator has, at the start of this section, called for inspiration on the god Quirinus, that is Romulus himself in his deified form. Ovid has set this up, in other words, as an explicitly partisan account, even a joke about Romulus' own attempt to shift the blame on to someone else.

None of this is Wiseman's territory. For his concern is with what he sees as the origin of the myth, and also with what he calls 'The Other Rome': the small city-state before it became the multicultural capital of a world empire, and before the era of the surviving literature that has defined its character in modern scholarship. That too is the concern of T. J. Cornell in *The Beginnings of Rome*. In many ways, this is as significant a book as Wiseman's, for it is the first major historical study of early Rome to integrate the results of recent intense archaeological activity in central Italy (often improving, it must be said, on the interpretations of the excavators themselves). It is almost bound to become a standard textbook, and rightly so. But writing the 'history' of a culture from which almost no contemporary writing of any sort survives has its own dangers; and the further back you go, the more acute those dangers are.

Cornell is committed (he has to be) to the idea that we can actually know something about earliest Rome; that the histories of the early city written by Romans centuries later are based on 'real information' that is, on documentary evidence still surviving, or at least on earlier historians who had access to evidence that was later lost. This commitment inevitably forces him into credulity, on a sometimes alarming scale. A case in point is the trustworthiness, or not, of the so-called consular *Fasti* (the same Latin title as Ovid's poem, but here referring to the list of consuls stretching back to the very foundation of the Republic, after the departure of the kings). If this list, as it was known in a canonical form to Romans in the first century BC, is an accurate guide to the chief magistrates of the city back into the sixth century, then it provides some kind of solid framework for a narrative account of Rome's history, even at an early period.

Of course, it almost certainly does not. Wiseman (who admittedly is committed to scepticism here, for the sake of his own argument) argues powerfully that a good deal of fixing, fudging and rationalisation by Roman antiquaries themselves lies behind the apparently neat list we have. He might have added that any document that has been worked on and emended with such intensity by modern scholars was probably (and it's a good rule of thumb) worked on equally enthusiastically by their Roman counterparts: a typical antiquarian creation. Cornell, on the other hand, claims that he can find no good reason for disbelieving its broad accuracy and the chronological framework it offers.

Cornell's problems are yet worse when he gets back to Romulus and the six kings who, according to myth, succeeded him. He seems clear enough at the outset that the foundation story of Romulus is 'legendary and has no right to be considered a historical narrative'. But before long we find that 'although Romulus is legendary, institutions attributed to him can be shown to be historical and to date back to the early regal period' which already goes a long way to reinstituting a regal 'personality', even if not necessarily on Livy's model. By the time he reaches the fourth and fifth kings, that personality is almost taken for granted: 'Ancus Marcius (641–617 BC) and L. Tarquinius Priscus (616–578 BC) are more rounded, and perhaps more historical, figures than their predecessors.' A few pages later, the issue has become how to make a mere seven kings fit into the 244 years traditionally assigned to their reigns (whether by supposing that there were in fact more than seven, or by shortening the chronology); and the historical mirage is completed by a neat family tree of the Tarquin dynasty (just to show that there is nothing inherently implausible about the relationships implied in the traditional Roman sources). Those of us who still need convincing that every single one of these kings is not a later Roman fiction (and all the more interesting for that) must long at this point for the inspired fantasy of a Wiseman.

But does any of this speculation on the prehistory of Rome matter very much? Matthew Fox, in the introduction to *Roman Historical Myths*, dares to raise the question of 'why the discourse of the (Roman) regal period should itself be interesting in the 1990s' conscious, maybe, that a great many historians (Moses Finley stridently among them) have thought it decidedly uninteresting. It is a great virtue of Cornell and (especially) Wiseman that they manage to convince the reader that indeed it might be interesting and matter; and in Wiseman's case he seems almost to have convinced himself as well. Characteristically, one of his sections opens with the sentence: 'The nineteen-seventies started unpromisingly for Remus.' This may or may not be a joke, smartly self-ironic or naively sincere. But, whichever way you choose to take it, it is typical of Wiseman's wry engagement with his subject; typical of this wild and wonderful book.

Review of T. P. Wiseman, *Remus, A Roman Myth* (Cambridge University Press, 1995); Matthew Fox, *Roman Historical Myths: the Regal Period in Augustan literature* (Clarendon Press, 1996); Gary B. Miles, *Livy, Reconstructing early Rome* (Cornell University Press, 1995); Carole E. Newlands, *Playing with Time, Ovid and the Fasti* (Cornell University Press, 1995); T. J. Cornell, *The Beginnings of Rome, Italy and Rome from the Bronze Age to the Punic Wars, c 1000–264 BC* (Routledge, 1995)

7

HANNIBAL AT BAY

The British Fabian Society takes its name from the Roman soldier and politician Quintus Fabius Maximus Verrucosus. He may seem an unlikely patron for a society of intellectual socialists. Born into one of the most aristocratic families of ancient Rome, Fabius is not known for his sympathy for the poor. It was his tactics in the war against Hannibal that inspired the society's founders in the 1880s.

During that war Rome was brought to the brink of disaster thanks to a series of rash and inexperienced generals who insisted on engaging the Carthaginians head on, with terrible consequences. The Battle of Cannae in 216 BC was the worst: our best estimates suggest that some 50,000 Roman soldiers were killed (making it a bloodbath on the scale of Gettysburg or the first day of the Somme). When Fabius held command, he took a different course. Instead of meeting Hannibal in pitched battle, he played a clever waiting game, harrying the enemy in guerrilla warfare, and scorching the earth of Italy (burning the crops, the homes and the hideouts); the strategy was to wear Hannibal down and deprive him of food for his vast army. Hence his later nickname 'Cunctator', the 'Delayer'.

This was exactly the waiting game that these late Victorian 'Fabian' socialists intended to play against capitalism: nothing so rash (or uncomfortable) as revolution, but a gradual process of attrition, until the time was ripe for change. As Frank Podmore (whose idea the name 'Fabian' was) wrote: 'For the right moment you must wait, as Fabius did most patiently when warring against Hannibal'.

Many more people in the 1880s than now would have known the

name of Fabius Maximus. But even then he did not match the popular renown of Hannibal, who so nearly managed to defeat the invincible power of Rome – and who pulled off the famous, if pointless, stunt of bringing his elephants across the snowy Alps. As Robert Garland observes, in a nice chapter on 'Afterlife' in his study of Hannibal, it has always been the Carthaginian's military tactics, especially at Cannae, that have intrigued modern generals (although George Washington did opt for a Fabian plan at the start of the American War of Independence). And it is Hannibal not Fabius who has become the subject of novels, operas and movies. In fact, the nineteenth-century mythology of Fabius often made him a frightful ditherer rather than a sophisticated strategist. 'Cunctator' could mean 'slowcoach' or 'procrastinator' just as well as 'canny delayer'.

It was exactly this side of Fabius that was picked up in a squib in the *Pall Mall Gazette* (the ancestor of the *London Evening Standard*) just after the Fabian Society was launched. Why on earth was a group of socialists calling itself after the 'dilatory' Fabius? 'Is it possible that the real name of the society is the Catilinarian Club [referring to the Roman revolutionary Catiline], and that the term Fabian is a mere humorous euphemism, a nickname by opposites, adopted so as not to alarm the British public?' A few days later an anonymous 'Fabian' wrote in to explain that it was not a joke: 'well-considered action' was the name of the game, not dilatoriness.

In ancient Rome too there had been a similar ambivalence about Fabius' achievements. On the one hand, the second-century-BC Roman poet Ennius, in his great epic on the history of Rome (which now survives only in snatches of quotation), credited him, single-handedly, with saving the city from Hannibal: 'one man alone restored the state to us by delaying (*cunctando*)'. But it is clear enough that for others the 'Cunctator' was a slowcoach, who dragged his heels in a way that was decidedly at odds with Roman ideas of bravery, virtue and military excellence.

In Livy's account of the Second Punic War, part of his 142-book history of Rome from its foundation (*Ab Urbe Condita*), written at the end of the first century BC, we find a carefully scripted debate about tactics set in 204, between the elderly Fabius and Scipio Africanus, the rising military star. Scipio plans to pursue Hannibal (who by this point was in retreat), and to defeat him once and for all in his home territory of North Africa; Fabius predictably argues for caution. Each man deploys a range of historical precedents to justify his proposed course of action. One of the more obvious is the disastrous Athenian expedition to Sicily in the middle of the Peloponnesian War, best known from the account of Thucydides (see Chapter 3). If Scipio here plays the role of Alcibiades in that earlier conflict, then Livy makes it quite clear that Fabius could be seen as the Roman Nicias – old, super-stitious, over-cautious and frankly not up to the job. In fact Scipio went on to succeed where Alcibiades did not. He decisively defeated Hannibal at the Battle of Zama in North Africa in 202, a year after Fabius' death. It was a victory for speed and military flair, not for delay – and in Garland's words 'a complete rout'.

If the figure of Fabius Maximus 'Cunctator' has faded from the popular imagination, whether as hero or slowcoach, that is partly to do with the fate of Livy's *History* itself. For much of the twentieth century this was relegated close to the margins of scholarly fashion; and although the wonderful stories of ancient Roman valour which it included ('Cincinnatus called from the plough', 'How Horatius held the bridge', and so on) made it a nineteenth-century favourite, it is now little read among a wider public, unlike Herodotus, Thucydides or Tacitus.

My guess is that even most professional classicists will not have read, in its entirety, the most detailed account of the career and policy of Fabius in the ten books of Livy (Books 21–30) that cover the Hanni-balic War. That is perhaps hardly surprising. True, there are some memorable highlights, such as the crossing of the Alps in Book 21, with its elephants, snow and the famous, surely apocryphal, story about Hannibal splitting open some rocks that lay in his path by heating them and then pouring vinegar on (a procedure which has launched all kinds of boy-scoutish experiments among classicists-turned-amateur-chemists). But most of Livy's story of the war is very hard going. As D. S. Levene admits in *Livy on the Hannibalic War*, 'keeping track of the story feels bewilderingly difficult'. There are so many different theatres of war (not just in Italy and Sicily but also in Spain and later Africa and the East), and it is hard to follow the thread from one time and place to another. Besides, as he goes on, 'we are confronted by a large set of faceless Carthaginians, most of whom seem to be called Hanno, Mago, or Hasdrubal, fighting against a varying cast of Romans who have a wider choice of nomenclature but scarcely anything more memorable in terms of attributes'. It is almost impossible to make any satisfying sense of the war, without a small library of works of reference to hand, including a very good atlas.

Add to this the fact that, on the orthodox view, Livy was a very poor historian indeed, whether by ancient or modern standards. He did no primary research, but relied exclusively on earlier histories. That was not necessarily unusual in antiquity, but Livy was worse than most: he often did not fully understand his sources or manage to reconcile them into a single coherent narrative. There are notorious occasions where he relates the same event twice, presumably because he found the same story told slightly differently in two different sources and did not spot that they were describing the same thing (so, as Levene notes, the cities of Croton and Locri are reported as falling to the Carthaginians twice, in two different years). And there are clear signs that his Greek was not good enough to understand properly one of his major sources, the Greek historian Polybius, who also covered the war in his account of Rome's rise to power in the Mediterranean. Enough of Polybius survives for us sometimes to be able to compare Livy's version with the text on which he depended. It can be a nasty surprise.

One notable Livian howler comes from his account of the Roman siege of Ambracia in Greece in 189 BC, after the end of the war. A complicated struggle is going on, within a series of underground tunnels, dug both by the Romans and the Ambracians. At one point, Livy refers to the fight going on 'with doors put in the way' (*foribus positis*). Where were the doors from? And what are they doing in the tunnels? If we go back to Polybius' text we find a significantly different story. He has 'shields' put in the way. The most plausible explanation is that Livy has mistaken the standard word for 'Roman shields' (*scuta* in Latin), which is in the original Greek (*thureous*) for a similar word (*thuras*) meaning 'doors'. To be fair to Livy, the words are etymologically related: the Roman shield was 'door shaped'. But it is still a basic error of translation that has made nonsense of the scene of fighting that he describes.

Despite all this, Levene wants to rehabilitate Livy. Joining a growing scholarly movement that sees, beyond the errors, considerable literary and historical sophistication in Livy's work, he sets out to show that the narrative of the war against Hannibal 'is the most remarkable and brilliant piece of sustained prose narrative in the whole surviving corpus of classical literature'. Does he succeed? Up to a point, yes. The project is not helped by his book's length or by his own prolixity

(Levene belongs to the 'never use just one example if you have five more that make the same point' school of literary criticism, and as with Livy himself, there is a lot to plough through). That said, he scores some powerful hits against the old dismissive orthodoxy and, after Levene, it should not be possible again to ignore these ten books.

He is excellent on challenging our modern expectations of reading and understanding a text such as Livy's. 'Put the atlas away' is his message. Ancient readers of Livy did not have a map beside them as they read this text, and in the end it may not be very important where every small town was actually situated (the ancient readers would not have known either). And he convincingly shows a range of literary subtleties that often go unnoticed. I particularly liked his demonstration that Livy partly constructs his description of the behaviour of the Roman general Marcellus in Sicily out of Cicero's speeches prosecuting Verres, the rapacious Roman governor of Sicily more than a hundred years later. Levene nicely argues that we are meant to see how Marcellus at the end of the third century BC already prefigures the worst character of Roman rule in the late Republic.

No less impressive is the way he shows that Livy seems determined to offer a different view of history and historical causation from the chilling rationalism of one of his main sources, Polybius. He is not merely diluting or misunderstanding his Greek predecessor; in some respects he is standing out against him. Levene points out, for example, that when, in Livy, Hannibal gives a speech of encouragement to his frightened soldiers before they make the crossing of the Alps, Livy puts into Hannibal's mouth some of the words used by Polybius in criticising the gullibility of his own predecessors. These historians, Polybius insisted, overestimated the danger of the mountains and told ridiculous stories about their danger, which were nothing short of falsehoods. So, says Livy's Hannibal, echoing Polybius, there are people who foolishly imagine that the Alps are so tall that they touch the sky. But there is a sting in the tail. For what did the soldiers find when, a few chapters later, they finally reached the mountains themselves? In Livy's words, they discovered that the 'snows all but mixed with the heavens'. The mountains really did reach to the sky, and Polybius' 'rationalist debunking of the terrors of the Alps is shown to be false, and the rumours which terrified his soldiers are true after all'. Like Fabius Maximus, who in addition to being a 'delayer' was also deeply respectful of the gods, Livy underscores the influence of the divine, the irrational and the unexpectedly strange on the unfolding of history.

Levene is a powerful advocate for Livy, while recognising some of his faults. He is not like some of those fashionable readers who put down every Livian inconsistency or repetition to artful emphasis, or to the ancient equivalent of postmodern 'destabilisation' (... it's not that Livy got it wrong in repeating the same incident twice, he is asking us to question the very nature of a linear narrative ...). Fortunately, Levene's Livy is not always super-sophisticated and is allowed to make mistakes, at the same time as making some powerful historical arguments. All the same, I retain a few doubts. Livy might have well-honed views about the over-rationalisations of his predecessors, and he might have had a subtle argument to make about historical causation. But how clever a reading of Polybius can we reasonably expect from a Roman historian who was unsure of the Greek word for 'shield'?

Review of Robert Garland, *Hannibal* (Bristol Classical Press, 2010); D. S. Levene, *Livy on the Hannibalic War* (Oxford University Press, 2010)

8

QUOUSQUE
TANDEM ...?

Marcus Tullius Cicero was murdered on 7 December 43 BC: Rome's most famous orator, off-and-on defender of Republican liberty and thundering critic of autocracy. He was finally hunted down by lackeys of Mark Antony, a member of Rome's ruling junta and principal victim of Cicero's dazzling swansong of invective: more than a dozen speeches called the *Philippics*, after Demosthenes' almost equally nasty attacks on Philip of Macedon, three centuries earlier. The chase had degenerated into an elaborate, occasionally comic game of hide-and-seek, with Cicero torn between holing up in his villa to wait for the inevitable knock on the door and making a speedy getaway by sea. Eventually the assassins caught up with him in his litter en route for the coast, slit his throat and packed off his head and hands to Antony and his wife Fulvia, as proof that the deed had been done. When the gruesome parcel arrived, Antony ordered that the remnants be displayed in the Forum, nailed to the spot where Cicero had delivered many of his devastating tirades; but not before Fulvia had taken the head on her lap, and – so the story goes – opened the mouth, pulled out the tongue and stabbed it again and again with a pin taken from her hair.

Decapitation, and its attendant embellishments, was something of an occupational hazard for front-line political figures in Rome in the hundred years of civil war that led up to the assassination of Julius Caesar. The head of Antony's own grandfather was said to have graced the dinner table of Gaius Marius in one of the pogroms of the early first century BC. A cousin of Cicero had his severed head ('still alive and breathing', in Cicero's words) presented to the dictator Sulla. And, in an even more baroque twist, the head of the unfortunate general Marcus Crassus, whose defeat by the Parthians in 53 BC counted among the worst Roman military disasters, ended up as a bit-part in a performance of Euripides' *Bacchae* at the Parthian Court. Some Romans drew an uncomfortable connection between the characteristic head-and-shoulders style of portrait bust that decorated their ancestral mansions and the eventual fate of so many of the sitters. The colossal portrait head of Pompey the Great, carried in his triumphal procession through Rome in 61 BC, would in time be taken as an omen of his death: severed on the shores of Egypt in September 49, his head was kept and 'pickled' (as Anthony Everitt frankly puts it in his biography of Cicero), to be presented to Julius Caesar when he arrived in Alexandria a few months later.

The story of Fulvia's violence against Cicero's severed head has implications beyond the routine sadism of Roman political life. She had been married to Cicero's two most bitter enemies (first the irritatingly charismatic Publius Clodius, who had forced Cicero into temporary exile only to be murdered himself by one of Cicero's henchmen; and later Antony) and she now had the chance of her own, woman's, vengeance. In rending his tongue with her hairpin, she was attacking the very faculty that defined men's role in the political process, and Cicero's power in particular. At the same time, she was transforming an innocent object of female adornment into a devastating weapon.

The sheer horror of Cicero's murder and mutilation contributed to its mythic status in later Roman literature and culture. His death was a popular subject for Roman schoolboys practising the art of speaking, as well as for celebrity orators in after-dinner performances. Learner orators were required to deliver speeches of advice to famous characters from myth and history, or to take sides in notorious crimes from the past: 'defend Romulus against the charge of killing Remus'; 'advise Agamemnon whether or not to sacrifice Iphigeneia'; 'should Alexander the Great enter Babylon, despite bad omens?' Two of the most popular exercises, repeated in countless Roman schoolrooms and at innumerable dinner parties, involved advising Cicero on the question of whether or not he should ask for Antony's pardon in order to save his own life; and whether, if Antony offered to spare him provided that he burn all his writings, he should accept the deal. In the cultural politics of the Roman Empire these problems were nicely judged – safely pitching one of the most brilliantly unsuccessful upholders of the old Republican order against the man who, as everyone came to agree, was the unacceptable face of autocracy; and weighing the value of literature against the brute force of life-or-death power. There was lustre, too, in the fact that Roman critics almost universally believed that Cicero had died an exemplary death. Whatever accusations of self-interest, vacillation or cowardice they might level at other aspects of his life, everyone reckoned that on this occasion he behaved splendidly: sticking his bare neck out of the litter, he calmly demanded (as heroes have continued to do ever since) that the assassin make a good job of it.

Judgements on the rest of Cicero's achievements, in politics and writing, have fluctuated wildly. Some historians have seen him as an able spokesman for traditional political values, as Rome fell deeper into civil war and, ultimately, one-man rule. Others have condemned him for meeting the revolutionary problems facing the Roman state with empty slogans ('peace with dignity', 'harmony of the social orders'). In the nineteenth century, reflecting on Cicero's constant shifts of allegiance (ending up as a puppet of the autocrats he claimed to abhor), Theodor Mommsen dubbed him 'a short-sighted egotist'. Everitt's biography, *Cicero: A Turbulent Life*, casts him instead as a sensible pragmatist, praising his 'intelligent and flexible conservatism'. For scholars of the Enlightenment, his philosophical treatises were a beacon of rationality. In an extraordinary fable told by Voltaire, a Roman embassy to the Chinese imperial Court wins the admiration of the sceptical emperor only after they have read him a translation of Cicero's dialogue *On Divination* (which carefully dissects the practice of augury, oracles and fortune-telling); while 'Tully's *Offices*', his treatise on duty (*De Officiis*), was the ethical handbook of many seventeenth-century English gentlemen. But this admiration did not survive the rise of intellectual philhellenism; and for much of the nineteenth and twentieth centuries Cicero's philosophy, all six modern volumes of it, was dismissed as no more than a derivative compendium of earlier Greek thought, valuable – if at all – for the hints it offered of the Greek material lost since antiquity. Even Everitt, who gives Cicero the benefit of the doubt wherever possible, can only praise him here as 'a populariser of genius', unoriginal, but a 'mature' synthesiser.

There is, however, one incident in Cicero's career that has always attracted more debate than any other: his suppression of the so-called Catilinarian Conspiracy during his consulship in 63 BC. For Cicero, this was his finest hour. In later life, he rarely missed an opportunity to remind the Roman people that in 63 he had single-handedly saved the state from destruction. And he attempted to immortalise his achievement in a three-volume epic poem, entitled *On the Consulship*. Only fragments of this survive, and it is now most famous for a line often regarded as one of the worst pieces of Latin doggerel to have made it through the Dark Ages ('O fortunatam natam me consule Romam' – a jingle with something of the ring of 'Rome was born a lucky city, when I as consul wrote this ditty'). Not surprisingly, from antiquity on, others have held different views about exactly how much gratitude the Roman people owed Cicero.

Lucius Sergius Catilina was a young aristocrat, and – like many of his peers – he was deeply in debt, as well as frustrated by failure to win election to the political offices he thought his due. Through various underground sources Cicero learned by the late summer of 63 that Catiline was plotting a revolutionary uprising that was to involve burning the city down and – the real horror for Roman conservatives – cancelling all debts. As consul, he put this information before the Senate, which declared a state of emergency. At the beginning of November, armed with further horrifying details and fresh, so he claimed, from a failed assassination attempt, Cicero denounced Catiline in the Senate and effectively drove him out of the city to his supporters in Etruria. A legion was despatched to deal with them – Catiline died in battle early the next year; the remaining conspirators in Rome were rounded up and, after a heated discussion in the Senate, were put to death without trial under an emergency powers decree. In triumph, Cicero shouted just one famous word to the crowds waiting in the Roman Forum: 'vixere' ('they have lived' – i.e. 'they're dead').

The fate of these prisoners instantly became a cause célèbre. One of the sharpest political debates of the first century BC centred (as it often has since in other political regimes) on the nature of the emergency powers decree. In what circumstances should you declare a state of emergency? What exactly does martial law, a prevention of terrorism act or – in Roman terms – a Final Decree of the Senate allow the state authorities to do? How far is it ever legitimate for a constitutional government to suspend the constitutional rights of its people?

In this case, the executions flouted the fundamental right of Roman citizens to a judicial trial (as Julius Caesar himself had recognised, when – with a characteristic stroke of imagination – he had argued in the Senate for the entirely unprecedented punishment of life imprisonment). For all his tub-thumping, for all his reliance on emergency powers, Cicero's treatment of the conspirators was bound to catch up with him; as it did four years later, when he was driven into temporary exile by Publius Clodius on the charge of having put Roman citizens to death without trial. While Cicero was languishing in northern Greece, Clodius drove the knife in even further: he knocked down Cicero's house in Rome and replaced it with a shrine to the goddess Liberty.

Other question marks hang over Cicero's handling of Catiline's conspiracy. Many modern historians, and no doubt a few sceptics at the time, have wondered exactly how much of a threat to the state Catiline posed. Cicero was a self-made politician. He had no aristocratic connections and only a precarious place in the top rank of the Roman elite, among those families who claimed a direct line back to the age of Romulus (or, in the case of Julius Caesar, back to Aeneas and the goddess Venus herself). To secure his position he needed to make a splash during his year as consul. An outstanding military victory against some threatening barbarian enemy would have been best: failing that (and Cicero was no soldier), he needed to 'save the state' in some other way. It is hard now not to suspect that the Catilinarian Conspiracy lies somewhere on the spectrum between 'storm in a teacup' and 'figment of Cicero's imagination'. Catiline himself may have been a far-sighted radical (cancellation of debts could have been just what Rome needed in 63 BC); he might equally well have been an unprincipled terrorist. We cannot now tell. But there is a fair chance that he was driven to violence by a consul spoiling for a fight – and for his own glory. The 'conspiracy', in other words, is a prime example of the classic dilemma: were there 'reds' under the bed, or was the whole thing a conservative invention?

It is not only historians who have found the story of Cicero and Catiline intriguing. For the last four hundred years at least, dramatists, novelists, poets, painters and film-makers have explored the ambiguities of the Catilinarian Conspiracy, with heroic sagas of a noble statesman saving his country from ruin matched by romantic tragedies of a misunderstood visionary brought down by the forces of reaction. Ben Jonson's *Catiline*, written only a few years after the

Gunpowder Plot, portrays its anti-hero in lurid colours, charging him with rape, incest and murder: in Jonson's Underworld, Charon has to demand a whole navy to ship Catiline's victims across the Styx. But his Cicero turns out to be a droning bore: so much so, that at the first performance a good proportion of the audience walked out during his interminable denunciation of Catiline to the Senate (Catiline's taunt in reply – 'insolent tongue-man' – must have called to mind Fulvia's horrible attack on Cicero's speaking parts). In complete contrast, Ibsen's *Catilina*, his first play, published under a pseudonym in 1850, writes Cicero out of the action entirely: he never appears on stage and is hardly mentioned by name. Instead, fresh from the revolutionary excitements of 1848, Ibsen portrays Catiline as a charismatic leader desperately challenging the corruption of the world in which he lives – only to die in the final scene, in a gory suicide pact with his noble wife. The twentieth century offered yet more versions of the story, from W. G. Hardy's whimsical tale of Catiline's affair with Publius Clodius' sister (in *Turn Back the River*, 1938), to Steven Saylor's enigmatically homoerotic protagonist (in *Catilina's Riddle*, 1993). And then there was Francis Ford Coppola's promised movie *Megalopolis*; it was never made, but according to its advance publicity, it was to have combined a utopian vision of a futuristic New York with the themes of the Catilinarian Conspiracy. Exactly how remains unclear.

What keeps the story of Cicero and Catiline more vivid than so many other episodes of Roman political history is the simple fact that the texts of Cicero's denunciations still survive. Inevitably, Cicero will have edited them before he put them into circulation, tidying up the loose ends, and inserting those brilliant one-liners that might have slipped his mind on the day itself. All the same, in the speech now known as *In Catilinam I* (the first speech 'Against Catiline'), we have preserved, as closely as we could ever hope, the exact words used by Cicero in the Senate, as he drove Catiline out of Rome in November 63. They have had almost as exotic an afterlife as the Conspiracy itself, particularly the opening sentence: 'Quousque tandem abutere, Catilina, patientia nostra?' ('Whither at length wilt thou abuse our patience?', to quote from Jonson's version of the speech, that so bored his audience in 1611). This is now probably the best-known Latin quotation after Virgil's 'Arma virumque cano ...' ('Arms and the man I sing'); and it is still widely used, parodied and adapted in ways that indicate a clear sense of its original meaning.

Its fame goes back to antiquity. The schoolboys whose exercises included advising Cicero whether or not to ask for Antony's forgiveness would almost certainly have been made to study this classic of Roman oratory very carefully indeed; they would probably have learned it by heart. So, too, would the schoolboy elite of the West from the Renaissance until about the middle of the twentieth century. Hence, again, the popularity of the slogan 'o tempora, o mores', which occurs a little later in the first paragraph of the same speech ('What an age we live in!' is a common translation; it literally means 'O the times! O the customs!'). More startling is the currency of the opening line even today in both Latin and modern language translations, when only a handful of students can have studied Cicero's oratory with any care. It may have something to do with the fact that since the eighteenth century the first paragraphs of *In Catilinam I* have been regularly used as the trial text for specimens of typesetting (and now of web pages). This may have kept the words somewhere in the cultural subconscious, but it can hardly be the whole explanation for its popularity.

From Africa to America, political frustration can still conveniently be framed in Cicero's terms – just put the name of your own enemy in place of 'Catilina'. The banners blazoning 'Quousque tandem' waved by Hungarian demonstrators in 2012 against their ruling Fidesz party were only the most recent in a long line. 'Jusqu'à quand Kabila abuserez-vous de notre patience?' demanded one member of the opposition to the new Congolese President in 2001. 'How long, José María Aznar, will you abuse our patience?' asked an editorial in *El País* in August 1999, criticising the Spanish Prime Minister for his unwillingness to bring Pinochet to trial. 'Quousque tandem abutere CRUESP patientia nostra?' chanted strikers in Brazilian state universities, not long after, to their Council of Rectors (CRUESP).

Outside politics, too, the phrase proves wonderfully adaptable to a range of enemies and circumstances. In a notorious attack, Camille Paglia substituted the name of Michel Foucault for Catiline. And in the closing days of the Second World War a disconsolate lover (Walter Prude), separated by the demands of military service from his new wife (Agnes de Mille, choreographer of *Rodeo, Oklahoma!* and *Gentlemen Prefer Blondes*), wrote: 'How long, O Hitler, will you abuse our sex life!'

The irony in all this is that the political dynamics of the slogan's original context have been consistently subverted. Cicero may have succeeded in writing himself into the political language of the modern world. But words which started life as a threat uttered by the spokesman of the established order against the dissident are now almost universally deployed the other way round: as a challenge from the dissident to the established order. Catiline should be smiling in his grave.

The fact that so much of Cicero's work survives – not only speeches and philosophy, but rhetorical treatises and hundreds of personal letters too – makes him an obvious subject for a biographer. And indeed, over the last two millennia there have been countless attempts to write his life story, in whole or in part. Cicero himself tried (unsuccessfully) to commission a well-known historian to produce an account of his consulship, exile and triumphant return. Just after Cicero's death, Sallust wrote a still influential monograph on the Catilinarian Conspiracy – using the incident as an exemplar of the moral decline of Rome in the late Republic. More to Cicero's taste, no doubt, would have been the biography composed about the same time by his ex-slave and secretary, Tiro, alongside a companion volume of Cicero's jokes. Neither of these has been preserved; but they almost certainly lie behind the surviving second-century biography by Plutarch (which includes a good number of jokes). Modern authors have taken up the challenge, with a rate recently, in English alone, of about one new biography every five years; each new attempt claiming some fresh angle, some plausible reason for adding to a biographical tradition that might seem crowded enough already.

Everitt's aim is explicitly 'rehabilitation', a reaction to what he sees as a consistent undervaluing of Cicero's political acumen: not as smart as Julius Caesar, maybe, but 'he had clear aims and very nearly realised them; he was unlucky'. Despite some nasty howlers in the Latin (why bother to use Latin words if you, or your editors, can't get them right?) it turns into a businesslike tale, told with a sometimes engaging enthusiasm for its subject and a good eye for the spicier detail of late Republican life. At the same time, like most modern biographies of Cicero, it is also consistently disappointing. Everitt's conventional 'back-to-the-ancient-sources' approach leaves him repeatedly at the mercy of the biographical and cultural assumptions of the one surviving ancient biography; hence his blithe assertion, following Plutarch, that at his birth Cicero's mother 'suffered few labour pains' – a shorthand in the ancient tradition for the birth of an extraordinary child. It also leaves him time and again trying to fill the inconvenient gaps left by the ancient evidence, or desperately over-interpreting Cicero's own words.

His letters from exile, for example, are taken to indicate that he was having a 'mental breakdown'; and from his large number of properties, we are asked to conclude that 'Cicero greatly enjoyed buying houses' (as if he was constantly scanning the property pages in the local paper). The result, almost inevitably, is a patchwork of ancient texts, sewn together with a thread of common sense, guesswork and sheer fantasy.

It is a missed opportunity. What we have been waiting for is not another 'straight' biography of Cicero; there are more than enough of those. Much more to the point would be a biographical account that tried to explore the way his life story has been constructed and reconstructed over the last two thousand years; how we have learned to read Cicero through Jonson, Voltaire, Ibsen and the rest; what kind of investment we still have, and why, in a thundering conservative of the first century BC and his catchy oratorical slogans. Why, in short, is Cicero still around in the twenty-first century? And on whose terms? *Quousque tandem?*

Review of Anthony Everitt, *Cicero: A Turbulent Life* (John Murray, 2001)

9

ROMAN ART THIEVES

On the wall of a now dilapidated house in the centre of the Sicilian town of Enna, there is a remarkable commemorative plaque. A carefully inscribed slab of marble, put up by the local council in 1960, reads: 'On this very spot stood the house in which Marcus Tullius Cicero lodged, the defender of Enna and the whole of Sicily against that plunderer of temples, Caius Licinius Verres, Roman governor of the island. The city of Enna, still mindful of his services twenty centuries later, erected this memorial'. Leaving aside the elements of fantasy (we have no idea at all where Cicero lodged when he visited Enna), it is vivid testimony to the enduring power of a Roman court case of 70 BC and to the memory of Cicero as defender of the province of Sicily against the depredations of its rogue governor.

Cicero was then an up-and-coming politician, keen to make a name for himself. So he had taken on the case of a group of Sicilians, who wanted to charge their governor with 'extortion'. It was a risky strategy. Verres was much better connected than Cicero, and it was anyway hard to secure a conviction for extortion in the provinces. Roman governors expected to come home considerably richer from their overseas postings, and juries at Rome (in 70 BC composed entirely of senators) almost inevitably saw it from the governor's side. For a prosecution to be successful, there had to be evidence of really outrageous crime and/or some overriding political advantage in delivering a guilty verdict. But Cicero, playing the combined role of prosecuting counsel and amateur detective, went off to Sicily and gathered together witnesses and detailed documentary evidence of

6. A shadow of its former glory? The spot in Enna where Cicero is
supposed to have lodged while investigating the case against Verres.

Verres' misdemeanours. His case for the prosecution is laid out in the
surviving speeches 'Against Verres'.

These document Verres' lifetime of crime. One speech concentrates
on his fiddling of the corn supply; another exposes his profiteering
when he was overseeing building work on the temple of Castor in the
Roman Forum (he tried to extract a vast payment from the contractor
on the grounds that the columns were not quite vertical). But the most
lurid and memorable parts of Cicero's denunciation concern Verres'
reign of terror in Sicily. The fate of Gavius from the Sicilian town of
Consa, who was flogged, tortured and crucified for being a spy, despite
the fact that he was a Roman citizen and so legally protected from such
treatment, has remained a powerful political symbol. Gavius died with
the words 'Civis Romanus sum' ('I am a Roman citizen') on his lips
– a slogan that was later adopted by Lord Palmerston when he sent a
gunboat in support of the British citizen Don Pacifico, who in 1847
had been attacked by an anti-Semitic crowd in Athens. It was famously
wheeled out again in 1963 by John F. Kennedy in Berlin: 'Two thousand

years ago the proudest boast was "civis Romanus sum". Today, in the world of freedom, the proudest boast is "ich bin ein Berliner'". Kennedy, presumably, did not know what happened to Gavius.

Another whole speech, and the focus of Margaret Miles's *Art as Plunder*, is devoted to detailing Verres' expropriation of the famous artworks of the province. As the commemoration in Enna hints, some of this came from sacred temples. In fact, his worst theft, according to Cicero, was of various venerable images, including a venerable cult statue of Ceres: 'this very Ceres, the most ancient and sacred of all, the fountain-head of all the cults of the goddess among all races and peoples, was stolen by Gaius Verres from her own temple and home'. But private property was not safe from his thieving hands. Gaius Heius, a 'successful businessman' of Messana, kept some rare masterpieces (including statues by Praxiteles, Polykleitos and Myron) in a shrine in his house. Verres soon forced him to sell them for a ridiculously low price. In general, for anyone in Sicily with valuables at home, the governor was a dangerous dinner guest. He was likely to leave with your gold and silver, your dinner service, or your rare Corinthian bronze, in his carriage.

These speeches against Verres are the only speeches for the prosecution to survive from the ancient Roman courtroom (speaking for the defence was usually seen as the more honourable trade). They now amount to six separate speeches (plus one from a preliminary hearing), or almost a quarter of all Cicero's oratory that has come down to us. It looks as if it must have been a long case – but it was not. Verres decided to scarper after listening to the evidence presented in the very first speech (a move which has usually been taken as an admission of guilt). He spent the rest of his days in exile in Marseilles, apparently still in possession of his art collection; almost thirty years later he was put to death on the order of Mark Antony, because he refused to hand over to Antony his favourite Corinthian bronzes – or so the suspiciously apposite anecdote, recounted by the elder Pliny, has it. After his flight from Rome Verres was condemned *in absentia*, and Cicero circulated a no doubt highly embellished version of the one speech he had actually delivered, and the five that had remained unused. Not only did these turn out to be a success in the Roman classroom and in the training of young orators; they also established the conflict between Cicero and Verres as an exemplary story of right versus might, and the cause of justice triumphing over violence and corruption. And so it still rings true in Enna.

The facts of the case are not, of course, so simple. As always, we only have Cicero's side of it. No one would seriously suggest that Verres was an entirely innocent victim of some vendetta on the part of Cicero and the Sicilians. But it is hard to know if he was very much worse in his conduct than other Roman governors at the time; and it is also hard to know how far the case was fired by Cicero's own eagerness to make a name. Recent studies have exposed many of the tactical obfuscations in Cicero's account of Verres' abuse of the corn supply. Besides, although his flight after Cicero's first speech in the courtroom may be an indication of Verres' guilt, innocent (or relatively innocent) men may also take to their heels. Sometimes they have just had enough.

Miles has no serious doubts that Verres was more or less guilty as charged. But in her study of his plundering of works of art, she does tease out some of the complexities that underlie Cicero's invective. In broad terms, we can detect a development in the ancient world from the idea of art as essentially a public or religious medium to the idea of art as the object of private collecting and connoisseurship. The late second and early first century BC in Italy was a particularly loaded moment in that transition, as the Romans came increasingly in contact with the artistic traditions of the Greek world, and works of art flowed to Rome from the eastern Mediterranean as the prize of conquest. Intensely debated were the role of Greek art within the 'native' traditions of Roman culture, the legitimacy of the private ownership of luxury arts, and how far it was appropriate for an elite Roman to fashion himself as a 'lover of art'.

Within these debates, almost anyone was a potential target. Gaius Mummius, who destroyed the city of Corinth in 146 BC, was ridiculed for being ignorant about art. One hostile anecdote tells how, when the treasures of Corinth were being loaded on to ships to be transported back to Rome, Mummius warned the sailors that if they damaged anything they would have to replace it. Yet to be passionately keen on Greek art could be presented as equally culpable – as Cicero makes clear in his attack on Verres. It was not just his crimes in acquiring all these statues and antiques that could be held against the accused, but his cupidity itself, his desire for art. Cicero, meanwhile, when discussing the famous statues owned by Heius of Messana, affects not even to be able to remember who exactly those renowned artists were ('... the sculptor, who was he? Who did they say he was? Ah yes, thank you, Polykleitos …'). Whether this was an attempt to distance himself from Verres' artistic passions, or (as Miles less plausibly suggests) an attempt to make fun of Verres' own 'pretensions to connoisseurship', it illustrates the perils for Romans of engaging – or refusing to engage – with art and its acquisition.

But there are other, bigger dilemmas at issue that Miles does not always pick up. For a start, the contested boundary between the cultured patron and the obsessive, rapacious collector is an almost universal one. This is nicely illustrated in Carole Paul's account of the display of the Borghese collection of paintings and antiquities in eighteenth-century Rome. In discussing the formation of the collection she devotes a short section to the seventeenth-century Scipione Borghese – a 'distinguished … patron of the arts', 'a great Maecenas'. It is only in the next paragraph that we learn that 'Scipione was also a remarkable – and ruthless – collector, who would stoop to confiscation and theft to obtain paintings, and even had artists imprisoned when they displeased him'. Same person, same habits: it all depended which side of Scipione's patronage you were on.

We can find very similar ambiguities in ancient Rome. In the fourth book of his poetry collection, the *Silvae*, published in the mid-90s AD, Statius praises one Novius Vindex, a connoisseur of art who has recently acquired a statuette of Hercules by Lysippos, once owned by Alexander the Great. Miles stresses how different the tone of this poem is from Cicero's treatment of Verres' art collecting. 'Unlike Verres', she observes, 'Vindex collects art honestly … not to further his ambitions and public career'. For her, there is 'an antithetical difference in character between the two men', and a chronological difference too. One hundred and seventy years after the Verrine case, there was now a positive role for the private collector in Rome. So there may have been, but surely more to the point is that we know of Verres from his enemy and Novius Vindex from his friend. If Verres had had a tame poet, he too would presumably have praised his cultured patron to the skies.

Even more crucially, the transfer, removal, or theft of art objects is almost always more complicated than any simple model of plunderer and victim suggests. This is certainly the case with Heius' collection of masterpieces, which he lost to Verres. How, we must ask, did a Sicilian 'businessman' acquire statues by Praxiteles, Polykleitos and Myron? Cicero stresses that they were inherited 'from his ancestors'; but that assertion, on its own, deflects rather than answers the question. The little we know of Heius suggests that he had been in business on the island of Delos, a major commercial centre of the Mediterranean and capital of the ancient slave trade. It is possible, though in my view unlikely, that he was 'an art dealer' of some kind. More probably, these fine statues were acquired with the profits from the ancient traffic in people. It could even be that the circumstances in which Heius acquired his prize works of art were not so very different from those in which Verres acquired his.

It was also the case that Verres bought rather than simply stole these famous statues. True, Cicero emphasises that the price was absurdly low – and, even if money did change hands, a coerced sale was coercion nonetheless, another version of theft. But inevitably the precise circumstances of the transfer of ownership are impossible to reconstruct now. (Just as it is impossible to know, in Paul's account, quite how willingly Camillo Borghese sold some of his collection to Napoleon; the pieces were not restored to him, with the other confiscated works of Italian art, after Napoleon's defeat.) Simply because the vendor later complains that he was forced into the deal does not necessarily mean that he was not a willing partner to the transaction at the time.

We tend now to imagine that most of the 'original' Greek works of art that ended up in Rome were the result of plunder and exploitation. Some of them certainly were. Triumphal processions in Rome were sometimes full of plundered masterpieces, the fruits of Roman victory. But, unless you take the extreme position that any trade whatsoever between the imperial power and its conquered territories was always coercive, there must have been some occasions on which the Greeks were happy to sell, or were even the leading partners in the transaction. The temple of Apollo Sosianus in Rome was refitted at the end of the first century BC, with antique sculpture that had once adorned an early fifth-century temple in Greece newly installed in its pediment. (The surviving fragments, now in the Centrale Montemartini Museum in Rome, leave no doubt whatsoever as to the date and general provenance – though most suggestions as to where exactly the stuff came from are no more than guesses.) This may have been the result of brute Roman rapacity. But it may have been a more collusive deal than that. It may even have been a deal driven by the original Greek proprietors, trying to make a profit out of some old sculpture they intended to replace anyway, and the Romans were gullible enough to buy.

On a more domestic scale, how, in Pompeii, did the terracotta frieze that originally decorated some temple in the city end up built into the garden wall of the rich 'House of the Golden Bracelet'? We can guess how Cicero would have excoriated the owner for using sacred sculpture to adorn his private property, Verres-style. And maybe Cicero would have been right. But maybe the owner was encouraged to buy them, at a high price, by the temple authorities. Or maybe he rescued them from the ancient equivalent of a skip.

The old idea of cultural plunder as 'rape' is more useful here than we might imagine. Just as few sexual rapes are violent attacks in dark alleys by unknown assailants, so in practice relatively few arguments about cultural property start from an invading army removing art treasures at the point of a gun. In any case, those are the easy ones to solve. Most rapes are some version of date-rape, where the issues turn on intention, (mis)understanding, competing memories and the fuzzy boundary between coercion, acquiescence and agreement. It is very hard to establish guilt or innocence; hence, in part, the very low rate of conviction. From Verres to Lord Elgin and beyond, disputes about cultural plunder normally follow the date-rape model. (Who gave permission? Did the owner really agree? And so on.) That is why they have proved so intractable to resolve.

Miles is keen to follow the themes of Cicero's attack on Verres through to modern debates on cultural property. She is particularly taken with Cicero's emphasis on the conduct of Scipio Aemilianus after the fall of Carthage in 146 BC. Under Scipio's aegis, those works of art which the Carthaginians had plundered from Sicily were sent back to their original homes in an unprecedented gesture of artistic repatriation – and a striking contrast to Mummius who, in the same year, was having all the masterpieces of Corinth sent off to Rome. Scipio's motives have been debated. Was this the virtuous act of a man of culture? Or a self-interested attempt to secure Sicilian support? And how far is Cicero's repeated stress on this action connected to the presence of one of Scipio's descendants on the jury? But Miles is mostly concerned to link this act of repatriation with the decision, centuries later, to send many of the works of art seized by Napoleon back to their original home (the campaign of repatriation in which Camillo Borghese lost out, because his pieces had technically been purchased rather than plundered).

The unlikely hero of the last part of the book is the Duke of

Wellington, who was instrumental in getting Napoleon's artistic plunder returned to Italy and elsewhere (despite the fact that there were many in England who had rather hoped to see the Laocoön and other prize pieces decorating an English museum). This was an important challenge to the traditional doctrine that art was a legitimate spoil of war – heralding the modern idea that cultural property is a 'special category that should be protected'.

Yet again it is more complicated than Miles appears to acknowledge. The most important point is that repatriation never restores the *status quo ante*: it is always another stage in the moving history of the art object. It is well known that the return of the Elgin Marbles would not restore them to the place from which they had been removed, but to the quite different context of a new museum. Less well known are some of the radical consequences of the repatriation of Napoleon's booty. True, many of the masterpieces were sent back to their country of origin, but they did not always go back to their original homes. The losers in the process included not only the Borghese family, but also the little churches of Italy, which did not in fact recover their beloved altarpieces. For these were usually 'returned' to the increasingly important Italian museum collections, such as the Accademia in Venice, or the Vatican in Rome. This act of repatriation was, in other words, a major step in turning them from sacred to museum objects.

We may try to regulate the movement of cultural property, but – licit or illicit – we cannot stop it. Nor would we wish to entirely (the idea of a world in which art was destined to stay in the place in which it was made is a terrible nightmare). One thing is certain: criminal prosecutions in this area tend to have a symbolic rather than practical importance, as the people of ancient Sicily found. Cicero may have won his case. In modern Enna the citizens may have decided to honour the man who defended their ancestors so stalwartly against the depredations of their governor. But the fact was that they did not get their statues back. Verres enjoyed them until his death.

Review of Margaret M. Miles, *Art as Plunder: The ancient origins of debate about cultural property* (Cambridge University Press, 2008); Carole Paul, *The Borghese Collections and the Display of Art in the Age of the Grand Tour* (Ashgate, 2008)

10

SPINNING CAESAR'S MURDER

The murder of Julius Caesar was a messy business. As with all assassinations, it was easier for the conspirators to plan the first blow than to predict what would happen next – never mind to have an exit strategy in reserve, should things go wrong. At a meeting of the Senate on the Ides of March in 44 BC, Tillius Cimber, a backbencher, gave the cue for the attack by kneeling at Caesar's feet and grabbing his toga. Then Casca struck with his dagger; or tried to. Clumsily missing the target, he gave Caesar the chance to stand up and defend himself by driving his pen (the only instrument he had to hand) into Casca's arm. This lasted just a few seconds, for at least twenty reinforcements were standing by, weapons at the ready, and quickly managed to dispatch their victim. But they had no time to take careful aim, and several of the assassins found themselves wounded by the ancient equivalent of friendly fire. According to the earliest surviving account, by the Syrian historian Nicolaus of Damascus, Cassius lunged at Caesar, but ended up gashing Brutus in the hand; Minucius missed too, and struck his ally Rubrius in the thigh instead. 'There must have been a lot of blood', as T. P. Wiseman crisply remarks in *Remembering the Roman People*.

Not just blood, but in the immediate aftermath there was chaos, confusion and, at moments, almost farce. That, at least, is the picture Wiseman reconstructs by carefully comparing the surviving ancient versions of the event. The main lines of their story, he argues, go back to an eyewitness account by some senator with a ring-side seat, transmitted perhaps in the lost history of Asinius Pollio – plus some later, less reliable elaborations taken from Livy, whose narrative of the year 44 BC is also lost. Wiseman may be too confident in the accuracy of this underlying account: an eyewitness is not necessarily the best historical guide to an assassination, and in any case it is harder to distinguish Livy's imaginative insertions from the earlier core than he allows. Nonetheless, his reconstruction of what happened is, by and large, compelling.

The watching senators, several hundred of them, were at first stunned by the attack. But, as soon as Brutus turned away from the body to address them, they regained their wits and took to their heels. In their flight from the Senate house, they must have almost bumped into the thousands of people who were just at that moment pouring out of a gladiatorial show in a nearby theatre. Hearing rumours of the murder, this crowd too panicked and ran home, shouting 'Bolt the doors, bolt the doors'. Meanwhile Lepidus, a leading Caesarian loyalist, left the Forum to rally the troops stationed in the city, just missing the blood-stained assassins who turned up there to proclaim their success – closely followed by three loyal slaves carrying Caesar's body home on a litter, with such difficulty (you really need four people to carry a litter) that his wounded arms trailed over the sides. It was two days before the Senate dared to meet again, and perhaps another two before Caesar's body was cremated on a bonfire in the Forum.

Shakespeare's version of the confusion, in *Julius Caesar*, is not far short of the truth – though the murder of Cinna the poet, which Shakespeare based on the Greek biographer Plutarch's account of events, does not pass Wiseman's scrutiny. For him, this ghastly case of mistaken identity ('I am Cinna the poet … not Cinna the conspirator', as Shakespeare put it) comes from one of Livy's additions to the story. Livy himself, he suggests, probably took it from some lost Roman drama on Cinna the conspirator and on the aftermath of the assassination more generally. Wiseman is renowned for 'reconstructing' lost plays to fill gaps or explain puzzles in the Roman historical narrative. Here he is typically ingenious, yet implausible. Intriguing as it would be to picture the ancient Romans themselves sitting down to watch a tragedy on Caesar's death, or to trace a memorable scene in Shakespeare back to a scene in an ancient Roman play, there is no evidence whatsoever for any such thing – beyond the fact that some incidents recorded in the historical accounts of the period are so vivid that it is easy to imagine them in performance or in dramatic form. But 'dramatic' writing exists both off and on stage. There is no strong reason here to suppose a direct reference back to the theatre at all.

What is certain is that, within a few months, the assassins managed to give this chaotic mess a positive spin, and to recast an almost bungled murder into a heroic blow against tyranny. In 43 or 42 BC, Brutus, who had negotiated an amnesty and safe passage out of Rome, issued what was to become the most famous Roman coin ever minted. It carried an image of two daggers, and between them a 'cap of liberty' or *pileus*, the distinctive headgear worn by Roman slaves when they were freed. The message was obvious: through the violence of these daggers, the Roman people had gained their freedom. Underneath was written the date, 'Ides of March'. Despite the political failure of the assassination in the medium term (Caesar's nephew Octavian soon established exactly the kind of one-man rule that the assassins had wanted to destroy), the Ides of March became as resonant a date in ancient Rome as 14 July in modern France. In fact, when Galba, the elderly governor of Spain, led a coup in 68 AD against the corrupt, murderous and possibly mad Emperor Nero, he issued a copy of Brutus' coin, showing the same two daggers and a 'cap of liberty', with the slogan 'The Liberty of the Roman People Restored'. Caesar's murder, in other words, offered a template for resistance to imperial tyranny more generally.

In *Remembering the Roman People*, Wiseman is not concerned with how the myth of Caesar's assassination was later exploited by the Roman governing class. His main reason for trying to get back to the truth about the events of 44 BC is to discover what the reaction of the ordinary people was to the assassination of Caesar. The prevailing modern view is that there is little reliable evidence to gauge the popular response, but that what there is hardly suggests a particularly hostile reaction to the murder from the crowd. In fact, writing less than a year later, Cicero could claim that the Roman people viewed the toppling of the tyrant as 'the most noble of all illustrious deeds'.

We should probably distrust this kind of conservative wishful thinking. A vociferous section of the political elite may have felt excluded, even humiliated, by Caesar's increasing control over the institutions of the state. But Caesar's reforms, from corn distribution to settlements for the poor overseas, were popular with most of the inhabitants of Rome, who no doubt regarded elite ideas of 'liberty' as a convenient alibi for self-advancement and for the exploitation of their less privileged fellow citizens. Wiseman unravels the various accounts of the murder's aftermath, to find plenty of evidence that the people as a whole had little sympathy with the assassins – even if occasionally he cannot resist using that 'lost play' about Cinna as a convenient way of disposing of material he wishes to bypass. 'This episode is immediately suspect', he writes of an alleged attack on Cinna's house, 'as the second act in our putative drama.'

This analysis of Caesar's murder is the last of a series of fascinating case studies that together make up *Remembering the Roman People*. In each of these Wiseman tries to unearth some aspect of the popular, democratic side of political ideology in the late Roman Republic, from the mid-second century BC on – whether public reaction to particular political crises, a forgotten hero of the popular cause, or a long-lost democratic slogan that was once the rallying cry of the Roman people. He has no time for the conventional view of Roman politics as 'an ideological vacuum', in which a small group of aristocrats fought for power without principles. And he has still less time for the view that Rome was a place where democratic ideals had no part to play, whether in its early history or in the violent century that led up to the assassination of Caesar. His aim, in short, is to put some ideology back into our understanding of Roman political life, and to bring the important democratic traditions of Rome to the surface once more.

Wiseman is not alone in challenging the modern orthodoxy. Fergus Millar, in particular, has already argued for a much more radically democratic element in the political institutions of the Republic (stressing, for example, the importance of popular elections and speech-making). But Wiseman is attempting something much more ambitious. He is trying to recover the popular heroes, symbols and myths that spoke for the democratic side of Roman political culture. What version of Roman history, he is asking, would the Roman people have told?

This is, of course, a very difficult question to answer, for the simple reason that the surviving Roman literature is so overwhelmingly conservative, and largely blind to the impact of democratic opinion. The task Wiseman has set himself is almost as formidable as searching for the ideology of the sans-culottes in the writing of Mme de Staël, or attempting to document the viewpoint of the English industrial poor through the novels of Jane Austen. In the case of Rome, the works of Cicero are so dominant among the surviving sources for the late

Republic that it has proved hard for modern historians not to see the Roman world through his conservative eyes. Cicero's devastating caricature of most radical politicians as crazed, power-hungry, would-be tyrants has regularly been taken as a statement of fact rather than a reflection of his political prejudice.

To find what he is looking for, Wiseman must read the sources against the grain, searching out hints of a different view of events, and looking for the cracks in the conservative story through which a glimpse of a popular tradition might be seen. He must look beyond the accounts of surviving ancient authors to the alternative versions that they were (consciously or unconsciously) concealing. In doing this, he not only depends on a rare familiarity with Roman literature, from the mainstream to its remotest byways, but also on a capacity for bold historical speculation that takes him right to the edge of (and in some cases beyond) what the surviving evidence can reliably tell us.

Sometimes he succeeds with panache. In the casual references of ancient writers to the equal distribution of agricultural plots to the earliest citizens of Rome ('seven acres of land'), he ingeniously detects one of the radical rallying cries of the late Republic – harking back to that mythical age of equality under Romulus and his successors which was, he suggests, central to later democratic ideology. Elsewhere, he carefully reconstructs the career of a certain Gaius Licinius Geta, the consul of 116 BC, of whom we seem at first sight to know almost nothing beyond a puzzling aside in a speech of Cicero. Geta, claims Cicero, was expelled from the Senate by the censors in 115 BC (the year after he had been consul), but was later restored and elected censor himself.

Starting from this unpromising skeletal information, Wiseman reconstructs a radical career for Geta, basing his argument partly on the traditions of Geta's own family (several of the Licinii are known to have introduced legislation in favour of the poor), partly on the links that he uncovers between Geta and Gaius Gracchus, the well-known reforming 'Tribune of the People'. Wiseman's hunch is that Geta also introduced popular reforming legislation during his consulship, or in some other way fell foul of the elite, and this caused the hard-line censors to take revenge the following year. But his exclusion from politics did not last long. We know that, in the years around 110, several conservative aristocrats were put on trial and condemned for corruption. That may well have been the context for the restoration of the popular Geta and for his own election to the censorship in 108.

7. Caesar stabbed to death: a nineteenth-century comic view.

Of course, much of this can be no more than speculation, and the picture of Geta's activities still remains very hazy. But thanks to Wiseman's detective work, we can begin to get a glimpse of a leading popular politician who became consul, then a victim of the conservative aristocracy, and finally bounced back. At the time he must have been a very significant figure in Roman politics, as both consul and censor, but he has been almost entirely lost to the historical record.

Some of Wiseman's reconstructions are far less plausible. Different readers will no doubt disagree about where to draw the line that separates his brilliant insights from his flights of fancy. For my taste, he is far too confident about what is to be found in the work of 'lost historians' and far too confident about his putative 'lost plays' – one of which (a tragedy on Licinia, the wife of Gaius Gracchus) finds its way into the story of Geta and is even trailed as one possible reason for his expulsion from the Senate. In short, he doesn't always know where to stop. But Wiseman can be inspirational too. The importance of his work lies not only in what he argues, but in how – and in the vision of the Roman past he invites us, with such enthusiasm and elegance, to share.

This book is ground-breaking for its simple suggestion that the ideology of Roman popular politics is not entirely lost to us, and for its virtuoso demonstration that, fragmentary, inadequate and intensively studied as our sources for the period are, they may still have more to tell us. Here as elsewhere, Wiseman offers us a view of late Republican Rome not preoccupied solely with elite self-interest, wealth and dignity – but where some voices still spoke out for equality, the sharing of wealth and land and for the rights of the common people. It is a far cry from a nearly bungled assassination of a people's champion by a group of disgruntled aristocrats in the name of (their own) liberty.

Review of T. P. Wiseman, *Remembering the Roman People: Essays on Late-Republican politics and literature* (Oxford University Press, 2009)

Section Three

IMPERIAL ROME
– EMPERORS,
EMPRESSES &
ENEMIES

This section turns the spotlight onto some of the most famous names of the Roman empire – from emperors, good and bad (starting with Augustus in Chapter 11, ending with Hadrian in Chapter 18) to enemies, both glamorous and ghastly (Cleopatra and Boudicca star in Chapters 12 and 16). One crucial question surfaces time and again. How can we write a life story of any of these characters, in the modern 'cradle-to-grave' sense? Or, to put it even more strongly, what do we really know about these emperors, empresses and their enemies, and how do we know it? In the case of every single one of them, there are vast gaps in the narrative – so that we find even some of the best modern biographers reduced to fantasising (and it is fantasy) about the toddler Cleopatra scampering through the colonnades of the Egyptian royal palace, or about what Hadrian's wife might have got up to in Britain while the emperor himself paid a visit to his Wall.

It may, at first sight, seem frustrating that any convincing year by year (or even decade by decade) story of these famous figures is quite beyond our grasp. But there is rich compensation for that in some extraordinary – sometimes eyewitness – glimpses of particular moments in their lives that do still survive and almost seem to take us back to the ancient world itself. Particular favourites of mine include a papyrus text, now in Oxford, of the speech given by the Roman imperial prince Germanicus, when he landed in Alexandria in 19 AD (as we find in Chapter 12, he complains about the journey and explains that he is missing his Mum and Dad!); the anecdote that reaches us, thanks to a mole in Cleopatra's kitchens, of the cooking arrangements and life below-stairs in her palace (also in Chapter 12); or the Jewish eyewitness account of the Emperor Caligula's passion for home makeovers, and his particular dislike of eating lamb (Chapter 14).

What is more, there is plenty of evidence to chew over, if we want to think about how the posthumous reputations of these different emperors have been formed. It is fairly clear, for example, that Nero (Chapter 15) was not always regarded as the monster of imperial depravity that he has become for us – and as he was for many historians in antiquity itself, who composed their accounts of his reign decades or even centuries after his death (notably Tacitus, whose terrifying denunciation of Roman autocracy is written, as I discuss in Chapter 17, in a style of Latin that is almost as difficult, or adventurous, as Thucydides' Greek). In fact, Nero was so missed in some quarters that, after his suicide, a series of people emerged across the Roman empire pretending to be him, still alive after a miraculous escape: not something you would do unless there was political capital to be gained from it. And, although for most Christians he was a cruel persecutor of their faith, there remains a trace of an alternative tradition that claimed that he actually put Pontius Pilate to death – making him something of a Christian hero.

But fiction and film also have an undeniable part to play in how the modern world imagines the Roman imperial cast of characters – in particular Robert Graves's novels, I, Claudius *and* Claudius the God *together with the famous 1970s television adaptation. These are very largely responsible for the stereotype we have of the Emperor Claudius, as an endearingly dotty old academic (not exactly what many people in the Roman world itself would have thought), and of Augustus' wife, the empress Livia, as a scheming and slightly camp poisoner. Chapter 13 explores how Siân Phillips in the television adaptation 'made' Livia – while taking a quick look also at a little known, and disastrous, attempt by John Mortimer to adapt the novels for the London stage (an attempt not helped by the appearance of Graves himself at the opening party).*

The British rebel, Boudicca, is even more a product of modern recreation than her Roman enemies. In the absence of almost any reliable evidence on her life story, character or aims, modern British writers and artists have for centuries tried to fill the gap. Chapter 16 looks at how they have done that – from Thornycroft's glamorous and proudly 'imperial' statue on the Thames Embankment, to the New Age spiritualist who is the heroine of a series of recent novels. To be honest, the real-life Boudicca would probably have been a much more unsettling character than either of these rather comfortable or quaint images suggest.

11

LOOKING FOR
THE EMPEROR

The ancient Romans liked an emperor who could take – and make
– a joke. Their first emperor, Augustus, was particularly renowned
for his sense of humour. In fact, even four centuries after his death, the
scholarly Macrobius devoted several pages of his encyclopedia *Satur-
nalia* to a collection of Augustus' bons mots, very much in the modern
'Wit and Wisdom' genre.

Some of these quotations expose a frustrating distance between
ancient humour and our own, or at least the difficulty of making good
oral quips work in writing. 'Do you think you are handing a penny to
an elephant' might have been a retort of inspired spontaneity to a man
who was nervously presenting a petition ('now holding out his hand,
now withdrawing it'); but it hardly seems worth the loving preservation that it has enjoyed. But other quips still work surprisingly well.
One of Macrobius' anecdotes is particularly revealing.

It concerns the period just after the Battle of Actium in 31 BC, at
which Augustus (then known as Octavian, or just plain Caesar) defeated
the forces of Antony and Cleopatra and effectively gained control of
the entire Roman world. He was met on his return to the capital by
a man with a tame raven, which he had taught to say 'Greetings to
Caesar, our victorious commander.' Augustus was so impressed that
he gave the man a substantial cash prize. But it turned out that the
bird's trainer had a partner who, when none of the 20,000 sesterces
came his way, went to the emperor and explained that the man had

another raven which he should be asked to produce. Predictably, the pair had been hedging their bets: this bird squawked 'Greetings to *Antony*, our victorious commander.' The emperor saw the funny side and did not get angry – but simply insisted that the prize money be shared between the two men.

The obvious point this story makes is that Augustus was a ruler with a human touch, not a man to take offence, and generous in his response to relatively innocent tricksters. But there is a rather more subversive political message here too. The pair of identikit ravens, with their nearly identical slogans, cannot help but hint that there was really very little to choose between Antony and Octavian/Augustus. Antony has gone down in history as a dissolute wastrel whose victory would have turned Rome into an Oriental monarchy, and Augustus as the sober founding father of an imperial system that would endure in some guise into the Middle Ages. But if you turn the clock back to 31 and to the end of the civil wars that had followed the assassination of Julius Caesar, the two antagonists look almost interchangeable. For most of the inhabitants of the Roman world, the victory of one or the other would require no more adjustment than the swapping of one talking raven for another.

In fact, this is exactly where the main historical problem in the career of Augustus lies. How can we understand his transition from a violent warlord in the civil conflicts of the Roman world between 44 and 31 BC to the venerable elder statesman who died safely in his bed (notwithstanding some conspiracy-theory rumours of poisoning by his wife, Livia) in 14 AD? How do we explain the metamorphosis of a young thug who was reputedly capable of tearing out a man's eyes with his bare hands into a serious-minded legislator apparently concerned to improve Roman morals, increase the birth rate, revive ancient religious traditions, and turn the capital (as he himself put it) 'from a city of brick to a city of marble', while at the same time success-fully repackaging the traditional political institutions to leave himself in the position of king, in all but title?

True, there are plenty of examples from all historical periods, including our own, of freedom fighters and terrorists being trans-formed into respected government leaders. But the case of Augustus is unusually extreme. As Octavian, he fought and schemed his way to victory over the course of a decade or more of bitter civil wars – in which the supporters of Julius Caesar first turned on those who had assassinated him in the name of 'liberty', before finishing the job by turning on one another. Octavian then dramatically reinvented himself. It was a change of image and substance marked by a change of name. In 27 BC he dispensed with 'Octavian' and its murderous associations. He flirted with the idea of calling himself 'Romulus' after the original founder of Rome, but that had some undesirable associations too: not only had he made himself king by killing his brother Remus (pp. 65–6) which might seem uncomfortably reminiscent of Octavian's fight with Antony, but according to one story Romulus had himself been murdered, just like Caesar, by a posse of senators. So instead he opted for 'Augustus', a new coinage, meaning something like 'Revered One'.

Anthony Everitt's aim in his biography of Augustus is predictable enough, even if (given the state of the evidence) over-optimistic: it is 'to make Augustus come alive', amid all the 'shipwrecks, human sacrifice, hairbreadth escapes, unbridled sex, battles on land and at sea, ambushes [and] family scandals' that characterised the period. Although anyone looking for the 'unbridled sex' is likely to be disappointed, he certainly offers some colourful stories from the emperor's life, robustly told. Sometimes, in fact, these are a little more colourful than the evidence allows, as in the introductory chapter, which opens with a look ahead to the very end of Augustus' long life and to the events surrounding his death.

Admitting that his reconstruction is partly 'imagined', Everitt happily embraces the rumours of poisoning reported by the third-century-AD historian Cassius Dio. This launches a lurid and highly dubious tale of Augustus' murder by his wife, Livia – contrived to ensure that the well-laid scheme for the succession of his heir Tiberius should not be disrupted by any unexpected recovery or undue lingering on the part of the sick and elderly ruler, and carried out with the victim's own tacit assent ('guessing what had happened, he silently thanked his wife').

Whether this is anything like what happened on 19 August, 14 AD (the month of Sextilis had been renamed in his honour some twenty years earlier), we cannot possibly now know. But the account here reads like a cross between the BBC's *I, Claudius* (which, as we shall see in the next chapter, memorably dramatised the final moments of the aged emperor) and the unsophisticated media management techniques adopted for the succession of British monarchs as late as the twentieth century. In 1936, as his doctor was in due course to admit, the death of George V was hastened by a lethal injection, administered partly to ensure that the news could be announced in the following day's *Times* rather than in the less august evening papers.

But the main failing of Everitt's *Augustus* is not its sometimes misplaced confidence in the ancient sources, or its over-imaginative reconstructions of key historical moments. It is that he fails fully to grasp the problem of the transformation of the emperor from thug to statesman, still less to explain how the transformed Augustus managed to put in place a radically new system of Roman government, replacing what had been a fraying democracy of sorts with one-man rule. These issues are as important a part of the project of 'making Augustus come alive' as the stories of murder, exile, adultery and family crisis.

The balance of the book points clearly to the avoidance of these big questions. More than half of its pages are devoted to the period between the emperor's birth in 63 BC (to Julius Caesar's niece Atia and her relatively undistinguished husband) and his defeat of Antony at Actium in 31 BC. As we know virtually nothing of his early life, beyond a few anecdotes revealing precocious signs of his future greatness, which were certainly invented later, this means that a large proportion of the biography is concerned with the years of civil war between 44 and 31.

The forty-five years of Augustus' reign as sole ruler of the Roman world are, in comparison, thinly treated. The reason for this is clear enough. Much more 'stuff happened' during the war to fill the pages of a biography, or to get recorded in the ancient sources on which Everitt depends. So he tells in some detail the packed and tortuous narrative of Caesar's assassination and its aftermath, when the young Octavian found himself, at eighteen years old, not only Caesar's main heir but also posthumously adopted in his will (it was this that enabled him, after Caesar's deification, to style himself 'son of a god'). Unable to dislodge Mark Antony, the other main defender of the Caesarian cause and twenty years his senior, he joined forces with him and together, after a short-lived truce with the assassins, they defeated the army of Brutus and Cassius in Greece in 42.

Nine further years of civil conflict were to follow, largely but not exclusively between the supporters of Octavian and of Antony, all of which also receive full coverage in the biography. This is an even more intricate tale, featuring rivalry, marriage alliances between the various parties, and brief periods of reconciliation (enormously hyped by ancient writers) interspersed with bouts of vicious fighting – until Antony, notoriously in partnership with Cleopatra of Egypt (who had earlier been the mistress of Julius Caesar himself), escaped from defeat at Actium, on the coast of northern Greece, to commit suicide in Egypt (see Chapter 12).

There is some vivid narrative here, and Everitt deploys some of the marvellously varied evidence for this period with a sharp eye for a good story. He gives, for example, a stirring account of the battle at Perusia (modern Perugia) in 41 BC between Octavian and Antony's brother Lucius, who was himself supported by Antony's then wife Fulvia, one of the most memorable characters in the entire conflict (and the woman who used her hairpins to pierce the tongue of the severed head of her husband's great enemy Cicero (p. 79) – a fair indication of the moral standards prevailing in this war). Octavian besieged the Antonians in the town and eventually forced them to surrender, before pardoning the leaders and sending Lucius off to be governor of Spain. But for once archaeology gives us a glimpse of how the siege was conducted on the ground. More than eighty lead sling-stones have been discovered at Perugia, left behind from the artillery of both sides in this campaign. On many of them rough and ready messages had been scratched – intended not so much, I imagine, for the enemy to read, but to convey something of the spirit in which they had been dispatched. They are mostly obscene: 'I'm after Fulvia's clitoris' and 'I'm after Octavian's ass' being typical examples. One, 'Lucius is bald', is regarded by Everitt as 'rather more feeble'. Given the obvious tone of the others, I rather suspect that it is a nice indication that baldness was seen as a greater physical imperfection in the Roman world than it is today.

It is a fascinating vignette, and a rare glimpse into the gendered prejudices, black humour, and basic emotions that drove ancient front-line combatants no less than their modern counterparts. But the overall conclusions that we can draw from this and the rest of the detailed narrative of the war are unsurprising. Like most successful warlords-turned-statesmen, Octavian owed his victory to the usual mixture of violence, good luck, treachery and shrewd judgement. The wealth of information that we have, expansively recounted by Everitt, hardly gets us much further than that.

The picture changes dramatically after the Battle of Actium. This later, and historically even more significant, period is marked by a relative paucity of known 'events', despite the fact that Augustus must then have been busy rewriting the politics of Rome and embedding a regime of imperial one-man rule in the place of republican government by the Senate and people. Everitt explains that he has been forced to abandon any attempt to give a straight chronological narrative, in favour of a more thematic approach. This is, of course, a consequence of the character of the surviving ancient evidence, which, in a narrowly historical sense, is now much thinner than for the period of the civil war. As Everitt laments, 'between 16 and 13 BC ... Augustus was in Gaul and Germany, but we have no idea where he went or where he was at any particular time.' Compare this with the sometimes almost day-by-day information that we have for his movements two decades earlier.

Part of our problem here is bad luck and the accidents of survival. Had, for example, the account of this period by Virgil's patron and one-time supporter of Antony, Asinius Pollio, or the final books of Livy's history *Ab Urbe Condita* (which originally went up to 9 BC – whereas the text we have stops in 167), survived the Dark Ages, we would almost certainly have a very different, more richly detailed story to tell. But it is not just that. For the long-term structural changes in politics and society brought about by, and under, Augustus are not easily or even usefully discussed in a linear narrative of significant events.

The establishment of the Augustan regime of one-man rule was not primarily a matter of momentary decisions or actions – however much many modern writers, as well as Dio, who provides the only surviving comprehensive ancient chronology of the reign, would like to pinpoint the major turning point in 27 BC (when Octavian changed his name and made some significant new arrangements for the administration of the Roman provinces). The regime was established much more by the gradual readjustment of political expectations among both the elite and the people, and by the gradual redefinition of the very idea of government and political activity. I strongly suspect, in other words, that even if the lost narrative of some thorough historian had been preserved, it would not have answered the most pressing questions we have of this period. It might well have told us more about Augustus' route through Gaul and Germany between 16 and 13 BC; it is extremely unlikely to have explained directly the conditions that made such an enormous political transformation possible.

The historical record has also been affected by the changing nature, and location, of political activity itself during the period of Augustus' rule. Under the Roman Republic's constitution, decisions were debated and made in public. Of course, private deals of all kinds must have been stitched up and plenty of behind-the-scenes haggling went on. But historians were able to record and sometimes to witness the debates and resolutions that affected the course of Roman history, whether elections of office holders or decisions to go to war or to distribute land to the poor. Political decisions were observable events.

With the advent of the rule of Augustus, the locus of power shifted decisively from public to private spaces. To be sure, many of the old institutions, including the Senate, continued to operate. But if any specific, individual decisions were crucial in the pattern of political change that Augustus inaugurated, these were most likely made not in the Senate house or Forum but in Augustus' own home (a relatively modest dwelling, a far cry from the vast palace that would later be built – but significantly part of the same complex as the Temple of Apollo, with all the resonance of divine power which that proximity brought). The political activity that mattered was now hidden from history.

This development was clearly seen by ancient writers themselves. Everitt quotes Dio on the lack of 'freedom of information' in Augustan Rome: 'Most events began to be kept secret and were denied to common knowledge .... Much that never materializes becomes common talk, while much that undoubtedly came to pass remains unknown.' Writing about a century after the death of Augustus, Tacitus, by far the sharpest and most cynical critic of Roman autocracy, pointedly compared the grand themes that could be addressed at will by those writing of the Roman Republic ('vast wars, cities stormed ... disputes between consuls and tribunes, land-laws and corn-laws') with the apparently trivial, monotonous and demeaning material available to a historian writing under and about a virtual monarchy. The paradox was, in Tacitus' eyes, that autocracy brought about the very conditions that made it difficult, if not impossible, for a historian to analyse it.

Everitt's decision, then, to treat the period after Actium more thematically is obviously the right one and, in view of the material, almost inevitable. Even so, he tends to shy away from facing directly the big questions of Augustus' success: what was the basis of his power? Why was it that he could succeed in supplanting the traditions of republican politics where Julius Caesar had failed? How did he manage to transform himself and his image from warlord to statesman? At times the version of Augustus that emerges from the second half of this biography is that of a sensible, efficient, and slightly 'Blairite' British civil servant. He was a careful drafter of speeches (in fact, he did not talk about important matters even to his wife without making notes first). He had a commitment to 'clean government'. He replaced the 'corrupt mechanisms of the Republic [with] ... something resembling an honest state bureaucracy'. He introduced 'orderly governance throughout the empire'. He 'held a sombre commitment to the public interest'. He took no steps to restrict free speech. 'No secret police knocked on the doors of dissident writers', for he 'understood that independence of spirit was central to a Roman's idea of himself'. He made the citizens feel more like 'stakeholders' than 'victims'.

Alternatively, you could see him as 'a chief executive of a large organisation'; and at his side was Livia, his trophy wife who made sure she stood by her man and looked the part. 'If guests were coming to dinner,' Everitt concludes at one point, 'she would need to look her best' – a trite piece of modernisation only slightly less jarring than his description of the vast basilicas that lined the Forum as 'shopping and conference centres'.

In fact, most of Augustus' aims sound so utterly unobjectionable as they are described here that it is hard to understand why there remain so many undeniable hints, even in generally pro-Augustan ancient sources, of potentially violent opposition. He deals briskly with what seems to have been a serious conspiracy in 24–23 BC. He passes quickly over the fact that when Augustus reviewed the composition of the Senate in 28 BC, he turned up, according to Suetonius, wearing armour beneath his tunic and had the senators frisked on their way into the meeting. As for that commitment to freedom of speech, the poet Ovid would presumably have responded to any such claim with a hollow laugh. For Ovid was exiled in 8 AD to the shores of the Black Sea. His precise crime remains a mystery, but the fact that Ovid himself refers in this connection to his *carmen et error* (literally his 'poem and mistake') strongly suggests that his punishment was somehow linked to the publication of his mock didactic poem *The Art of Love*. This consisted of three books of risqué lessons for boys and girls on how, where, and when to pick up a partner: hardly 'on message' with the emperor's programme of moral reform.

Whatever the exact circumstances that lie behind any of these incidents, together they suggest that Augustus' monopoly of power provoked much more serious opposition than Everitt (or, to be fair, most recent historians) care to admit. Violence, or more often the lurking threat of violence, must have been a constant undercurrent in the Augustan regime. It is in this setting perhaps that we should understand the continuing circulation of the stories of the emperor's ruthlessness, if not brute sadism, during the civil wars. However benign an image he might choose to present in middle age, it did his power no harm for everyone to know that he had once been capable of blinding a man with his own hands. Scratch the surface and perhaps he still was. As in many political systems, the economy of force operated through anecdote and rumour, as much as through the spilling of blood.

But the most frustrating aspect of Everitt's book is that he does glance fleetingly at a number of the major issues that might have thrown clearer light on how the Augustan regime worked and what underwrote its ultimate success. But he does not stop long enough to draw out their importance or their implications. He has a few pages, for example, on the visual imagery sponsored by Augustus and his advisers, a brief reference to the famous Altar of Peace, to the vast sundial erected with an Egyptian obelisk to cast the shadow, and to the quip about finding Rome a city of brick and leaving it one of marble. Yet it would be hard to guess from this just how crucial in the establishment of the Augustan regime worldwide such images were.

Augustus was the first Roman politician to realise that power in part stemmed from visibility, or at least to act on that realisation. More portrait statues of him survive than of any other Roman ever, and they have been found throughout the empire – often, it seems, made from a model distributed from Rome. And in the capital itself, he repeatedly stamped the cityscape with his own image in various forms. Everitt has only a few words for what is probably his key monument, the so-called Forum of Augustus. This was a vast development in gleaming marble, adjacent to and towering over the old Roman Forum, which had been the political centre of the traditional Republic. Its decorative programme did not simply underline the power of the emperor (whose statue probably appeared in a triumphal chariot in the middle of the central piazza); it also demonstrated his direct descent from Rome's two mythical founders, Romulus and Aeneas. If he didn't actually take the name of Romulus, he certainly found other ways to convey the idea that he had re-founded Rome, and to identify his own destiny with that of the city.

But the Augustan regime was not based on myth and image-making alone. As I have already hinted, the deployment and control of force went hand in hand with the softer side of political domination. Everitt clearly recognises that Augustus' control of the Roman army was absolutely central to his power base. But again, he does not press the point long or far enough. As the civil wars that brought Augustus to power themselves illustrate, the Republic collapsed in part because Roman armies were semi-private institutions, owing loyalty to their own commander rather than to the state. Augustus nationalised the armies and directed their loyalty to himself. He did this by a vast programme of structural reform: regularising recruitment, conditions of service, and pay (from the state treasury), and providing a generous retirement package at the end of a fixed period of service, sixteen years by the end of the reign. The importance that Augustus must have given to this is indicated by the vast financial outlay that it entailed. One estimate has it that army costs alone devoured more than half the annual tax revenue of the whole Roman Empire.

Such financial commitments certainly left a legacy of problems for his successors. Significantly, the first main incident that Tacitus recounts at the beginning of his *Annals* (a history of Rome from the reign of Augustus' heir Tiberius to the death of Nero) is a mutiny in Pannonia, a province in central Europe. Soldiers complained, among other things, that they were being kept under arms longer than the agreed term and that their retirement package was not forthcoming. The reason for this is clear: Augustus had overextended himself; there was simply not enough money in the treasury to cover the costs; the easiest way of economising was not to discharge the troops (after all, the longer they were in service, the fewer payouts there would have to be at the end).

But Tacitus' starting point is significant in another way too. Critics have often wondered why his *Annals* dissects the history of Augustus' successors, but not (apart from a few paragraphs of retrospective review) the reign of the first emperor himself. Was it that Tacitus intended to return later to examine this (as he himself hinted at one point)? That it was too large a subject to be combined with his successors? Or that it was too risky to take on? My hunch is that it was none of these, and that we have grievously misunderstood his *Annals* if we imagine that it is *not* about Augustus.

For, of course, it is exactly that, as its dark opening sentence ('The city of Rome has been the possession of kings from the beginning') hints. As we shall see again in Chapter 17, this is a far more complex claim than it may seem at first sight. For it is partly to say that, despite the democratic interlude of the Republic, monarchy was embedded in the history of Rome from Romulus onwards. But, so far as Augustus himself is concerned, by omitting a narrative account of his life Tacitus may be suggesting that his reign is only comprehensible if we understand it through his dynastic successors. Or even, from Tacitus' position a century later, that Augustus' reign existed primarily as a mythic origin of the new traditions of one-man rule – a vacant space to be reinvented and refilled by each succeeding successor, every one of whom, significantly, took the title 'Augustus'; in a way each emperor through the centuries became Augustus anew.

Everitt sees part of this complexity. In fact, he refuses to describe Augustus as an 'emperor' on the grounds that the nature of the regime became established only when its dynastic aspirations were fulfilled under Tiberius. But neither he, nor the rest of Augustus' would-be modern biographers, have taken the lessons of Tacitus sufficiently to heart.

Review of Anthony Everitt, *Augustus: The Life of Rome's First Emperor* (Random House, 2006)

12

CLEOPATRA: THE MYTH

In 19 AD, almost fifty years after the death of Cleopatra, the Roman prince Germanicus paid a visit to Alexandria, the city that had once been the capital of her kingdom, and was now the administrative centre of the Roman province of Egypt. According to the historian Tacitus, the ostensible purpose of this imperial visit was to relieve the famine then afflicting the country (which he did by simply opening up some granaries where grain was stored). But the real reason, Tacitus insists, was sight-seeing – for the monuments of the Egyptian pharaohs, already thousands of years old in 19 AD, were almost as much an attraction to Roman visitors as they are to modern tourists.

In fact, Germanicus took an antiquarian cruise up the Nile, visiting the 'vast ruins of Thebes' and the Valley of the Kings, just as his great-grandfather Julius Caesar had done in the company of Cleopatra herself in 47 BC. Germanicus' trip, however, did not go down well with his adoptive father, the reigning Emperor Tiberius, since the young man had broken the rules by going to Egypt without the emperor's express permission. This was the only province of the Roman Empire to which such travel restrictions applied. Vast, rich, fertile, and unstable, it offered a potential power base for rival claimants to the throne. Even without a turbulent queen, Egypt was always liable to be trouble.

A fragment of papyrus excavated from the rubbish dumps of the Egyptian town of Oxyrhynchus gives a precious glimpse of Germanicus' visit. This contains a verbatim account of the speech he gave, in

Greek, to the welcoming crowds on his arrival in Alexandria. In it, he complains about his long sea journey and the fact that he has been 'torn from the embrace of my father and grandma and mother and brothers and sisters and children and intimate friends'. It's a rather cosier view of imperial family life than Tacitus offers – and especially striking when you recall that his 'grandma' was the notoriously scheming empress Livia (whose alleged crimes are explored in the next chapter).

Germanicus goes on to compliment the Alexandrians on the spectacular beauty of their city, tactfully including a passing tribute to Alexander the Great, who had founded it ('the hero who is your founder', as he put it). Cleopatra's dynasty of the Ptolemies had taken over the city on the death of Alexander in 323 BC. The first King Ptolemy, a Macedonian Greek, had been one of 'the hero's' leading generals – and the one who had managed to hijack his body for burial in Alexandria (p. 43), an ancient publicity coup, intended to blazon forever the otherwise brief association of this new city with the ancient world's greatest conqueror.

To judge from the papyrus, Germanicus was given a boisterous reception by the Alexandrians. The crowd kept interrupting him with cries of 'Hurrah', 'Good Luck', and 'Bravo', and – scarcely concealing his impatience – he was driven to tell them to calm down and let him finish what he had to say: 'Men of Alexandria … wait till I have completed the answers to each of your questions before applauding.' Maybe this was a common problem for ancient speakers addressing mass audiences; certainly, Greek and Roman oratory can hardly have been the sedate affair that it seems now, when we read it on the printed page. Nonetheless, the Alexandrians had a reputation for being particularly rowdy. Later in the first century AD, the Greek philosopher and orator Dio 'Chrysostom' ('the Golden Mouth') explicitly took them to task for their jibes and their laughter, their fisticuffs and frivolity. 'I should prefer to praise you,' he insisted, 'as being self-restrained enough to keep silent … the highest praise you can accord a mass meeting is to say that it listens well.' By all accounts, this did not make much impact on the Alexandrians whose riots and unruliness were notorious well into the Christian period (and provide the backdrop to the Spanish director Alejandro Amenábar's movie *Agora*, which is set in fourth-century-AD Roman Egypt).

In *Cleopatra: A Life*, Stacy Schiff vividly captures the glamour and larger-than-life reputation of ancient Alexandria. In the reign of

Cleopatra (51–30 BC), before the large-scale investment in building, art and culture in Rome itself at the end of the first century BC, Alexandria was the jewel of the Mediterranean. Anyone sailing from Alexandria to Rome in 46 BC (when Cleopatra herself made that journey to visit Julius Caesar) would have felt, to use Schiff's apt comparison, rather as if they were going from eighteenth-century Versailles to eighteenth-century Philadelphia. Alexandria was a place of star-studded luxury, laid out with parkland, colonnades and wide thoroughfares (according to Schiff, its main street 'could accommodate eight chariots driving abreast'). Rome at the time, despite its enormous population and its political and military dominance over most of the Mediterranean, looked more like a provincial backwater, for the most part 'a jumble of twisting lanes and densely packed tenements' – its public buildings decidedly unimpressive by Alexandrian standards.

The prestige of the Egyptian capital had a lot to do with its famous monuments and tourist sites. The tomb of Alexander was only one among many highlights, though it was a particular favourite with visiting Roman generals (p. 43). When Augustus (then still known as Octavian) made his pilgrimage to the tomb in 30 BC after he had finally defeated Cleopatra and Mark Antony, he actually broke off a piece of Alexander's nose, in his enthusiasm to touch the mummified body – or so one Roman historian alleged. But the early Ptolemies were great builders on a much wider scale. The enormous lighthouse, commissioned by Ptolemy I at the beginning of the third century BC and standing more than three hundred feet tall at the city's harbour entrance, was one of the wonders of the ancient world. The famous library, which housed the biggest collection of ancient texts ever assembled, stood near the royal palace, and right next door to the Musaeum ('place of the Muses') – a kind of pleasure gardens, research institute and dining club rolled into one.

The Alexandrians themselves were a good match for their city. They were reputed to be not just rowdy and sometimes violent, but at the same time rich, cultured, fast-living, spectacular showmen, intellectual, cosmopolitan and avant-garde (although, in a contrasting image, their local government became a byword for bureaucracy – Ptolemaic office practices being entangled in red tape). It all sounds more like the melting pot of New York than the showy decadence of Versailles.

True, Alexandrian cultural brilliance may have waned somewhat by the reign of Cleopatra; the leading intellectual of her palace was a second-hand compiler by the name of Didymus, who was credited with writing more than 3,500 treatises (and was nicknamed 'the book-forgetter' since he could not remember what he had said in his earlier books, so was always contradicting himself). Nonetheless, Cleopatra and her contemporaries could look back over the last couple of centuries to all kinds of extraordinary achievements, often powered by migrants from the rest of the Mediterranean world. For there had been the ancient equivalent of a brain drain to Ptolemaic Alexandria. The library is supposed to have been organised by Demetrius of Phaleron (a suburb of Athens), who was himself a pupil of Aristotle. One of the most famous men to work there, in the early third century BC, was the poet Callimachus, originally from Cyrene (in modern Libya). Between them the library and the research institute in the Musaeum attracted people such as the mathematician Euclid and Herophilus from Chalcedon (in modern Turkey), the scientist who first identified the difference between veins and arteries.

The intellectual achievements of Ptolemaic Alexandria are well known to us, and indeed a good deal of its literature and scientific writing still survives – rather more, in fact, than has come down from the glory days of fifth-century classical Athens, and much more varied in character. Admittedly, we have only a few scraps of the work of Didymus (probably not a great loss). But the galaxy of surviving Alexandrian literature includes some of the 'hymns' of Callimachus (not liturgical texts, but fantastically learned, highly crafted poems on the subject of the gods – and one of the touchstones of 'difficult' writing in antiquity); the brilliant multivolume epic on Jason and the Argonauts (the *Argonautica*) by Callimachus' pupil and great rival Apollonius; and the pastoral idylls of Theocritus, which were the inspiration of Virgil's *Eclogues* and the origin of the whole later tradition of pastoral poetry, through Spenser and Milton to Matthew Arnold and beyond. And this is not to mention a wealth of writing on technology, geography, mathematics and medicine, some of which now survives only in Arabic translation.

It is, however, much harder to get a clear picture of Alexandrian society more generally, partly because it is now almost impossible to decide which of the ancient stories about Ptolemaic extravagance and spectacle are more or less true, and which are the product of the ancient 'myth of Alexandria' – a city in which, as many ancient writers (Alexandrian and others) loved to fantasise, everything was dazzling, expensive, and brilliantly out of proportion. One particularly puzzling case is a famous procession in honour of the god Dionysus, sponsored in the early third century BC by one of Cleopatra's predecessors on the throne, Ptolemy II 'Philadelphus' ('sister-lover'). We have a detailed account of this, originally written by a historian about a hundred years after the event, now surviving only as a quotation in a vast literary encyclopedia (*Deipnosophistae*, or *Philosophers at Dinner*) compiled at the end of the second century AD by Athenaeus, who himself came from a town near Alexandria.

The description of this procession oozes with amazement at the extraordinary spectacle. Each of the floats required hundreds of men to pull them along, partly because of the ingenious, mechanical – and presumably very heavy – displays that they carried. One of the highlights, and a triumph of Alexandrian engineering, was an eight-cubit-tall (approximately twelve feet) statue that 'stood up mechanically without anyone laying a hand on it and sat back down again when it had poured a libation of milk.' Another attraction was the chariots not pulled by men or horses, but by ostriches. Another was the 'wine-sack made of leopard skin and holding 3,000 measures', which gradually released its contents onto the processional route.

Like most other modern writers, Schiff takes this account as vivid testimony of the extravagant pageantry that was laid on by the Ptolemaic court. But we should probably be more sceptical. If the splendour of the show seems almost beyond belief, that is most likely because it is not to be believed. Take, for example, that leopard-skin wine-sack, whose contents dribbled out along the road (presumably, we are meant to imagine, into the cups and flagons of the spectators). On the most reliable calculation of '3,000 measures', this would mean a leopard-skin sack of a volume roughly equivalent to three modern tanker trucks. Even the richest Ptolemaic monarchs were surely not capable of constructing that. So is the description an exaggeration? Speculation? Or sheer fantasy? We do not know.

Part of the problem in trying to assess the myth of Alexandria against the likely historical truth is that most of the Ptolemaic city now lies beneath the sea, inundated by the fourth century AD, after a series of earthquakes and tidal waves. In Rome, determined excavation in the ground can give us a clue to the character of the ancient city, and to how it changed from the rabbit warrens of the first century BC to the much more impressive (or aggressive) imperial capital of the first century AD. In Alexandria we must rely on heroic archaeology under water. This produces dramatic photographs of barnacle-infested sculpture emerging from the sea, but does little to give a clear chronology of the ancient city – still less to give a picture of what it would have looked liked, and quite how lavish it really was.

Ironically, one of our most powerful, albeit indirect, connections to Cleopatra's Alexandria are the two obelisks known as 'Cleopatra's Needles', one of which now stands in Central Park, the other on the Thames Embankment. Originally pharaonic obelisks made about 1450 BC, they were later transferred, perhaps by Augustus, to form the entrance to the shrine of Julius Caesar in Alexandria, which had almost certainly been planned and inaugurated by Cleopatra before her death. They ended up in New York and London at the end of the nineteenth century, thanks to the usual combination of generosity, antiquarianism and imperial exploitation.

The life of Cleopatra VII, the last monarch of the Ptolemaic dynasty, is even more 'mythical' than the story of Alexandria, and the real queen is even harder to excavate than the remains of her capital. This is, in part, thanks to the inventive traditions of modern drama, from William Shakespeare to Elizabeth Taylor, which have indelibly fixed a languorous and decadent queen bathing in ass's milk in the popular imagination. But these modern versions draw on an ancient mythology that goes back ultimately to the propaganda campaigns of the Emperor Augustus, whose own reign was founded on the defeat of the 'Egyptian' Cleopatra (in truth she was, almost certainly, ethnically Greek) and Mark Antony. It was irresistible for Augustus to demonise Cleopatra as a dangerously seductive Oriental despot, living a life of extravagance entirely at odds with the down-to-earth traditions of Rome and Italy, which he himself claimed to represent. Several of the most renowned poets of his reign chimed in enthusiastically with the official Augustan line on this 'demented queen ...with her polluted mob of retainers' (as Horace put it in a famous poem on her defeat).

In fact, we now take this image so much for granted that it comes as a shock to discover different versions of the 'Cleopatra myth', from different sides. Egyptian historians, for example, have long conscripted her into their own national story, as a heroine and public benefactress. Al-Mas'udi in his tenth-century history, *Prairies of Gold*, records a brilliant subversion of the canonical Roman account. His Cleopatra not only goes to enormous trouble to acquire the snake with which to kill herself, but she also manages cleverly to conceal it in some aromatic plants, so that it bites Octavian as well when he comes to discover her body. Instead of going on to reign over Rome for more than forty years, in al-Mas'udi's history, Octavian died in Alexandria from the venom – though it took a full day to work, during which time he wrote a poem about what had happened both to himself and to Cleopatra.

To be sure, there are one or two pieces of vivid historical testimony, occasionally more or less first-hand, buried within these stories. My own favourite is the tale told by Plutarch, writing at the turn of the first and second centuries AD, about the procedures in the kitchens of Cleopatra's palace when she was entertaining Antony sometime in the 30s BC. Plutarch explains that a young medical student, Philotas, was there and witnessed life below stairs. Noticing eight boars being cooked, he assumed that a very large party was being catered. But no, there were only about twelve guests; as the kitchens did not know exactly when the party would want to eat they had different boars put on the spit, to be ready at different times. So how did Plutarch know this? Was it just a cliché of royal extravagance? In part maybe, but it was not *just* that. For Plutarch claims to have heard the story, embellished or not, from his grandfather Lamprias, who had been a friend of Philotas himself. We have here, in other words, a direct connection right back to an eyewitness in Cleopatra's kitchens, more than two thousand years ago.

For the most part, however, we have no knowledge of many of the most basic facts of Cleopatra's life. Her famous end is perhaps well enough served, with some further eyewitness testimony (however biased or unreliable it may be, and all from her enemy's side). Of the beginning of her life we know almost nothing. She was the daughter of Ptolemy XII 'Auletes' ('flute player,' the nickname said to refer to his chubby cheeks), but the identity of her mother is a mystery, as is the date of her birth. Schiff follows many other modern writers in placing it in 69 BC, relying entirely on Plutarch, who writes in his biography of Mark Antony that she was thirty-nine when she died in 30 BC. But this means overlooking the fact that almost the very next thing Plutarch goes on to claim (that she had 'ruled together with Antony for more than fourteen years') is without doubt numerically wrong. It is almost certain that she did not even meet Antony until 41 BC, which would give a period of nine years at most, even on the most generous interpretation of 'ruling together'. Whatever accounts for the error in

Plutarch's text (maybe a medieval copyist simply miscopied the figure, or maybe Plutarch himself got it wrong), the standard scholarly confidence that Cleopatra was born in 69 is just one of the many examples where modern biographers cherry-pick the parts of an ancient text that suit them and turn a blind eye to those that do not.

Schiff's approach to the story of Cleopatra is, in part, sceptical and businesslike. She has a refreshing, outsider's perspective on this period of Mediterranean history, and plenty of pithy phrases to match. Occasionally these bons mots come rather too thick and fast for my taste. But her summary of the atmosphere in Rome after the assassination of Julius Caesar ('a lively market opened for defamation and self-justification. There was a run on self-congratulation') captures the politics of the period more aptly than the many pages written by specialist historians; and she gets Roman ambivalences toward extravagance exactly right when she observes that 'luxury is more easily denounced than denied.'

The fairly traditional picture she paints of Cleopatra – as a powerful, independent queen, strategising to serve her own best interests, and manipulating a succession of Roman grandees with her sexual and intellectual wiles – is not necessarily wrong. But it is worth observing that the English historian Adrian Goldsworthy in his double biography *Antony and Cleopatra* reached precisely the opposite conclusion – that she was an unimportant sideshow in Roman power struggles that she could hardly influence, the last in the line of a once glorious but now very faded dynasty – on exactly the same evidence. Frankly, we shall never know.

But what of the myth? When she reflects on how to handle the fictions that have grown up around Cleopatra and how to write a historical biographical account, Schiff writes about 'peel[ing] away the encrusted myth' and 'restor[ing] context'. Here she is at her weakest. This is partly because, despite some sharp flashes of insight, her grip on the history, culture and law of the Greco-Roman world is not always as firm as it might be. Where on earth did she get the idea, for example, that Roman women in the first century BC had 'the same legal rights as ... chickens'?

Schiff's problem lies more in the nature of the project that she has set herself: namely to write the biography of an ancient character as if it were possible to tell a reasonably reliable story from cradle to grave (on the model of her earlier excellent studies of Antoine de Saint-Exupéry and Mrs Vladimir Nabokov). To be fair, she is not alone in this. There have been at least five biographies of Cleopatra in English in the last five years (in that she well outranks even Cicero, p. 86); and the appetite on the part of readers and publishers for life stories of ancient characters seems insatiable. Even when these are reasonably well documented by ancient standards, there are always huge gaps in the evidence. As Schiff herself admits, 'childhood was not a big seller in the ancient world', by which she means that for most biographical subjects there is an almost total void to be filled before the age of twenty or thirty. For Cleopatra there are also periods of several years later in her career when we know next to nothing of her life or whereabouts. It is here that 'context' tends to substitute, misleadingly, for biography.

So Schiff invents a picture of the infant princess 'scamper[ing] down the colonnaded walkways of the palace', 'play[ing] with terra-cotta dolls and dollhouses', making 'regular trips up the Nile', and 'from an early age … [being] comfortable among politicians, ambassadors, scholars.' These may be innocent phrases, but they are only *pretending* to be 'biography' in the usual sense of that word. Typical too is the 'contextual' approach we find later when Schiff comes to the birth of Cleopatra's son by Julius Caesar, Caesarion. 'We know as little of the actual birth as we do of the intimacy that preceded it', she writes. That is certainly true; in fact, we do not even know in which year the child was born (or if he was really Caesar's son). But her honest profession of ignorance is the prologue to several paragraphs on what birthing procedures and infant care *would have* been like at the time (including cutting the umbilical cord with an obsidian knife and the qualities of midwives) – and then on whether Cleopatra *would have* had access to reliable contraception had she so chosen.

This information is drawn from any ancient source that can conveniently be brought into the picture, all jumbled together: the second-century-AD doctor Soranus, who provides most of the information we have about ancient obstetrics (including the detail of the obsidian); a papyrus letter from five centuries earlier (on what to look for in a midwife); and a considerable variety of writers on the principles and practice of contraception, from the Hippocratic corpus to the Roman satirist Juvenal. It is a useful assemblage of references to women's medicine in antiquity, but has nothing at all to do with Cleopatra.

The truth is that 'peel[ing] away the encrusted myth' of Cleopatra reveals that there is very little underneath the ancient fictional surface, and certainly nothing that can be the stuff of a plausible life story – unless it is padded out with half-relevant background that is, in a sense, fiction of a different kind. In this case the rich evidence on papyrus that survives from Greco-Roman Egypt hardly helps. For Cleopatra, there is nothing as vivid as those few lines of Germanicus' speech uttered as he stepped off the boat. In her case the best we have is a possible 'signature' on a document authorising tax concessions and the report that in her final days she muttered again and again, 'I shall not be led in triumph' (whether the surviving fragments of writing on cosmetics, dandruff and weights and measure, attributed to a 'Cleopatra', are by her or not is now anyone's guess). As for the fragmentary, difficult, and disputed archaeology of Alexandria, it continues to produce new theories on the possible site of her palace or her tomb, each one as implausible (and newsworthy) as the last. In the end, we should probably resist the allure of biography and stick with the Augustan myth and Horace's 'demented queen'.

Review of Stacy Schiff, *Cleopatra: A Life* (Little, Brown, 2010)

13

MARRIED TO
THE EMPIRE

The Emperor Augustus used to boast, it is said, that his clothes were made at home by his devoted wife, Livia. In the cosmopolitan culture of first century Rome, where silks and fine linen were the more usual attire of grandees, the emperor himself paraded his attachment to homespun woollens. We have no idea how often the charade of the noble empress sitting at her loom, or sewing basket, was literally acted out in the imperial residence. But if the intention of the boast was to convince contemporaries and posterity of Livia's humble and self-effacing virtues (as well as of Augustus' own modest habits), it was a signal failure. From the first century AD to Robert Graves and beyond, Livia has appeared to play a much more crucial role in the power politics of Empire than the image of resident seamstress would suggest. At best, she has been portrayed as a key mediator between the emperor and various different interest groups in his Empire (the historian Cassius Dio, for example, scripts a long – and implausible – discussion between the empress and her husband, in which she successfully persuades him to show mercy to a man suspected of treason). At worst, she has been seen as a serial poisoner, the *éminence grise* of the Augustan court, determined to destroy any obstacle to her ambitions – including, in the end, her husband. As Graves himself put it, in *I, Claudius*, 'Augustus ruled the world, but Livia ruled Augustus'. The origins of the darkest version of Livia's character go back to the historian Tacitus, writing in the early second century AD almost a

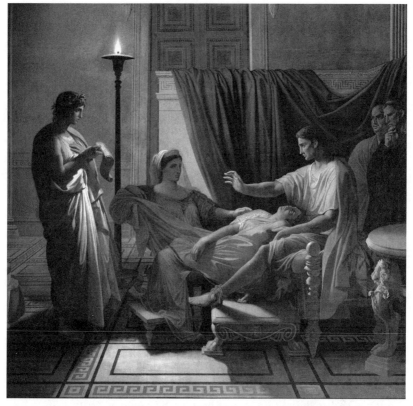

8. Ingres' view of the home life of the imperial family. Virgil
reads his epic poem to Augustus, Octavia and Livia.

hundred years after her death in 29. He, at least, is the earliest
surviving author to insinuate that she might have had a hand in the
death of Augustus, driven by her fears that the ageing emperor was
about to prefer a rival candidate as his heir, over Tiberius, her own son
by a previous marriage. 'Some suspected his wife of foul play', Tacitus
wrote with typically unsettling and unspecific innuendo. And there
are similar hints about her role in the unexpected death of the young
prince Germanicus a few years later, the golden boy of the Roman
court, poisoned – or so we are led to believe – at her nod, if not her
direct instigation.

This hostile image has had a vigorous afterlife, including a chilling
portrait by Ingres, *Virgil reading the Aeneid to Augustus, Octavia and
Livia*. This painting shows Augustus' sister Octavia swooning as she
listens to Virgil reading aloud from his new poem – the lines, we

must imagine, that refer to her dead son Marcellus, another of Livia's victims according to some ancient accounts. The empress herself pats Octavia's shoulder with the icy detachment that you might expect of the consummate murderer. Seneca, court philosopher and tutor to the young Emperor Nero, once famously praised Livia's self-control compared with the emotional excesses of Octavia. Ingres here shows us just how disturbing that 'self-control' might be.

The most powerful image of Livia's villainy for the modern world comes from the 1976 BBC television series of *I, Claudius*, which featured Siân Phillips as the twentieth-century face of the scheming empress. The adapter, Jack Pulman, recast Graves's novels (both *I, Claudius* and *Claudius the God*) much more radically than is usually recognised, in particular making Livia the dominating, evil presence of the first half of the series. Graves himself had taken a much more Tacitean turn. Livia is rarely in the foreground of the book. Her sinister hold over Augustus is explained at the very beginning of the novel by Claudius, the narrator ('The truth is the marriage was never consummated ... Augustus, though capable enough with other women, found himself impotent as a child when he tried to have commerce with my grandmother'). But as the story unfolds, her evils are rarely emphasised; instead they are archly insinuated in one-line hints and asides. It is only retrospectively, when Claudius has a final dinner with his dying grandmother, that he gets the truth out of her: the list of victims is almost as long as Graves had hinted, and does include her husband Augustus ('yes, she had poisoned Augustus by smearing poison on the figs while they were still on the tree').

Pulman's television version, by contrast, makes Livia's murders the articulating thread of the early episodes, with a whole succession of lurid scenes of death-by-poisoning. Livia herself is brought out of the background to become the memorable, if slightly camp, anti-heroine, with a ghastly line in stage irony for viewers-in-the-know to relish (the ambiguities in the word 'food-poisoning', for example, are richly exploited). Pulman even hands her lines that resonate with those of other 'bad women' of film and fiction. 'It's very good of you', croaks the young prince Marcellus, as she nurses him to death; 'No, no my dear, goodness has nothing to do with it' she replies. Or as Mae West later put it in *Night after Night*: 'Goodness, what beautiful diamonds', 'Goodness had nothing to do with it, dearie.' One of the most striking scenes of all has no direct link whatsoever to the original novel. The close-up face of the helpless, dying Augustus (Brian Blessed) monopolises the screen for several minutes, while Livia's voice-over taunts and reproaches him: 'You should have listened to me more ... I've been right more often than not and because I am a woman you pushed me into the background. Oh yes, yes you did.' As she leaves the deathbed, to stage-manage the succession, she issues a hesitant reminder to Tiberius, who has arrived conveniently to take over the throne: 'Oh, by the way, don't touch the figs.' Modern historians have found it very hard to evaluate the role of the real life Livia and the extent of her political power. It is not, for once, simply a question of the lack of surviving evidence. In fact, on some aspects of Livia's life we have much fuller information than for almost any other woman in the Roman world. Thanks to the discovery, for example, of the large burial chamber used by members of her slave household, we have an extraordinary glimpse on to the composition of her domestic entourage. She was equipped, as their epitaphs tell us, with catering officers, cooks, secretaries, accountants, wardrobe mistresses, hairdressers, masseuses, menders, furniture polishers, goldsmiths, plasterers and footmen, not to mention a small retinue of personal doctors (whose malign presence at the bedside of her relatives was always a sure sign, in the fictional world, of an imminent death).

There is also a wide range of more or less revealing anecdotes attached to her name. A fourth-century medical writer preserves a recipe for one of Livia's own concoctions for sore throats and another for nervous exhaustion (without any hints of sinister side effects). And from the vast compendium of useful knowledge assembled in the elder Pliny's *Natural History*, we learn that she put her longevity down to drinking wine from Friuli (a claim still used to advertise the vintage); and we glean hints of an unlikely rivalry between Livia and Augustus' granddaughter Julia over who owned the smallest dwarf (Julia won the male competition with a specimen of two foot five inches, Livia the female – height unspecified).

But if material of this kind sheds rare light on the social and cultural life of the early imperial palace, it gives very little help with what, for many historians, has been the central question: what kind of influence did Livia wield, and how? For this the evidence is ambivalent, elusive and almost impossible to interpret. As Tacitus, and other ancient writers recognised, historians are by definition excluded from the decision-making that takes place behind the closed doors of an autocracy. Women close to the man in power may, of course, capitalise on that proximity to promote their own interests. At the same time, they also provide the analyst with a handy – and untestable – explanation of why the man acts as he does. Just as the modern press has found Nancy Reagan or Cherie Blair convenient explanatory tools, when all else fails, in accounting for their husbands' policy decisions, so ancient historians could always fall back on Livia or other imperial women when it came to making sense of the vagaries of the emperor's actions. There is no way of telling if they were right. Charges of poisoning are a particularly loaded example of just this problem. Women – from Livia through Lucretia Borgia to Harriet Vane – have always been victims of accusations of this type (a typically sly female crime, and a neat perversion of the woman's role as cook and housekeeper). But who could tell whether a poisoned mushroom was really that, or just an innocently unrecognised toadstool? And should we always assume that sudden deaths were brought about by those who ultimately benefited from them? Such assumptions produce tidy history, but they may not be correct.

The upshot is that exactly the same evidence has been used to justify wildly different positions on Livia's role in Augustan politics. At the one extreme are the views of Theodor Mommsen and others that Livia, eventually at least, gained a quasi-official status in the political hierarchy of imperial Rome. At the other is the no-nonsense position of Moses Finley who discussed just this problem in a Radio Three talk, broadcast in the 1970s, shortly after the *I, Claudius* television series. Despite the impression you might get from Robert Graves, he assured listeners, none of these imperial ladies featured in the novel 'had any influence on Roman history whatsoever'. Anything that suggested the contrary was 'just gossip'.

In his biography, *Livia: First lady of Imperial Rome*, Anthony Barrett struggles hard and scrupulously with much of the disputed evidence. It is a first-rate collection of material; but it will almost certainly disappoint anyone wanting to get to the bottom of the historical Livia, as no clue to her power and influence ever turns out to bear the weight of interpretation we might wish to rest upon it. In one poem, for example, purportedly written as a 'consolation' to Livia at the death of her son Drusus in 9 BC, she is addressed as 'Romana princeps' ('first lady' – and the female equivalent of one of the titles used by Augustus himself, *princeps*). Is this a sign of a recognised, even if not strictly 'official', public status? Or is it a much more elusive kind of poetic hyperbole characteristic of Roman court poetry? Do the public buildings erected in her name attest to her active input into city planning, including its financial support? Or are they largely to be seen as a particularly lavish example of the Roman tradition which encouraged wealthy men to endow building schemes in the name of their female relatives (who probably took very little active part in the planning)? And so on. In general, Barrett keeps his head through these ambiguities, albeit at the cost of offering a rather sketchier view of Livia's position than some readers might hope. But even he nods from time to time. In one of his lapses he tries to argue that her horticultural interests and, in particular, the 'distinctive type of fig which bore her name, the Liviana … may have contributed to the tradition that she eliminated Augustus by specially treated figs'. The opposite is infinitely more likely: that the Liviana derived its name, jokily, from Livia's reputed fondness for figs as a vehicle for poison.

It is hard to resist the conclusion (though Barrett himself does) that we will not get much further in understanding Livia until we have changed the nature of the questions we are asking. Perhaps it is for this reason that some bona fide classicists have recently turned to take a closer look at the modern image of the empress on stage and screen, through *I, Claudius* in particular. The BBC series was not the first to adapt Graves's novels. There was a famous, aborted attempt in 1937 to film the books, starring Charles Laughton as Claudius and Flora Robson as Livia (the surviving rushes were stitched together into a BBC documentary, *The Epic That Never Was*, in 1965). Much less well known is the unfortunate stage version by John Mortimer, which ran for a couple of months in the West End in 1972.

Apart from a warm tribute in the *Observer* (where Mortimer himself was a regular theatre critic), most reviews placed this production somewhere on a scale between feeble and horrendous. Aidan Higgins in *The Listener*, for example, pilloried the dreadful lines ('You don't miss the brothel, do you, Calpurnia?'), the production effects ('The Sybil of Cumae … performing awkward gyrations half nude on the lower parts of the great ugly scaffolding that fills the stage') and the character of Livia herself ('poor Freda Jackson … made-up like the Witch in Disney's Snow White'). To be fair, Mortimer was well aware of how bad it was. As he explained in *Murderers and Other Friends*, the play's disastrous reception was presaged by the disastrous pre-opening party. Graves himself turned up, bored the celebrity guests with silly stories about Jesus Christ living to the age of eighty and discovering spaghetti and presented Mortimer with a 'magic stone' which, he claimed, would ensure good notices. It didn't.

These, and other recent Roman spectacles, are the subject of an excellent collection of essays, *Imperial Projections: Ancient Rome in modern popular culture*. It includes a wonderful exploration of *Carry On Cleo* and its brilliant send-up of the epic *Cleopatra* (part of the laugh was that the Carry On team used many of the actual costumes and sets left over from the Burton/Taylor extravaganza). And there is a sharp dissection of both the Broadway and cinema version of *A Funny Thing Happened on the Way to the Forum* (1966). The film's success came from a powerful blend of the Roman comedies of Plautus, New York Jewish humour and Jérôme Carcopino's famous book on *Daily Life in Ancient Rome*, first published in English in 1941, and even now still in print. The ironic twist, for the history of a show with such strongly Jewish roots, is that Carcopino had been Minister of Education in Vichy France and, among other things, had signed the order banning Jews from French archaeological institutes abroad. For all its now classic status, on a careful reading the ideological roots of the book still show through.

But the outstanding contribution to *Imperial Projections* is Sandra Joshel's essay on *I, Claudius*. Starting from the original context and impact of Graves's novels in the 1930s, Joshel traces its history through Mortimer's version (briefly) and on to the BBC series. But she does not stop with its British reception in 1976; she takes the story on to the repackaging of the series for an American audience, the following year. Featuring as part of the aggressively upmarket *Masterpiece Theater* productions, sponsored by Mobil on Public Service Broadcasting, it was trimmed of some of its more raunchy scenes, and introduced each week by the urbane Alistair Cooke, acting as a mediator of this very British version of Rome for American viewers. The secret of Joshel's success lies in her ability to play off all these very different contexts, both chronological and geographical, and to show how they produced radically different versions of *I, Claudius*. Even the very same series, shown in successive years, proves to have had a quite different significance on different sides of the Atlantic.

The Claudius novels themselves range widely; they take the reader from the recesses of the imperial palace to the remotest regions of the Roman Empire (namely Britain). Graves was partly engaged in a wry debunking of the schoolboy heroic values implicated in Roman imperialism – hinting, in fact, that it was among the 'barbaric' Britons that the stalwart virtues of the classic old Roman heroes were to be found. It was presumably for this reason that T. E. Lawrence found the tone of *I, Claudius* 'sickening'. The television changed all that. Filmed on a tight budget ('cheap thrills in the financial as well as the salacious sense', carped an unenthusiastic review, again in *The Listener*) and entirely within a studio, very few minutes of the full thirteen hours of the series feature any location other than an imperial palace or villa; even the scenes at the games show only the imperial box, with enthusiastic crowd noises off.

This produces an image of Rome quite different from the novel or the would-be big screen spectacular of 1937. The television *I, Claudius* was 'domestic' in more than one sense: it brought the home life of the Roman court into the ordinary sitting room; and with its emphasis on conversation between the main characters, lingering facial close-ups and sex, it exploited the conventions not of epic extravagance, but of family soap opera. As the promotional material for the American series made explicit, it was a show about 'the family whose business was ruling the world'.

But the political impact of this domestic scene was much more pointed in the USA. Of course, British audiences were well aware of contemporary relevance of the *I, Claudius* story to debates on power and its corruption. Even those who were dubious about the Mortimer adaptation had noted that 'the play's relevance to the present age is as obvious as it is frightening'. But audiences in the United States in the 1970s found particularly powerful and precise resonances. Reviewers repeatedly saw links between the series and the suspicious 'atmosphere of post-Watergate America' – prompted, in part, by the promotional material itself, which emphasised that there was little 'difference between the malpractice in government revealed in today's headlines and the corrupt practices of ancient Rome'. There were right-wing resonances too. For those in the Moral Majority who saw women's growing power as a key factor in American decline, the behaviour of the imperial women in *I, Claudius* offered historical justification. The figure of Livia was the dominant symbol in all this. American reviewers harped on her Machiavellian ways: 'power hungry', planning 'death as coolly as most women would take a trip to the supermarket'. And the face of Siân Phillips accompanied almost every newspaper account of the series. But the intervention of Alistair Cooke, as host of each episode of the series, pushed her capacity for evil on to an entirely new level. As Livia's murder of Augustus approached, Cooke intervened to explain to the American audience the first Roman emperor's political significance: 'He wrote a constitution which, through the channel of Roman law, passed first to Britain and then to America, as a model, an outline of our own constitution ... most of all he reconciled the old nobility and the new republicans and merchants and middle classes to a system of government that was fundamentally republican.' This is historical nonsense. But it casts a role for Livia far more pernicious than Tacitus or Graves ever hinted at. In this American version, in murdering Augustus, she is not simply a scheming menace, Joan Collins writ large, with a fondness for poison and getting her own way. In Cooke's interpretation, Livia is guilty of destroying the political foundation of the American State.

Review of Anthony A. Barrett, *Livia: First Lady of Imperial Rome* (Yale University Press, 2002); Sandra R. Joshel, Margaret Malamud and Donald T. McGuire Jr (eds.), *Imperial Projections: Ancient Rome in Modern Popular Culture* (Johns Hopkins University Press, 2001)

14

CALIGULA'S SATIRE?

King Canute has had a raw deal from history. He took his throne down to the beach in order to show his servile courtiers that not even a king could control the waves (that was in God's power alone). But, ironically, he is now most often remembered as the silly old duffer who got soaked on the seashore because he thought he could master the tides. When, for example, Ryan Giggs, celebrity footballer, tried to use a super-injunction to stop the swell of news about his private life, he was hailed as 'the King Canute of football'.

For the German classicist Aloys Winterling, the Emperor Caligula offers another case of the Canute problem. He has generally gone down in history as a mad megalomaniac: so mad that he gave his favourite horse a palace, lavish purple clothing, a retinue of servants, and even had plans to appoint it to the consulship, the highest political office below the emperor himself. In fact (so Winterling argues) his extravagant treatment of the animal was a pointed joke. Caligula was satirising the aims and ambitions of the Roman aristocracy: in their pursuit of luxury and empty honours, they appeared no less silly than the horse.

Caligula occupied the Roman throne for just four years, between 37 and 41 AD. He was the son of the glamorous imperial prince Germanicus (who died in mysterious circumstances in Syria in 19 AD), and spent much of his childhood on military campaigns with his father. Hence his name: although he was born Gaius Caesar Germanicus (and his official title was the Emperor Gaius), the soldiers nicknamed him 'Caligula' or 'Little Boots', after the mini-military uniform, boots included, in which he used to be dressed – and it stuck. At the death of the elderly Emperor Tiberius, he was eased onto the throne, aged 24, ahead of Tiberius' natural grandson, who was murdered not long afterwards. The popularity of his father – plus the fact that, through his mother, Agrippina, he was a direct natural descendant of Augustus, the first emperor – provided a convenient veil for what must have been a nasty power struggle, or coup. But another coup soon followed. Four years later Caligula was assassinated, and the throne passed to his uncle Claudius, found, as the story goes, hiding behind a curtain in the palace, so terrified was he in the confusion that followed the murder.

Caligula's reign may not have started too badly. There was perhaps one of those brief honeymoon periods that regularly accompanied a change of ruler in ancient Rome. In *Caligula: A Biography*, Winterling points to a range of conciliatory measures in the early months. Incriminating documents relating to treason trials under Tiberius were put on a bonfire in the Forum (though it later emerged that Caligula had secretly kept copies). A system of popular elections for magistrates was (at least temporarily) reintroduced, while generous cash handouts were paid to the people of Rome and to the soldiers. In his first major speech to the Senate, he denounced the unpopular actions of his predecessor and promised he would behave better. The canny senators, suspecting that he might forget his promises, ruled that the speech should be recited annually (it looked like a tribute to the new ruler's oratory: in reality it was an attempt to hold him to his pledge of good behaviour).

Even so most of the ancient accounts of Caligula's reign focus on his cruelty, his excesses and (following Suetonius, who wrote the classic biography of the emperor almost a hundred years after his death) his clinical insanity – an unpredictable mixture of fits, anxiety, insomnia and hallucinations. A whole range of stories tells how he claimed to be a god, to hold conversations with Jupiter and to sleep with the moon goddess. He is said to have built a bridge to link his palace on the Palatine hill with the major temples on the nearby Capitoline hill, as if to unite secular and religious power in the state. There is also plenty of talk about his ridiculously extravagant lifestyle (from serving food covered in gold leaf to draping his wife in jewellery that was worth a good deal more than the total fortune of the average Roman senator) and, of course, about his capricious sadism. There was, for example, Suetonius' story (pp. 55–6) that he forced a father to watch the execution of his son and then, later that day, to dine with him at the palace. He is also supposed to have used criminals as food for his wild beasts when beef became too expensive. On one occasion, after recovering from an illness, he insisted that a loyal citizen who had vowed to offer his own life if the emperor survived, should stand by his vow and die.

Modern versions of Caligula in film and fiction have been even more lurid. The most famous is the 1979 movie, funded by Bob Guccione and *Penthouse*, with a script by Gore Vidal. It starred Malcolm McDowell as a convincingly bonkers young emperor, backed up by a group of A-list actors, including Gielgud and Helen Mirren, who were said to have been unaware of the soft porn enterprise in which they were involved. (Did they really think that Guccione was bankrolling serious historical drama?) Much more shocking was the portrayal of Caligula in the BBC's *I, Claudius* (Chapter 13). In his novels, Robert Graves had exploited the ancient allegations that Caligula had a suspiciously close relationship with his sister Drusilla. The inventive Jack Pulman, author of the screenplay, went even further. In a terrifying scene that has no source either in ancient accounts or in Graves's narrative, he has Caligula (John Hurt) take on the guise of Jupiter and cut the baby Drusilla is carrying from her belly and – on the model of some versions of divine gestation and paternity in Greco-Roman myth – eat the foetus. The 'Caesarian' itself was not shown on screen, but Caligula's very bloody mouth was. Deemed too much for American audiences, the scene was cut out of the PBS version of the series.

A few elements of the standard version of Caligula's excesses are at least partly confirmed by archaeological evidence and the occasional eyewitness account. No certain trace has ever been discovered of the supposed Palatine-Capitoline bridge. But the recovery, sponsored by Mussolini, of two vast pleasure barges from Lake Nemi (one explicitly identified, on some internal piping, as Caligula's property) gives an idea of the luxury of his court life. They were apparently equipped with hot and cold running water, richly decorated with sculpture and mosaics, and roofed with gilded tiles, almost all sadly destroyed by Allied bombing during the Second World War, and not discussed by Winterling (a few remaining fragments are on show in the Palazzo Massimo Museum in Rome).

Caligula's preoccupation with a high standard of living accommodation is also implied by the philosopher Philo's wonderfully vivid account of visiting the emperor in 40 AD on an embassy on behalf of the Jews of Alexandria. He was at his 'garden estates' (*horti*) on the edge of Rome, and – according to Philo – the envoys were forced to trail around after him as he inspected his property ('examining the men's rooms and the women's rooms … and giving orders to make them more costly') and commissioned the ancient prototype of window-glass. 'He ordered the windows to be filled up with transparent stones resembling white crystal which do not hinder the light, but which keep out the wind and the heat of the sun.'

In the midst of this imperial *Homes and Gardens* scene, Philo hints at the difficulties of doing business with Caligula and at the autocratic style of his rule. The envoys were careful to bow low to the ground in greeting him, but Caligula's response was merely to taunt them with sacrilege ('You are haters of god, as you do not think that I am a god, I who am already acknowledged to be a god by every other nation'); he went on to ask them why Jews don't eat pork: a question which caused a rival embassy, also seeking to influence the emperor, to laugh out loud. The Jews attempted to say that different people have different habits: 'Some people don't eat lamb', one Jewish envoy said. 'They're quite right, it's not very nice', Caligula replied. By this time he was mellowing slightly, and although the embassy left dissatisfied, the emperor's parting shot adopted a tone more of pity than anger: 'These men,' he said as they went, 'do not appear to me to be wicked so much as unfortunate and foolish in not believing that I have been endowed with the nature of god.' It would be hard to miss, in Philo's indignant tale of this encounter, some of Caligula's well-known trade-marks: ridicule, humiliation, extravagance and whim. But it is some way from the monstrosities that dominate most ancient and modern accounts.

It is now very hard to write a convincing biography of any Roman emperor, even those who have not become mythologised in the way that Caligula (or Nero, or Commodus) has. But Winterling has succeeded much better than most others who have made the attempt. This is largely because he doesn't share the usual biographical *horror vacui* which drives modern writers to tell a full life story, even where there is no surviving ancient evidence at all. Winterling doesn't invent what we don't know, but instead concentrates on the evidence there is. The result is a well-founded, and slim, volume.

His main question is: what went wrong? Whatever the murky circumstances of the succession, it appears that the reign started reasonably well, but quickly degenerated first to a stand-off between emperor and Senate, and before long to murder. Why? Winterling's answer is partly to be found in that story of Caligula's favourite horse, and in the serious point he believes the emperor was trying to make.

The focus of his book is the dissimulation and hypocrisy that lay at the heart of Roman imperial politics, and had in a sense been the foundation of the governmental system established by Augustus. In making one-man rule work successfully at Rome, after almost half a millennium of (more or less) democracy, and establishing a 'workable entente' between the old aristocracy and the new autocracy, Augustus resorted to a game of smoke and mirrors in which everyone, it seems, was play-acting. 'The senators,' Winterling suggests, 'had to act as if they still possessed a degree of power that they no longer had, while the emperor had to exercise his power in such a way as to dissemble his possession of it.' As others too have recently emphasised, the politics of the Empire were founded on double-speak almost as much as on military force: no one said exactly what they meant, or meant exactly what they said. It is no surprise that, on his deathbed, Augustus is supposed to have quoted a line, in Greek, from a comic drama, comparing his own role to an actor's: 'If I've played my part well, clap your hands – and send me off the stage with applause.'

On Winterling's model, successful emperors after Augustus were those who managed to exploit the double-speak, and turn it to their advantage; the unsuccessful were those who fought against it. Caligula's predecessor, Tiberius, 'never grew into' the role. He 'took it all at face value', refused to master the game of 'ambiguous communication', and in the process repeatedly revealed the autocratic reality of imperial rule underneath the carefully constructed democratic veneer of the Augustan system. So, for example, according to the Augustan principles, stable relations between Senate and emperor demanded that the Senate continue to debate issues apparently freely – but always in full knowledge of the outcome desired by the emperor. Tiberius, however, insisted that the Senate decide important issues of policy without making clear to them what his own view was. He then became angry 'when they reached decisions counter to his wishes'. Ultimately, relations between the emperor and the traditional governing class broke down so badly that Tiberius spent the last decade of his reign on the island of Capri, governing Rome from a distance and through a series of more or less vicious henchmen.

Caligula also resisted imperial double-speak, but – according to Winterling – in a subtly different way. He tried to fight the ambiguity of political communication that had become the norm in the imperial regime and to counter not only its insincere flattery and apparent emptiness, but also its systematic corruption of meaning. That is the message which underlies the story about the man who had vowed his own life if Caligula recovered from his illness. The intention of this public vow, we must assume, was to draw attention to the man's deep loyalty to the emperor, and so attract a handsome reward for his devotion; it was no indication of the man's real readiness to die. 'The explicit wish – for the emperor's recovery – did not match the unstated wish: to be rewarded for their flattery.' By taking it at face value, Caligula is 'outing' the insincerity, and showing that he would 'abjure this form of communication'.

The campaign against imperial double-speak turned out to have disastrous consequences. The story of the honours given to the favourite horse already hints at these, in the sense that it was not seen as a cautionary tale, but as an instance of the very lunacy it may have been trying to critique. There was in ancient Rome – as there always is – a grave danger in insisting on the 'face value' of communications, however honest it might at first seem. Such insistence can work in two diametrically opposite ways: it can reveal the absurdity of empty flattery, but it can also serve to make the absurd claims of the flatterer seem literally true. To develop Winterling's argument a little: in Caligula's world, the rejection of coded language and double-speak had the effect of validating the truth of his absurd, extravagant, even divine, claims about imperial power. It didn't expose the suggestion that the emperor was a god as empty rhetoric or subtle metaphor, and so in a sense defuse the deification. Quite the reverse: if words must always mean what they say, then Caligula *was* divine.

What is more, the aristocracy was humiliated in the process. There had been an important point to 'empty flattery' in the Augustan system. As the story of the senators requesting an annual recitation of Caligula's speech shows, it was sometimes used by the flatterers themselves as a mechanism of control over the object of their flattery. More often the very emptiness of it allowed the senators to play their part in praising the emperor without having to believe all they said. Strip the flattery of its emptiness, and the senators ended up looking ridiculous, as if they were committed to the words they were speaking.

It was this humiliation, in Winterling's view, that soon led to the violent rift between Caligula and the aristocracy – a rift that ended in his assassination.

Caligula: A Biography offers a sharp analysis of political communication in imperial Rome and faces the central question raised by many ancient writers themselves: the question of how language functions under an autocracy. It is an eloquent and compelling study of Roman imperial history, and especially of the difficult relations between the imperial monarch and the traditional aristocracy. Whether Winterling also has the answer to the particular problems of Caligula's reign and can provide the explanation of its apparently rapid decline into tyranny is another matter.

For a start, he doesn't tell us – or not very convincingly – why Caligula felt the need to attack the rhetorical conventions of imperial rule in the first place. He is also repeatedly forced to adjust a good deal of unpromising, or even conflicting, evidence to fit his basic scheme. Too often, he takes some bizarre anecdote supposedly illustrating Caligula's madness and ingeniously reinterprets 'what actually happened', to end up with yet another example of Caligula's resistance to (or exposure of) imperial double-speak and hypocrisy.

Take the story about a commercial brothel established by the emperor on the Palatine, to raise money for the imperial treasury (according to Suetonius). Installing Roman matrons and respectable boys in a lavish suite in the palace, he sent heralds out to invite anyone to come and enjoy them and lent customers money for the fee – at substantial interest. Winterling puts this story together with a passage (selectively excerpted, it must be said) from the *History* of Cassius Dio, describing the enforced lodging of some leading Roman families in the palace, almost as hostages. After a few pages of rather one-sided argument, the brothel disappears altogether from Winterling's version, and the story becomes another example of Caligula exposing the insincerity of the aristocracy. In this case, he pretends to take their protestations of friendship seriously and so installs their wives and children close to him in the palace. 'What actually happened' turns out to be far away from anything recorded in Suetonius, or even in the (non-excerpted) account of Dio. Rather too far for comfort, in my view.

But we are still left wondering how we should understand the extraordinary tall stories told by ancient authors about Caligula's crimes. If we don't believe them to be literally true, and if we cannot rationalise them all into a single model of conflict between emperor and Senate, what sense do we make of them? Here Winterling has another explanatory weapon in his armoury. He rightly insists that the problems of succession define not only imperial history, but also historiography.

Augustus had answers to many of the problems of governing the Roman Empire: from the carefully nuanced – even if hypocritical – balance of power between monarch and aristocracy to his wholesale nationalisation of the Roman army, so more or less ensuring its loyalty to the state rather than to series of unscrupulous political leaders (p. 114). But he conspicuously failed to set up a reliable system of monarchical succession. That was partly because there was no generally recognised Roman principle of inheritance (such as primogeniture). And it was partly due to bad luck: Augustus and his long-term wife, Livia, each had children with earlier partners, but none together. The result was that the Roman Empire came into being with a question mark over who was likely to succeed, and over the centuries the succession was repeatedly fought out by murder, or by allegations of murder (witness the suspicious death of Caligula's father, Germanicus). As Walter Scheidel has recently shown, the Roman Empire has a bloodier record in the transfer of power than any other monarchy in the history of the world. In fact there were allegations, true or false, that every single one of the first dynasty of Roman emperors was murdered – from the poisoned figs that were said to have finished off Augustus (p. 128) to Nero's forced suicide after a military coup deposed him.

Winterling is right to point to the impact of these bloody transitions of power on the written history of the Empire. Most senators during most reigns were collaborators (as most people are under most systems of power, however brutal); and when regimes changed they made every effort to reposition themselves, usually by excoriating in speech and writing, in ever more gory detail, the dead emperor who had once been their friend. That writing is the Roman imperial history we have inherited. And it determines our view not only of the brief reign of Caligula, but that of almost every Roman ruler. Even the most hard-headed and cynical of ancient Roman historians are implicated. Tacitus, who devastatingly exposed the corruption of the regime of Domitian (81–96 AD) after the emperor's death, had himself been a beneficiary of Domitian's patronage during his reign and had been rapidly promoted by that 'monster' in the Roman imperial honours race.

Just occasionally Roman writers themselves recognised that survival in Roman imperial politics depended on the ability to reinvent oneself at regime change. In the nicest example, Pliny told of a select dinner party with the Emperor Nerva in the 90s AD, where the conversation turned to one Catullus Messalinus, a notorious hatchet man under the previous emperor, Domitian (who had recently been assassinated after what was said to have been a reign of terror). 'I wonder what he would have been doing now, if he was alive today?' Nerva mused naively. 'He would have been eating here with us', piped up a brave and honest soul.

Whatever the ups and downs of double-speak, the fact is that most of Caligula's senatorial friends and enemies survived his years in power to denounce him after his death. Their vitriol is our legacy.

Review of Aloys Winterling, *Caligula: A Biography*, translated by Deborah Lucas Schneider, Glenn Most and Paul Psoinos (University of California Press, 2011)

15

NERO'S COLOSSEUM?

The most lasting memorial to the Emperor Nero is the Colosseum, even if that was not the intention. In fact, the new Flavian dynasty which took control of Rome in 69 AD erected this vast pleasure palace for the people precisely in order to obliterate Nero's memory. It was a calculated decision to build a public amphitheatre on the site of the artificial lake that had been one of the most infamous features of Nero's palace, the Golden House: what had been private imperial property was here seen to be given back to the citizens of Rome. But even this was not enough to dislodge Nero from the city and its 'sites of memory'. By the Middle Ages, the amphitheatre was being called the Colosseum. Not just because it was very big, though its sheer size must be one factor in explaining why the nickname has stuck. It was named after the Colossus, the 120-foot bronze statue commissioned by (and perhaps originally representing) Nero that was part of the display of the Golden House and continued to stand near the amphitheatre at least into the fourth century. Nero and the Colosseum have in modern times come to belong so closely together that most film-makers manage to persuade their audiences that Nero slaughtered Christians there, even though the amphitheatre was not yet built and – while some religious martyrs presumably did meet their death there – there are no genuine records of any Christian dying in its arena.

Both the Colosseum and the Colossus offer important lessons in how ancient Rome remembered its past emperors, and how the physical layout of the city was adjusted to changing dynasties and changing views of what was worth remembering. Simple obliteration was usually a double-edged sword. The harder you tried to wipe an emperor's monuments off the face of the landscape, the more you risked drawing history's attention to what you were trying to remove. Even without its medieval name, the Flavian amphitheatre was always liable to be remembered as the monument that stood on the site of Nero's lake. The Emperor Trajan erected a vast set of public baths over another part of the Golden House: these are remembered not as Trajan planned, but as a building that has preserved Nero's palace in its foundations.

The story of the Colossus reveals even more complex realignments across the centuries. There is a good deal of dispute about the origins of the statue. Was it finished before Nero's death? Was it meant to stand in the vestibule of his palace, as many people – but not all – have taken Suetonius, Nero's biographer, to be suggesting? Did it represent the Sun God, or Nero, or Nero as the Sun God (how would you tell the difference)? However it began, Roman writers refer to repeated attempts to fit its imagery to new circumstances. Several imply that, while they may have left the statue in place, the Flavian dynasty made efforts to remove its Neronian associations (perhaps changing Nero's facial features to be more unambiguously those of the Sun God; although some people, we are told, detected a resemblance to the Flavian Emperor Titus).

Hadrian later moved the whole statue closer to the amphitheatre to make room for his new Temple of Venus and Rome (so, probably, encouraging the twinning of statue and building). The Emperor Commodus, it is said, looked back more warmly to Nero and found propaganda value in giving the Colossus another makeover, inserting his own features in the face and dressing it up as his favourite deity, Hercules. But, with the fall of Commodus, it was soon back as a sun god. The famous slogan, quoted by Bede in the eighth century – 'So long as the Colisaeus stands, Rome also stands, when the Colisaeus falls, Rome will fall too' – probably refers to the statue, not, as it is usually taken (partly because it makes a better prediction), to the amphitheatre.

Edward Champlin's *Nero* is both more and less than a biography. Champlin's main focus is on Nero's later Roman reputation: how the now orthodox image was constructed and how it is reflected and debated in ancient literature, architecture and visual imagery (he includes several trenchant pages on the Colossus). The problem that launches the book is a relatively simple, and familiar, one. The picture of Nero presented by the three main surviving ancient accounts of his reign (by Tacitus, Suetonius and the third-century historian Cassius Dio) is more or less uniformly hostile. Nero slept with and murdered his mother; he killed his step-brother, two of his wives (the second, Poppaea, by kicking her in the stomach when she was pregnant), not to mention a substantial swathe of the Roman elite; he may well have started the great fire of Rome in 64 AD, to help make space for his new palace; his megalomania extended to his imagining himself to be a champion athlete, a talented theatrical performer and singer, even a 'new Apollo'. Jewish and Christian tradition chimes reassuringly with this, painting Nero as a demon or the Antichrist. It is surely no coincidence that, as many have calculated, the numerical equivalent of the Hebrew letters which spell 'Neron Caesar' adds up to 666.

Yet – and this is where the problem emerges – scratch the surface of the tradition, or look outside the main historical accounts, and a much more favourable image of Nero can be glimpsed. Most obviously, after Nero's supposed death a rash of people tried to cash in on his legacy by claiming to be the emperor, still living after all. Unless they were entirely inept politically, this suggests that Nero enjoyed considerable support in some quarters. Champlin has done an excellent job in pulling together other, less familiar examples of the emperor's posthumous popularity. He cites the more than life-size statue put up in Tralles, an important city in Asia Minor, a century after his death, and some second-century mirrors decorated with Neronian coins. This isn't the treatment usually accorded to a monster. Even more striking is the story from the Babylonian Talmud which has Nero converting to Judaism, marrying, and becoming the ancestor of one of the greatest second-century rabbis, Rabbi Meir. Christians too, on occasion, could imagine Nero in a very different mode from the Antichrist. The sixth-century historian-cum-fantasist John Malalas gives him the honour of executing Pontius Pilate: 'Why did he hand the Lord Christ over to the Jews,' his Nero asks, 'for he was an innocent man and worked miracles?'

How, Champlin asks, can we account for these discordant versions? Why was it that some people in antiquity paid 'allegiance to an image of the emperor quite different from the one etched by our mainstream sources, an image which is at bottom favourable to him'? He is not the first to have raised such questions. Classicists have often been much more troubled than most modern historians or political analysts about conflicting judgements on major political figures. (Imagine being puzzled that there were very different assessments of the premiership of Margaret Thatcher or the presidency of Barack Obama.) They have also been more confident than most that some kind of accurate calibration of monstrosity versus political virtue is attainable. Hence there has been a long series of worthy studies reaching the unsurprising conclusion that Nero was probably not as bad as he is painted in the dominant tradition.

As we have seen with Livia (Chapter 13), any number of people said to have died of poisoning might not have been poisoned at all; and charging Nero with torching the city may be no more than the ancient version of blaming the government. Side by side with such injections of cold water or common sense, has come the equally unsurprising suggestion that Nero's mistake was to offend the wrong people. The chances are – or so this argument runs – that his teenage antics, plus his enthusiasm for street-life, shows, spectacles and horse racing, appealed greatly to the mass of the Roman people. It was the traditional elite who did not like them, and who were closest to the notorious crimes that took place within the palace; and it was the traditional elite, by and large, who wrote or influenced our mainstream histories.

Champlin is more sophisticated than this. He stresses at several points that he is not concerned to rehabilitate Nero or to justify his actions. His interest, he claims, is in the construction of the image, not with 'whether Nero was a good man or a good emperor, but with how he might be seen as such'. His study, in other words, is more historiographic than narrowly historical. This, too, belongs to a long scholarly tradition, going back to the ancient world. Tacitus, reflecting on very much this issue, explained different treatments of the same reign as the consequence of the politics of literary production. 'The histories of Tiberius and Caligula, of Claudius and Nero, were falsified while they were alive through cowardice; after their deaths they were composed under the influence of still rankling hatreds.' In other words, you could trust neither a contemporary nor a later historical account.

There is something in this simple analysis, at least so far as the later accounts are concerned (dismissing contemporary praise as 'flattery' is itself a product of 'still rankling hatreds'). A new reign, and even more a new dynasty, regularly saw elite historians, even the apparently unbending Tacitus (Chapter 17), scurrying to distance themselves from the previous ruler – by sincerely denouncing his villainies, or cannily inventing them. The end of Nero's reign must have seen just that kind of realignment, as the new Flavian orthodoxy chose to justify the monster's fall on the grounds of his monstrosity.

This cannot, however, entirely explain the discordance between the different images of Nero, which does not divide neatly on chronological lines. Champlin argues that the dominant tradition has consistently misunderstood or misrepresented the purpose and logic of Nero's behaviour. This is not a question, as it may have been with Caligula (Chapter 14), of overlooking the serious political purpose behind some of the emperor's lunacies. In the case of Nero, Champlin argues, both ancient and modern historians have failed to see the wit and artful humour that underlay some of his most notorious excesses. So, for example, his game of dressing up as a wild animal and then – as reported by Suetonius – attacking the private parts of men and women who stood bound to stakes is, for Champlin, 'not (or not just) the whim of a demented tyrant'. The historians who decry its obscenity have not spotted that this 'joke or prank' is 'a would-be artistic rendering of the standard legal punishment called *damnatio ad bestias*, in which bound criminals were exposed, often naked, to mauling by wild beasts'.

Similarly, some of the more horrifying actions that are regularly ascribed to Nero, such as kicking his pregnant wife to death, may be the result, Champlin suggests, of the emperor's attempts to spin accidental events into an elaborate replica of earlier history and myth. With the death of Poppaea, he may have found an ideal occasion to cast himself as a new Periander, the semi-legendary tyrant of Corinth in the seventh century BC, who made his city great but also killed his pregnant wife with a kick. Presenting himself as a mythic Greek hero (Nero cashed in on Orestes and Oedipus, too) revealed 'a daring new conception of Roman power'. It was hardly his fault if the symbolism got read too literally. This is less silly than it sounds. Champlin has a keen eye for the parallels between Neronian history and the mythic inheritance of Greco-Roman culture, though those parallels, in my view, are more likely to be the result of the conscious or unconscious interpretative framework of the elite historians than any public relations campaign by Nero himself (that is to say, it wasn't that Nero set out to link himself to Periander, but rather the learned historians who wrote about the death of Poppaea had the actions of the Greek tyrant at the back of their minds as they wrote).

There is much else in the book that is the fruit of careful and astute analysis. Champlin is excellent, for example, on the various forms of triumphal or pseudo-triumphal celebrations in Nero's reign, especially the 'triumph' for the emperor's athletic victories in Greece, in which he is supposed to have blended a traditional Roman military ceremony with the Greek ceremony of the victorious athlete's return. Yet overall, Champlin's suggestions raise more problems than they solve. In particular, in attempting to expose the logic and purpose of Nero's actions, he is drawn increasingly, and perhaps inevitably, to those issues about the 'real' emperor's behaviour that he set out to avoid. Over the course of the book, history of a rather narrow type decisively wins out over historiography. So much so that we repeatedly find Champlin passing judgement on the truth and falsehood, rights and wrongs of Nero's alleged crimes.

The murder of Poppaea? Never mind the precedent of Periander, the verdict here is innocent (or at least manslaughter: 'a tragically domestic incident: a wife in discomfort nags her husband, perhaps he has had a bad day at the races'). Arson at the fire of Rome? Guilty. This was, among other things, part of a plot to represent himself as a new Camillus, the hero who re-established Rome after the sack of the city by the Gauls in 390 BC. And so on. In the concluding chapter, Champlin sums up the Nero 'who has emerged in the preceding pages': 'Whatever his many faults as an emperor and a human being may have been, [he] was a man of considerable talent, great ingenuity and boundless energy.' Much the same could be said of Jesus, Nelson or Stalin.

There is, however, a bigger question raised by Champlin's *Nero*, and by any biographical study, ancient or modern, of a Roman emperor: just how influential on the wider developments of Roman history was an individual ruler? Imperial biographers are professionally committed to the idea that the emperor is crucial, and Champlin does his best to demonstrate that there was a significant imperial programme at work during this reign that can be traced back to Nero himself. This approach would, no doubt, draw support from Tacitus' comments on the influence of changing rulers, the fear and flattery they provoked, on the pattern of Roman history writing. But Tacitus could also be taken to support almost exactly the opposite position: namely, that so long as the right words were mouthed, praise and blame delivered in the expected quarters, business could go on as usual from reign to reign, no matter who was on the throne. Even if you had been an elite ally of the last emperor, all that was required was some well-honed denunciation of the previous regime to keep your place in the new hierarchy.

That, after all, is the message of the story of the great Colossus. True, some minor readjustments might have been necessary from time to time, but essentially this was a statue by, or of, Nero that lasted throughout the imperial regime and could be used to symbolise the power of any emperor at all – both good and bad.

Review of Edward Champlin, *Nero* (Harvard University Press, 2003)

16

BRITISH QUEEN

When Edmund Bolton proposed in 1624 that Stonehenge had been built as the tomb of Boadicea he was solving, at a stroke, two of the key archaeological questions of his day: what on earth was the vast stone circle on Salisbury Plain for? And where had the famous British rebel been laid to rest after her defeat and (according to the Roman historian, Cassius Dio) 'costly burial'? Bolton's attractively economical hypothesis lingered on for more than a century. As late as 1790, Edward Barnard, writing his *New, Comprehensive, Impartial and Complete History of England*, still flirted with the idea that 'Stonehenge was erected as a monument to commemorate the heroism of Boadicea'.

Other options, however, soon looked more attractive, if not plausible. Never mind the changing views on the date and function of Stonehenge; a series of rival claimants for the title of Boadicea's last resting place followed. One nineteenth-century fantasy had her buried at Gop Hill in Flintshire (where there have been sightings of her ghostly chariot). A long-standing theory, also mentioned by Barnard, placed her tomb in a small tumulus in Parliament Hill Fields in London – an idea which did not survive a full-scale excavation of the site in the 1890s and the awkward revelation that it was of Bronze Age date, centuries before Boadicea. But London has other possible locations to offer. There are those, even today, who think that she lies somewhere deep under Platform 8 at King's Cross Station.

Ever since Polydore Vergil in the sixteenth century, the British queen who rebelled against the Roman occupation in 60 (or 61) AD has been the subject of elaborate scholarly theorising – from the causes and aims of her rebellion, through the effects of the uprising, the location not only of her tomb but also of her major battles, to the correct spelling of her name (a strange academic obsession, since one certainty in the whole story is that Boadicea/Boudic(c)a herself could neither read nor write, let alone spell). The reason for the intense debate is partly nationalistic zeal, but partly the existence of two highly coloured ancient accounts (one by Tacitus, the other by Cassius Dio) which conjure up a marvellous picture of this Amazonian warrior, but differ from one another in all kinds of significant details. Dio, for example, has his 'Boudouika' – not one of the favoured modern spellings – react mainly to the economic exploitation of Roman rule, and particularly to the ruinous effect caused by the philosopher Seneca calling in the vast loans he had made to the islanders (Stoic philosophy was no bar to usury in the ancient world). Tacitus, on the other hand, suggests that the rebellion was sparked by the flogging of Bouducca/Boodicia (manuscript readings differ) and by the rape of her daughters after the death of her husband, King Prasutagus of the Iceni, a character and a tribe not mentioned by Dio. Tacitus' queen kills herself with poison after a set-piece battle in which 80,000 of her troops die – as against just 400 Romans. Dio's is an altogether nastier piece of work (her army's worst atrocity is to cut off the breasts of the Roman women and sew them into their mouths 'in order to make the victims appear to be eating them'); but his version of the final battle is a closer-run thing and the queen's death – before that 'costly burial' – a matter of sickness not suicide. It is hardly surprising that for centuries historians and archaeologists have tried to get to the bottom of the story.

In their study of the tradition of the rebel queen, Richard Hingley and Christina Unwin capture some of the more extraordinary modern histories of Boadicea with considerable verve. Before the firm identification of the sites of 'Camolodunum' and 'Verulamium' (both said by Tacitus to have been destroyed in the revolt) as Colchester and St Albans, the main arena of conflict ranged widely around the British Isles. Polydore Vergil himself thought that 'Voadicia' (another spelling that has not caught on) was a Northumberland girl and that Camolodunum was the Roman name of Doncaster or Pontefract. At about the same time, Hector Boece in his *Chronicles of Scotland* was pushing the story even further north. His Camolodunum was somewhere near Falkirk and he reconstructed two generations of Boadicea: 'Voada', the widow of Arviragus, who killed herself after defeat in battle; and her daughters, one of whom was married off to the Roman who raped her, the other 'Vodicia' who continued the struggle and fell in combat. It was not until the work of William Camden (1551–1623) that the rebellion was definitively brought south again to St Albans (correctly identified) and Maldon in Essex (incorrectly). But even Camden peddled the myth that coins of Boadicea survived; these are now known to be the issues of a rather less glamorous Iron Age chieftain, Bodvoc, from what is now Gloucestershire.

It is easy to be smug about these wildly inaccurate attempts to pin down the story of Boadicea. And Hingley and Unwin occasionally are: although they let Polydore Vergil off with only a minor reprimand (he 'was writing at a time prior to the development of any serious anti-quarian interest in the ancient monuments of Britain and his failings should be seen in this context'), they have a general tendency to treat modern archaeology ('careful and thorough excavation') as if it is likely to offer authoritative answers in contrast to the woeful errors of the past. In fact, their detailed account undermines this optimism. For they reveal with devastating clarity that, despite all their scientific advantages, modern archaeologists have not done much better in the study of Boadicea or her revolt than their antiquarian, or pre-antiquarian, predecessors.

True, there are a number of archaeological remains that have been associated with the rebellion. Skulls from the Walbrook stream, on display in the Museum of London, have been said to belong to some of her Roman victims. A tombstone of a Roman cavalryman, Longinus Sdapeze, at Colchester has been thought to have been mutilated by the rebels. A large enclosure recently discovered at Thetford has been hailed by local archaeologists as the 'palace of Boudicca'. But, as Hingley and Unwin must repeatedly point out, none of this quite adds up. The skulls, which cannot be precisely dated, probably belong to a long tradition of depositing such objects in the stream. The tombstone was actually mutilated by the archaeologists who excavated it in the 1920s (the missing bits have recently been found). And the grandly named 'palace' is only one of a number of similar structures in the east of England whose function is a matter of open speculation. Whatever the temptation to assign finds to the 'Boudiccan period', there is only one single piece of clear archaeological evidence for the rebellion. Still impressive, this is the thick (1–2 feet) black or red 'destruction layer' in London and Colchester, and to a lesser extent in St Albans, which is the residue of the torching of these Roman settlements and the subsequent collapse of their buildings.

Archaeological evidence is, of course, notoriously difficult to link with specific historical events. More to the point, perhaps, the wider pre-Roman Iron Age background to the rebellion – which might give us some clearer direction on the aims and motivations of the rebels – remains also very hazily understood. There have been a number of recent claims of a 'revolution' in our knowledge of this period ('the Late Pre-Roman Iron Age', or LPRIA as it is known in the trade). And Hingley and Unwin are largely upbeat about the possible counter-weight that recent archaeological work may offer to the old-fashioned schoolbook image of tribes of 'primitive barbarians' waiting innocently for the 'gifts of peace and civilisation' that the Romans brought (or the penalties of slavery and economic exploitation, depending on your point of view). There are hints that Boadicea's world was a more complicated, outward-looking place, with social, commercial and political relations with cultures across the Channel.

But what do these hints amount to? Hingley and Unwin's first chapter in *Boudica* is right up to date in its approach to the Iron Age, but their honest measured account exposes just how little we still know. That 'Iron Age society was characterised by communities who lived in settlements of varying sizes' is not, I imagine, a conclusion that will surprise many readers. Nor will the idea that 'carts were probably a common form of transport'. Meanwhile, the 'revolution' in Iron Age studies has not made much of an inroad into many of the old controversies and uncertainties. Even after decades of excavation, we still do not know what the characteristic Iron Age 'hill forts' (such as Maiden Castle in Dorset) were for. Were they principally places to store the wealth and agricultural surplus of a community? Or were they habitation sites – either on a long-term basis or just in times of danger? And why are they not found in certain parts of the country (even when likely hills are available)?

These uncertainties have a serious impact on our understanding of Boadicea. Even the straightforward claim, drawn from Tacitus, that she was the widow of Prasutagus, King of the Iceni tribe, is far less straightforward than it might appear. What, for example, was this 'tribe'? Though we tend to take for granted 'tribal groupings' (whatever that means) as the main form of social organisation in pre-Roman

Britain, and though we are used to a map of the British Isles which neatly divides the territory into different tribal sectors (the 'Cantii' in Kent, 'Silures' in South Wales, and so on), once again the evidence is extremely flimsy. For a start, most of the standard names given to the tribes are attested only in the later Roman period (as the titles of regions of provincial government).

When Julius Caesar invaded Britain a century before the Boadicean revolt, the only 'tribe' mentioned in his autobiography that we hear of later is the Trinovantes (of Essex). The others in his list – 'Cenimagni, Segontiaci, Ancalites, Bibroci and Cassi' – are complete mysteries to us, unless the Cenimagni are a garbled version of the Iceni (or vice versa). Besides, the spheres of tribal influence that form the basis of the map are inferred only from the spread of different types of Iron Age coinage. These coins do not regularly mention any tribal affiliation, although they do sometimes include the name of a 'king', which may occasionally – plausibly or implausibly – be matched up to a name known in literature. Whether the hand, and name, of Prasutagus is to be seen behind the coins found in East Anglia and stamped 'SUBRI-IPRASTO' (if that is what it really says) is frankly anyone's guess. In short, the evidence for these 'primitive' British tribes just as easily supports the idea (as some archaeologists have suggested) that they were largely a later construction by the Romans – a mechanism of provincial government maybe (or maybe not) loosely based on some pre-existing, if less defined groups. 'Boadicea widow of King Prasutagus of the Iceni tribe' is in almost every sense a Roman creation. Predictably enough, this evidential vacuum has been filled for centuries with fictional recreations of the queen. Hingley and Unwin have collected a good array of these: from John Fletcher's terrifying *Bonduca* (a play first performed in the early seventeenth century) through Thomas Thornycroft's imperial vision of the queen, in his statue near Westminster Bridge ('I like to think she's advancing on Parliament', as Fay Weldon put it, '... but I fear she's stuck where she is') to a host of modern novels, websites, museum displays and (usually appalling) television documentaries. Sadly, however, they have nothing to say about the most substantial literary treatment of the rebellion (substantial in length at least): Manda Scott's four-novel *Boudica* cycle.

This is a trick not missed in Vanessa Collingridge's *Boudica*. Hailed on the jacket as a 'ground breaking biography', this is in fact a rather more racy and rather less reliable trawl over the ground covered by

Hingley and Unwin: the Iron Age background to the rebellion, the scanty evidence for what happened, plus a good deal on the fascinating afterlife of the rebel queen (not much 'biography' here). Collingridge seems to have done quite a lot of her research by long-distance phone calls or steaming round the country talking to 'experts'. Richard Hingley was one of these sources ('"It's a beautiful part of the country in which to work", mused the archaeologist, Richard Hingley, as we walked across the campus at Durham University. I had made the three-hour journey to interview him by train ...'); so was the Director of the Colchester Archaeological Trust ('"I definitely think there was someone out there called Boudica", mused Philip Crummy in one of our long phone conversations ...'); so too was Manda Scott. As reported by Collingridge, at least, Scott comes over as something of a nutter: 'she now practises and teaches shamanic dreaming and spirituality' and 'she firmly believes her subject was given to her by the spirits: "I asked them, 'What do you want of me?' and the answer I received was specifically to write these books about Boudica. They are about the whole culture and the spirit of the late Iron Age which must represent the apex of British indigenous spirituality as it then stopped with the Romans".'

After this warning, Manda Scott's *Boudica: Dreaming the Hound,* the third volume in her series, comes as a relief (or at least the spirits were sensible enough to finger someone who could write). Despite the irritating New Age tinge throughout, the book at its best crafts an engaging and sometimes moving version of the early years of the Roman occupation. 'The Boudica' ('Bringer of Victory'), real name 'Breaca', now for the first time in the series meets her husband of history, Prasutagus (real name "Tagos' – the 'Prasu' was added to impress the Roman Governor), and we follow the story through the King's death up to the flogging of Breaca herself and the rape of the daughters. 'Tagos is particularly well drawn: a one-armed collaborator with the occupying power, who embarrassingly apes Roman ways (his bodyguards have taken Roman names and he serves wine at dinner). As the story progresses, he comes to see the extent of Roman corruption – especially when the new tough procurator arrives on the scene and Seneca calls in his loans – and eventually dies in a skirmish with some Roman slave traders. But Scott is also good at evoking the complex relations between Romans and natives which must have marked the Roman, no less than any other, imperial encounter (and there is a fine cameo role for Longinus Sdapeze, he of the (un)mutilated tombstone). This is a world in which Romans and British mix and depend on each other, and it is hard to be certain exactly which side anyone is on. But even if there is a smattering of good Romans and bad natives, there is no doubt at all which side the *reader* is meant to be on. I found myself not so sure. Scott makes it impossible to back the Romans, who – as an occupying power – rape, pillage and exploit. But at the same time Breaca's shamanistic weirdos (not beyond some horrible acts of violence themselves, when it suited) only confirmed my view that life in Britain under the rebels, had they been successful, would not have been much fun either. All too often, even the most glamorous rebels are just as unappealing, under the surface, as the imperialist tyrants themselves.

Review of Richard Hingley and Christina Unwin, *Boudica: Iron Age Warrior Queen* (Hambledon, 2005); Vanessa Collingridge, *Boudica* (Ebury Press, 2005); Manda Scott, *Boudica. Dreaming the Hound* (Bantam Press, 2004)

17

BIT-PART EMPERORS

The Emperor Nero died on 9 June 68 AD. The Senate had passed the ancient equivalent of a vote of no-confidence; his staff and bodyguards were rapidly deserting him. The emperor made for the out-of-town villa of one of his remaining servants, where he pre-empted execution by committing suicide. An aesthete to the end, he insisted that marble be collected to make a decent memorial, and as he lingered on the choice of suicide weapon, he repeated his famous last words – 'Qualis artifex pereo' ('What an artist the world is losing by my death') – interspersed with some appropriately poignant quotes from Homer's *Iliad*. Or so the story goes.

Whatever Nero's popularity may have been among the grass roots, he had sufficiently outraged elite opinion that by 68 almost every army commander and provincial governor had an alternative candidate for the imperial throne – or harboured ambitions to run for the office himself. Four contenders came forward in turn. Galba, the elderly governor of Spain, had been hailed as emperor before Nero's death. He arrived in the capital sometime in the autumn of 68, only to be murdered in mid-January 69 in a coup that handed the throne to Otho, one of his already discontented supporters. But Otho didn't last long either. He was defeated by the forces of Vitellius, governor of Lower Germany, who was himself crushed a few months later, in the autumn of 69, by a coalition backing Titus Flavius Vespasianus, the general who had been directing the Roman campaigns against the Jews. Vespasian's propaganda tried hard to suggest that he had been propelled somewhat unwillingly to the throne by the urging of his troops, and out of a sense of duty to save his country from yet more carnage. It is much more likely to have been a brilliant piece of calculation: Vespasian bided his time while the other major contenders fought it out, then moved in to 'save the state'. Either way, the result was a new imperial dynasty: the Flavians.

'The Year of the Four Emperors', as it is euphemistically called in modern accounts, as if to avoid the term 'civil war', marks a crucial turning point in Roman history. Nero was the last of the Julio-Claudian dynasty. With him died not only an artist, but the very idea that claims to imperial power could be legitimated by direct or indirect genealogical connection with the first emperor. Augustus' own arrangements for succession had been a weak point in his regime. For the rest of imperial history, what made an emperor – or what gave one candidate for the purple a better claim than another – would be an even more intense matter of dispute. And, as Tacitus sharply observed, in the conflicts between rival provincial governors with their rival armies in 68–69 AD, one 'secret of empire' had been let out of the bag: 'It was possible for an emperor to be created somewhere other than Rome.'

The first contender of the four seems to have presented a very different image from Nero; hence, no doubt, his appeal to his aristocratic supporters. Galba was already over 70 when he claimed the throne from Spain; Nero, by contrast, had been only 31 at his death. Galba was no golden boy with artistic leanings, but a self-consciously old-fashioned senior citizen, with the kind of physical disfigurements (including a particularly unsightly hernia which required a truss) that might still count as marks of distinction to those who valued the no-nonsense, Republican, warts-and-all style of political leadership. He was also renowned for his economic prudence. Nero and his advisers had unashamedly adopted a financial strategy of boom and bust, but Galba seems from the start to have taken a firm grip on public spending – notoriously refusing to pay out expected benefits to the army. This might have been a sensible policy in the long term, but in the short term it backfired disastrously. Prudence was taken, maybe correctly, for meanness; and as soon as they had the chance, Galba's troops deserted to Otho, with all his promises of bonus payments.

In other respects, though, Galba was not so different from Nero. He claimed an ancestry no less distinguished. Indeed, the family tree, painted – as was Roman custom – on the walls of the atrium of his house, apparently traced his line back to Jupiter on one side and on the other, rather more riskily (given the sexual oddities involved), to Pasiphae, the legendary wife of King Minos and mother of the Minotaur. This must have been seen as a fair match for the Julio-Claudians' claim to be the descendants of Venus through her son Aeneas. Yet, if his ancestral past was glorious enough, the future of Galba's line was more doubtful. Like Nero, he had no living heir. To rectify this problem, on 10 January 69, when he got wind of the uprising of Vitellius in Germany (he still hadn't seen that the more imminent danger lay with Otho at home), he adopted a young aristocrat to be his successor: Lucius Calpurnius Piso Frugi Licinianus. Piso was murdered, with Galba, five days later.

The adoption of Piso is the first major event in Tacitus' *Histories*, which opens with the beginning of the year 69 and originally – though much has been lost – told the story of the Roman Empire through to the end of the reign of Domitian, and with it the end of the Flavian dynasty, in 96. Tacitus is now generally seen as the most acute, cynical and hard-headed ancient analyst of Roman political power, although there is little evidence to suggest that his books were widely read in the ancient world (and quite a lot to suggest the reverse). Born around 56 AD he prospered in a senatorial career under some of the emperors he would later denounce, and seems to have turned to history in the late 90s. After a series of short monographs (including a surviving biography of his father-in-law, Agricola, one-time governor of Britain), he was at work on the much more substantial, multi-volume *Histories* by the first decade of the second century. So, at least, we can deduce from the famous eyewitness letters of the younger Pliny describing the eruption of Vesuvius in 79, which were written to Tacitus sometime in 106 or 107, when he was presumably gathering material for that part of his narrative. After the *Histories*, he embarked on another project now known as the *Annals* (both *Histories* and *Annals* are Renaissance titles), which deals with an earlier period, from the death of Augustus in 14 AD to some point around the death of Nero. We do not know exactly when it finished because the end of the work, among other sections, has not been preserved; and it may be, in any case, that Tacitus did not live long enough to complete what he had started.

The *Annals* has attracted much more modern attention than the *Histories*. It has been the key text in most of the recent studies of the rhetoric of history in Rome, and in attempts to understand the nature of imperial autocracy, in culture as well as politics. Even Roland

Barthes, who only rarely made forays into classical antiquity, wrote a short article on 'Tacitus and the Funerary Baroque', examining scenes of murder and suicide in the *Annals*, and exposing a Tacitean world in which the act of dying is seen as the only vestige of humanity left to the free man living under the tyranny of Empire. (The original five-page typescript of this gem was on sale not so long ago for $2500.) Among professional classicists, books and articles on the *Annals* consistently outnumber those on the *Histories* by as many as ten to one.

There are several reasons for this disparity. First, though neither come to us complete, much less of the *Histories* survives: just the first four-and-a-bit books out of an original 12 or 14 (compared with roughly nine out of a total of 16 or 18 for the *Annals*). Second, those four books of the *Histories* cover only the first two years of Tacitus' chosen period, 69 and 70, and are much concerned with the brutal but extremely complicated fighting and infighting of a series of bit-part emperors who, as individuals, made little impact on Roman history, politics or culture. Many readers have found it hard not to regret the loss of the later, and presumably much juicier, books on the reign of the monster Domitian. At the same time, it has proved difficult not to prefer the *Annals*, with its star billing of many of the popular heroes and villains of the Julio-Claudian period and their unforgettable scenes of crime, horror and (as Barthes saw) frequent death: the murder by poisoning and/or magic of the charismatic prince Germanicus; Nero's bungled attempt to do away with his manipulative mother in a collapsible boat; Seneca's histrionic, Socrates-style suicide after he was discovered plotting against the emperor. Third, there is the common view that the *Annals* is the culminating and most distinctively 'Tacitean' of all his works. From this perspective, the *Histories* represents only a step on the way to what Tacitus was to become as a writer; for the real 'Tacitus experience', you need to read the *Annals*. Certainly, his characteristic extremes of language, the extravagant neologisms, the insidious puns, the abandonment of syntax, are at their most extreme in the later work. It is here that we see his most daring attempt to find a new Latin language for the analysis of the corruption and the disintegration of morality that imperial autocracy heralded. It is this that makes the *Annals* uniquely challenging and disturbing. But it also has to be admitted that, perhaps even more than Thucydides (Chapter 3), it is very difficult to read: expecting a student with two or three years' Latin to take on the *Annals* is in some ways like offering *Finnegans Wake* to a non-Anglophone equipped only with a Basic Proficiency Certificate in English.

Yet this relative neglect does not do the *Histories* justice. Even the apparently unremarkable first line of the first book ('The beginning of my work will be the consulship of Servius Galba, for the second time, and Titus Vinius') raises significant ambiguities and important questions concerning the nature of the imperial regime. Some modern critics have queried Tacitus' choice here. Why begin his story with 1 January 69 (the new consuls took office at the beginning of the new year), when the crucial political break had surely been in June 68, with the death of Nero and the end of the Julio-Claudian dynasty? But that is precisely Tacitus' point. By parading (as he does elsewhere in both *Histories* and *Annals*) the framework of the old Republican consular year, Tacitus is highlighting the tension between Roman tradition and the political realities of the imperial regime: the reigns of emperors could not be made to fit the patterns of Republican office-holding which gave the Romans their age-old system of dating ('the year in which X and Y were consul'). Autocracy, in other words, destroyed the foundation of Roman time itself. But there are other hints in this single sentence of major themes to come in the book. The casual, almost formulaic, reference to the fact that this was Galba's second consulship certainly prompts a reader to wonder about his first. In fact, that had been a whole generation earlier, in 33 BC, way back under Augustus' successor, the Emperor Tiberius. Galba, as this opening sentence insinuates, was a man who literally belonged in the past; one of the problems of the opening weeks of 69 was that a time-expired neophyte was occupying the imperial throne.

An even stronger flavour of Tacitus' style of history comes with the scene of the adoption of Piso, where he puts into the mouth of Galba a lengthy speech justifying not only his selection of a successor, but the whole principle of adoption as a means of finding an heir to the throne. It is a speech full of high-minded expressions of patriotic responsibility. Galba praises Piso's star-studded lineage stretching back into the 'free' Republic, and emphasises his blameless record to date. He piously regrets that the restoration of traditional democratic government is no longer an option; adoption, however, is the next best thing, he argues, allowing a ruler a free choice of the best man to rule the state. Many critics have detected in this speech a clear reference to later events in Roman history. For in 97, when Tacitus may well already have been at work on his *Histories*, the elderly, uncharismatic and childless Emperor Nerva (who had succeeded the murdered Domitian) adopted Trajan as his successor – no doubt mustering many similar arguments. But if this speech was intended as a compliment to Nerva and Trajan, it was a double-edged one. For, as Cynthia Damon points out in her edition of *Histories* 1, beneath the lofty sentiments, Tacitus' Galba gets almost everything wrong. Far from there being 'consensus', as he claims, behind his choice, it is the adoption of Piso that finally pushes Otho to make his challenge. His assertion that only his childlessness is denting his popularity shows him deaf to the complaints of the soldiers demanding their benefits. And his idea that Piso's aristocratic background and blameless record amount to a sufficient qualification for ruling the Empire is naive at best. Besides, Piso was blameless only because he had been exiled under Nero, had held no political office in Rome and had hardly had a chance to put a foot wrong; and, inauspiciously, his aristocratic forebears (as Galba is made to note) included Pompey the Great, whose defeat by Julius Caesar in the civil wars of the 40s BC heralded the advent of one-man rule.

The adoption scene, in other words, makes a wonderfully suggestive opening to a narrative whose next stages will principally be concerned with imperial succession. Scratch the surface of Galba's speech (Piso, significantly, says nothing) and many of the dilemmas of succession are revealed: not just who to choose, but how – and what arguments could ever count as good when picking a man to rule the world. It is a set of dilemmas picked up a few chapters later in Tacitus' famous post-mortem summary of Galba's career: 'omnium consensu capax imperii, nisi imperasset' ('by universal consent capable of being emperor, had he not been one'). Further into Tacitus' narrative of 69, the dilemmas are acted out yet more horribly in the appalling massacre of the civilians of Cremona who get caught in the crossfire between rival camps. Even bit-part emperors can wreak havoc.

Some of the pleasures of Tacitean history, however, are not always easily accessible. As we saw with Thucydides, the violently radical use of language – particularly, but not only, in the *Annals* – defeats almost all translators. The excellent Latinist Tony Woodman has recently tried to give us a version of Tacitus that is faithful to the original Latin: the result is as unappealing as it is accurate. More often translators start by wringing their hands and lamenting the impossibility of their task in an apologetic preface. Kenneth Wellesley, for example, in his introduction to the Penguin *Histories,* talks of his 'guilt and remorse', and fears – not unreasonably – that he may 'prove to have butchered his victim'. But, apologies over, they get down to business, smoothing out the Latin into something approaching standard English, but a very long way from the original.

It is, without doubt, a daunting assignment. To take just one very straightforward example, I have never seen any translation (even Woodman's) capture the subversive ambiguity of the very first line of the *Annals*: 'The city of Rome has been/was the possession of kings *a principio*' (above, p. 115). *A principio* can mean both 'in the beginning' and 'from the beginning', and the double meaning is significant. Is Tacitus' meaning simply that 'in the beginning' Rome was ruled by kings (Romulus and co)? Or is he also encouraging us to wonder if autocracy and the city of Rome have actually gone hand in hand 'from the start'? It is hard to see what a good and readable (and saleable) English translation of this or much else of the *Annals* might look like. But something must be better than the ever-popular Penguin by Michael Grant ('When Rome was first a city, its rulers were kings'), which over its fifty years of publication has probably launched more misapprehensions of the character of Tacitus and his historical rhetoric than any other single book.

The good news, though, is that some of Tacitus' most characteristic and insightful themes shine through even the dreariest of translations. The figure of Piso, 'the four-day Caesar', raises one of the most striking of these: namely, the danger of living in the penumbra of the imperial family; the particular peril of being too well connected to be ignored, or trusted. The classic case of this in the *Annals* is the family of the Junii Silani, whose misfortune it was to be directly descended on the female side from Augustus himself. Every Julio-Claudian emperor anxious about his own legitimacy on the throne would take the precaution of disposing of the nearest Silanus – for Tacitus, a Silanian murder was almost part of the coronation ritual. Even total indolence (or a display of it) was no protection. Nero's mother, Agrippina, made sure that one of the laziest of the family, nicknamed 'The Golden Sheep', was done away with on her son's accession; 'the first death of the new reign', is the way Tacitus ironically routinises the crime in the opening sentence of the thirteenth book of the *Annals*.

Piso's family faced similar problems. They were not merely well connected but, as we have seen, dangerously descended from Pompey the Great, who had become one of the most powerful symbols of Republican liberty in the face of autocracy. To be born into this family was to be born onto a killing field. One of his brothers – who had dared to adopt Pompey's title of 'Magnus' – was married to a daughter of the Emperor Claudius but accused of some crime and summarily executed in 46. (Seneca joked that Claudius had 'given him back his name, but nicked his head'.) The same witch-hunt also saw the deaths of both Piso's parents. Another brother fell to Nero and an elder sibling must have been a later victim, for Tacitus ghoulishly jokes: 'Piso had at least this advantage over his elder brother, that he was the first to be killed.' For Tacitus these families represent almost alternative dynasties whose role in the imperial power games was to be slowly annihilated.

We shall never know in any detail their own side of the story. But in Piso's case we do have a glimpse, for a lucky archaeological discovery in the late nineteenth century threw up material from his family tomb. The epitaphs of Piso and his brother Magnus are masterly examples of discretion, or euphemism. Piso himself is commemorated simply with his name and the title of a priesthood he held; recorded with him is his wife, Verania (who survived into the reign of Trajan, when she was apparently tricked into giving a legacy to a man reputed in 69 to have gnawed the severed head of her dead husband). There is no mention of adoption by Galba, no allusion to his nasty end. Magnus is commemorated as the son-in-law of Claudius, despite his execution on the emperor's orders. Only a statue bust, very likely found in the same archaeological assemblage, offers any hint of a family ideology that would fit the Tacitean narrative. It is the magnificent portrait (now in the Ny Carlsberg Glyptotek in Copenhagen, Fig. 2) of Pompey the Great.

Were it not for the discovery of this statue with the family memorials, we might well have considerable reservations about the history of Piso's family as told by Tacitus and (rather less acidly) by other Roman historians. After all, if dynastic murder flourishes under autocracy, so also do accusations of dynastic murder; sudden death may often have been conveniently explained as the work of the emperor, or better still the emperor's mother or wife. As many modern critics have recognised, part of the corruption at the heart of Tacitus' picture of the Empire must have been the gloss, if not the outright invention, of the historian himself. An alternative version of this family's story could hardly deny Piso's bloody end at the hands of the Othonian faction, but might easily be suspicious about exactly how suspicious some of the other deaths were; at the same time, it might have reason to question how far families such as these paraded their rival claims to political power or acted as rival dynasties in waiting. The presence in the tomb, however, of an image of Pompey – with all its Republican ideological baggage – does seem to support a broadly Tacitean view. So does the later history of the family. Piso himself may only have been a 'four-day Caesar', but a century on, one of his relatives, Faustina, was married to the Emperor Antoninus Pius, and her nephew became the Emperor Marcus Aurelius. They made it to the throne in the end.

Review of Cynthia Damon (ed.), *Tacitus: Histories I* (Cambridge University Press, 2002)

18

HADRIAN AND
HIS VILLA

The Emperor Hadrian once went to the public baths and saw an old soldier rubbing his back against a wall. Puzzled, he asked the old man what he was doing. 'Getting the marble to scrape the oil off,' the old man explained, 'because I can't afford a slave.' The emperor immediately presented him with a team of slaves and the money for their upkeep. A few weeks later, he was in the baths again. Predictably, perhaps, he found a whole group of old men ostentatiously rubbing their backs against the wall, trying to cash in on his generosity. He asked the same question and got the same response. 'But haven't you thought,' replied the canny emperor, 'of rubbing each other down?'

This anecdote is preserved in an extraordinary 'fantasy biography' of Hadrian put together sometime in the fourth century AD, over two hundred years after Hadrian's death, by a man writing under the pretentious pseudonym of 'Aelius Spartianus'. It is an anecdote that must have been told about any number of Roman emperors; the fact that here it happens to be attached to the name of Hadrian probably has no significance at all. What is significant is the glimpse it gives into some Roman assumptions about what made a 'good' emperor. He should be generous, far-sighted (note the grant for the slaves' upkeep: Romans knew that even free slaves did not come cheap) and, above all, smart, not the kind of man to be taken for a ride. He should also have the nerve to come face to face with his people: not for him the elite seclusion of some private bathing establishment, but mucking in with all-comers at the public baths. The Roman emperor should be one of the lads, or at least pretend to be.

Most of the anecdotes that cluster around Hadrian tell the more ambivalent story of someone who prompted awkward questions about the fragility of imperial virtues. Romans might, for example, admire an emperor who was well versed in the Greek literary classics, or one who could tell his Stoics from his Epicureans. It was less clear, however, that their admiration extended to an emperor like Hadrian, who not only grew a beard, Greek-philosopher style, but even flaunted a young Greek boyfriend. And not just a boyfriend, but one whom the besotted emperor embarrassingly made into a god, after his mysterious death on the Nile. Similarly, Romans might admire a ruler who took the trouble to get to know conditions in the provinces. But what of an emperor who became such a professional traveller that he was almost never at 'home' (wherever that was)? Could Hadrian get away with breaking the links that bound the emperor to the city of Rome, or not?

And what of his passion for hunting? Hadrian was reputedly a master of this ancient sport of kings: according to Spartianus, he founded a whole town called Hadrian-otherae ('Hadrian's hunt') to commemorate a particularly successful trip. There was a sneaking suspicion, however, that he might have exercised his hunting prowess at the expense of real military virtues: playing at combat, not combat itself. When, for example, his favourite hunting horse died, Hadrian erected a lavish tomb, complete with memorial poem: an elegant reference, perhaps, to the elaborate commemoration that Alexander the Great had laid on for his favourite horse, Bucephalus, but an inevitable reminder also of how things had changed – in the good old days favourite horses were used to conquer the world, not to spear a few boars.

Similar problems are raised by Hadrian's great 'villa' at Tivoli, some twenty miles outside Rome. 'Villa' is an understatement, for this was the biggest Roman palace ever built, covering an area more than twice the size of the town of Pompeii (it was almost as large as Hyde Park). It was not just a single building, more a city in itself – combining grand entertainment suites, bathing complexes, libraries, theatres, dining rooms, kitchens, service quarters and fantastic pleasure gardens. A visit to the site today captures little of the original impression; most of it is still not properly excavated and the standing ruins are very ruined indeed. (The fact that it is now the fourth most visited state monument in Italy probably has less to do with the surviving remains or the fame of Hadrian than with the presence of the second most visited monument – the Villa d'Este – just up the road.) But the literally hundreds of statues from it, dug up in the eighteenth century, sold on the Grand Tour antiques market and now adorning the Western world's museums (including the British Museum), are evidence enough of its almost unbelievable riches; while the various attempted reconstructions, from Piranesi on, combined (as we shall see) with some strange remarks in Spartianus, help to fill out the picture of luxury on a colossal scale. The Villa at Tivoli looks like a monument to megalomania, whether on the part of Hadrian or of his architects, or (more likely) of both.

The question is partly where (or how) to fix the dividing line between the upmarket elegance of an emperor and the decadent vulgarity of a tyrant. This is a problem insistently raised by many of the Villa's 'amenities': for example, the Water Dining Rooms, where the guests reclined around a pool of water and (so one reconstruction has it) steered the delicacies round to each other on a fleet of tiny boats. (Slaves would be on hand, of course, to rescue the beached pickles.) The best-known and most photographed monument on the site, the 'Canopus', with colonnade, canal and miniature temple, once thought to be a monument to Hadrian's beloved boyfriend, Antinous, is now interpreted as one of these dining areas; here the diners took their fill, stretched out in front of the water on couches set in a replica of a famous shrine of the god Serapis. Either learned pastiche for sophisticated diners, or the Roman equivalent of McDonald's serving Big Macs in a look-alike Sistine Chapel (tarted-up with ornamental fountains and fairy lights).

There is also the bigger question of what the Villa as a whole might be taken to represent. Spartianus writes of it as a microcosm of the Roman Empire itself: Hadrian 'actually gave to parts of it the names of provinces and places of the greatest renown, calling them, for instance, Lyceum, Academy, Prytaneum, Canopus, Poikile and Tempe'. In other words, the philosophical schools, as well as some of the most famous monuments of Athens and the Eastern Mediterranean, were somehow given a presence in Hadrian's palace. Spartianus was not necessarily any better informed than we are about the emperor's intentions, but it is certainly the case that some of the Villa's features (like the Canopus) seem to mimic these great buildings or famous features. It is hard to resist the conclusion that the Tivoli palace and its designers were making a statement about imperial possession, that they were strategically conflating imperial territory with the emperor's private estate. To put it another way, the Villa meant that Hadrian could be 'abroad' even when he was 'at home'.

At the same time, the similarities between the image of Hadrian and that of the monster Emperor Nero, half a century or so earlier, are very striking. In both cases, the anecdotal tradition stresses their un-Roman devotion to all things Greek. (Nero is said to have enjoyed a magnificent royal progress round Greece, competing – and winning – in all the major festivals that were re-scheduled to coincide with his visit, before finally and ostentatiously granting the country its 'freedom'.) They also shared a passion for palatial building, Nero's Golden House being an obvious precursor of the palace at Tivoli (Nero's place covered a relatively modest 120 acres, but equipped with state-of-the-art revolving ceilings and a colossal bronze statue – probably of the emperor (p. 144) – in its entrance hall).

Why, then, was Nero overthrown and demonised, while Hadrian died safely in his bed and escaped with nothing more damning than an awkward question mark over his aims and motives? Partly, no doubt, because Hadrian walked the tightrope of imperial image-making more deftly than Nero. The Golden House caused offence because it monopolised the heart of the city of Rome itself ('Romans flee to Veii – your city has become one man's house' was a well-known joke against Nero's building schemes), whereas Hadrian's yet more grandiose Villa was at a discreet (enough) distance from the capital. Partly, the question provides its own answer: most Roman rulers were not overthrown because they were demons or demonised (my guess is that assassinations were more often the result of self-serving rivalries within the palace than of political principle or moral outrage), they were demonised because they were overthrown. If one of the many attempts on Hadrian's life had been successful, he, too, would most probably have been written into history as a tyrannical maniac. Instead, whatever the truth about his regime, his loyal and chosen successor, Antoninus Pius, made sure that posterity did not treat him as badly as it might have done – or (who knows?) as he might have deserved.

Anthony Birley does not have much time for problems of this kind. His biography of Hadrian deals with the Villa at Tivoli in little more than a single page (mostly concerned with the names of other people of Spanish origin, like Hadrian, who might, or might not, have owned villas nearby). He devotes no space at all to wider questions: how imperial reputations were formed, or even how to evaluate the rich anecdotal tradition that goes on telling almost exactly the same stories about a whole series of different emperors. Birley's method is not much more than blind faith: quoting a well-known anecdote about Hadrian's encounter with a peasant woman (Hadrian said he was too busy to speak to her; 'then stop being emperor', she retorted, so he turned back), he admits that it is also told about a number of earlier Greek rulers; but he still manages to summon up enough credulity to assert that in this case 'it is likely to be genuine for all that.' If he feels any doubts about what a modern biography of a Roman emperor is *for*, about what it should contain or, indeed, whether a modern model of a 'life story', still less a 'personality', is an appropriate one to foist on the Romans, he certainly does not share them with the reader.

Birley adopts a no-nonsense approach. Starting at the beginning, he charts the course of Hadrian's life until his dying breath. He asks: what offices did Hadrian hold, who advanced his career, who were his friends (and enemies), where did he go, who did he go with, how did he get there, what did he do when he had arrived, what did he do next? These are harmless enough questions: the problem is that there is virtually no evidence from which to answer most of them. True, there are plenty of anecdotes about Hadrian, there is an enormous quantity of visual material, and not only at Tivoli (he sponsored the grandest building programme in Athens since the development of the Acropolis under Pericles); and a good deal of contemporary philosophy and rhetoric, as well as some startling poetry – including fragments of a mini-epic of Hadrian and Antinous hunting in Africa. What is missing, crucially, is any substantial narrative of Hadrian's life or reign that attempts to lay out the events within some kind of chronological framework. All we have, for a reign of twenty years, are the 20-odd pages of Spartianus (an ideological fantasy composed centuries after Hadrian's death) and about the same amount of Byzantine excerpts from Cassius Dio's account of the period, written in the third century. How, then, has Birley constructed such a long and detailed chronological narrative of Hadrian's life from this unpromising material? Where has all the information come from? Quite simply, how has he filled the pages?

The way historians of the ancient world have always done, by a combination of scholarship, conjecture and fiction. It does not take long, as you read *Hadrian*, to spot the favourite tactics for expansion. First, Birley extracts a 'fact' from Spartianus or Dio: for example, that Hadrian went to Germany (or Britain, or Greece, or Asia). Next, he reflects on the range of personnel who *might* have been involved. This can last up to a page: 'Bradua seems to have accompanied Hadrian on his travels ... it might be that he first joined the Imperial party at this stage'; 'Sabina's presence was deemed advisable, no doubt'; 'other senators were probably in the party as well ... slaves and freedmen would have been in attendance, too.' When this line of conjecture is exhausted, he turns to the route. How might Hadrian have travelled from A to B? 'He cannot have been in this part of Asia without visiting Pergamum'; 'it is hard to deny Hadrian a call at the famous oracle of Apollo at Claros'; 'it is hard to believe he did not take the chance of visiting Olympia'; 'it is easy to envisage the energetic emperor climbing the triple peak of the Eildon Hills to survey the Tweed valley.'

The wilder the speculation, the greater the panoply of scholarship. Fragmentary inscriptions are dissected in detail (largely because Birley conveniently assumes that an inscribed dedication to Hadrian in town X means that Hadrian actually visited town X – when there are plenty of other reasons to account for such displays of local loyalty). Poetry is grilled for 'facts' that it could never yield. In one horribly memorable argument he takes a fragment of an epigram by the poet/historian Florus ('I don't want to be the emperor/Strolling about among the Britons') as evidence to support his claim that Hadrian made his first inspection of Hadrian's Wall on foot. Almost equally memorable is Birley's invention of a summit conference on the River Euphrates in the mid-120s between Hadrian and the Parthian king, each supported by their respective (conjectural) friends and 'with each side coming across in turn for dinner': this exercise in fantasy stems from just one phrase in Spartianus, recording that the emperor halted a war with Parthia 'by negotiation' ('conloquio').

To be fair to Birley, he does signal his conjectures, guesses and inferences for what they are. Obsessively so. His text is littered with the technical terminology of 'careful' ancient history: 'presumably', 'one may readily postulate', 'the odds are that', 'it is no more than a guess', 'no doubt', 'in all likelihood', 'on this hypothesis'. Such phrases occur literally hundreds of times throughout the book. The problem with this method is not its dishonesty (though readers should be warned that many of Birley's terms are used in their narrowest academic sense: 'no doubt' means 'this is an extremely dodgy speculation'). The real issue is that this veneer of scrupulous scholarship ('I shall claim nothing as fact that I cannot firmly authenticate') turns out to act as a brilliant alibi for outright fiction: 'I am at liberty to spin any line I fancy, provided I admit that it is conjecture.' A biography of Hadrian (or of almost any Roman emperor) stretching over four hundred pages is bound to be largely fiction. Birley's problem, *it may be conjectured*, is that he is pretending (to himself, *no doubt*, as much as to anyone else) that it is not.

Publishers like biographies, because – so we're led to believe – they sell. But it cannot have been mere commercial pressure that induced the immensely knowledgeable, careful and scholarly Birley to concoct his *Hadrian*. The problem also has to do with ancient history itself, as a discipline, and with what modern historians of the ancient world think it is worth studying and writing about. Contrary to popular opinion, we are not starved of evidence: enough material survives from the Roman world alone to last any historian's lifetime; and if you include relevant material from Judaism and early Christianity, the problem is one of excess, not shortness of supply. Yet historians still start their books with a ritual lament about 'the sources' and their inadequacy. The lament is not entirely insincere (though it is something of a self-constructed problem): the sources often *are* inadequate for the particular questions that historians choose to pose. But that is part of the ancient-historical game: first pick your question, then demonstrate the appalling difficulty of finding an answer given the paucity of the evidence, finally triumph over that difficulty by scholarly 'skill'. Prestige in this business goes to those who outwit their sources, prising unexpected answers from unexpected places, and who play the clever (sometimes too clever) detective against an apparent conspiracy of ancient silence. This is true right across the discipline: as much for radical young social historians of the ancient family as for bluff traditionalists like Birley.

The sad thing is that, as *Hadrian* shows, it is all a missed opportunity. Instead of fantasising about the route Hadrian took to get to Bithynia or where Sabina went (a ladies' trip to the local spa bath?) while her emperor-husband visited his Wall, Birley could have stopped to think harder about some of the material we do have and know: the extraordinary writing, for example, of one of Hadrian's own freedmen,

Phlegon of Tralles, who produced a famous *Book of Marvels*, a wonder-fully evocative Tales of the Ancient Supernatural (as it is, Phlegon appears in Birley only to testify to the emperor's route around the East); or the series of surviving portrait sculptures of Hadrian that projected a distinctive, and in some ways strikingly new, image of the Roman emperor across the world.

In fact, the book is a missed opportunity on a bigger scale than even this might suggest. Seen in a wider context, the reign of Hadrian marked the start of a 'velvet revolution', the first moment, after its conquest of the Greek world, when the nature of Roman imperi-alism was comprehensively revised. It was a period of startling new strategies for integrating the Greek and Roman cultural traditions, when 'Roman', 'Greek' and 'citizen of a world empire' came to mean something radically new. Even Hadrian's constant travelling may suggest something more than mere personal *Wanderlust* – in fact it signalled a major change in ideas of where the emperor 'belonged'. Meanwhile, Birley is worrying about the quickest route between Spain and Antioch.

Review of Anthony Birley, *Hadrian: The Restless Emperor* (Routledge, 1997)

Section Four

ROME FROM THE
BOTTOM UP

This section wonders what Rome looked like from the point of view of ordinary Romans – from the slaves to the squaddies who patrolled Hadrian's Wall (or, for that matter, the provincials they were trying to keep in order). What can we say about how those who were not rich, powerful or famous spent their lives?

The answer is: we can say rather more than you might think. It will come as no surprise that it is even less possible to write a biography of any ordinary Roman than of an emperor. Nonetheless, a whole variety of material survives that brings the world of the poor, the humble, and the disadvantaged back to life. Chapter 20 looks at what the bones of the victims of Pompeii can tell us about how those people lived, as well as exploring some forgotten texts that lift the lid on the day-to-day worries of the average inhabitant of the Roman empire. Pride of place must go to an ancient fortune-teller's kit, which answered such perennial questions as 'Am I about to be caught as an adulterer?' or 'Will the one who is sick survive?' (not to mention some less perennial ones, such as 'Am I going to be sold?' or 'Have I been poisoned?'). Chapter 22 celebrates the Roman letters and documents that over the last couple of decades have been discovered at the fort of Vindolanda near Hadrian's Wall – from a lady's birthday party invitation to lists of food consumed in the officers' mess; and it wonders what they tell us about a Roman squaddie's life in the frozen north (for one thing, it was much more 'family friendly' than we often suppose).

But thinking about life beyond the elite also raises big questions that are still debated about the infrastructure of the Roman world, and how it actually functioned. One of the most important, and puzzling, issues is Roman slavery

(Chapter 19). Why did the Romans free so many of their slaves? What differ-ence did it make to Roman society in general that so many free people were ex-slaves, or descended from them? And, once Rome's major wars of conquest were over, where did all the new slaves come from to replace those that had been freed or died? Should we imagine large-scale people-trafficking on the margins of the empire?

Big questions are also raised about Roman imperialism and militarism. Chapter 21 confronts some current debates on just how keen on war Rome, or the average Roman, was. Were they really as committed to brutality as they have often been painted? And what view did people living in the generally peaceful centre of the empire have of the wars fought in their name hundreds of miles away? Chapter 22 brings some of those issues down to earth in Roman Britain, by asking how violent the Roman conquest and occupation of the province was, what the scale of casualties might have been. But it also asks, more generally, how we should understand the interactions between the invaders and the British people. How 'Roman' did the province ever become? Did Roman culture in some form reach down to the average 'bloody Brits' (Brittunculi, *as the Romans sometimes called them)?*

Another aspect of Roman imperialism is language – not just how far Latin wiped out the other languages it met in its path, but how communication actually took place between the Roman governors, military officials and their staff, and the provincial populations. In the eastern part of the Roman empire, that problem was less marked, as many elite Romans were fluent in Greek, which more or less acted as a lingua franca of Roman rule. But how would a Roman senator have coped when he got off the boat in Britain for a short stint governing the province? And in what language did the Roman squaddies deal with the 'bloody Brits'? The final chapter in this section looks at bilingualism in the Roman world: not just the Greek that could be written and spoken by Romans at the top of the social spectrum, but the bits of foreign languages (the ancient equivalent of 'holiday French') picked up by many people in the multicultural world of the empire. We have evidence for Romans who could 'get by' in Carthaginian Punic, and for potters in Gaul dealing in Latin with their Roman bosses. But the most vivid and touching exhibit of all is a tombstone from Roman South Shields, put up by a man from Palmyra, in Syria, to his wife, (an ex-slave) called Regina (Fig. 12). She is commemorated on the stone, bilingually, in both Latin and Aramaic. One has to wonder how many people in Roman South Shields knew Aramaic – or much Latin, for that matter.

19

EX-SLAVES AND
SNOBBERY

On a dirty patch of grass next to a tram terminus in modern Rome
is one of the most intriguing monuments to have survived from
the ancient world. It is the tomb of a Roman baker, Marcus Vergilius
Eurysaces, who died around the middle of the first century BC. Over
30 foot high, it is a visual joke. Its strange shape and decoration mimic
on a grand scale the various tools of the baker's trade, from mixing
bowls to kneading machines; in a way, the whole tomb can be read as
an image of a bakery, or a vast bread oven. And, just to make it explicit,
around the top (originally on all four sides of the monument, but one
has been lost), run detailed sculpted friezes showing different stages
in the bread-making process: from the buying of the grain, through
grinding, mixing and baking, to the loaves being weighed and sent
out to be sold. It offers an illustrated handbook of the Roman bakery
business, and a wonderful document of pride in the job (as well as –
given the tomb's size and splendour – the profits to be made from it).

Eurysaces was both lucky and unlucky in his choice of site for his
memorial. Unlucky, because he had purchased a prime and (presumably) expensive position where two main roads met, just outside the
city limits. But within a few decades his monument was completely
overshadowed – indeed, practically hidden – by a huge new aqueduct,
which ran into the city hardly more than a few feet away from it. Lucky,
because the aqueduct was later incorporated into the city wall, and
eventually the fortifications of one of the city gates (the present Porta

9. The idiosyncratic baker's tomb is now overshadowed
by the Roman aqueduct and later city gate.

Maggiore) were built around Eurysaces' tomb, preserving it almost
perfectly until it was brought to light again in the nineteenth century –
giving the baker more lasting fame than he could ever have dreamt of.

But that fame was two-edged. Modern scholars have been very
struck by the monument – and also very snobbish about it. The usual
assumption is that the baker was an ex-slave (the text on the tomb
does not actually state that explicitly, but at this date a Greek name
such as 'Eurysaces' generally indicated slave origins). As such, so the
familiar argument runs, he may have had plenty of money, but not
much taste. However cute we may now find it, the tomb was frankly
vulgar by Roman standards – 'an egregious monument', as one architectural historian described it.

This is, in fact, how art sponsored by ex-slaves in the Roman world
is regularly judged. The wonderful paintings from the so-called House
of the Vettii in Pompeii (including the famous picture-postcard cupids,
playing at grape-treading, cloth-working, racing and the like) would
be hailed as masterpieces if they had been found on the walls of the

imperial palace in Rome. But 'the Vettii' were very likely a pair of ex-slaves, in a provincial backwater to boot, and their decoration tends to be sniffed at by art historians: it's all a bit nouveau, a bit over the top.

Henrik Mouritsen develops this theme in the introduction to *The Freedman in the Roman World*, his wide-ranging study of ex-slaves (*liberti* in Latin, 'freedmen' in the usual modern scholarly jargon – which is taken to include 'freedwomen'). As he points out, there is a puzzling contrast between, on the one hand, the overwhelmingly sympathetic treatment given to Roman slaves in modern writing, as innocent victims of a terrible human wrong – and, on the other, a decidedly disparaging attitude to ex-slaves, who had been granted (or bought) their freedom. No writers today quite echo the strident complaints of early twentieth-century historians who regularly decried the Roman practice of 'manumission' (that is, the formal process of freeing slaves) and lamented the dilution of the true Italian stock with the foreign blood of freedmen, whose origins often lay in the East. But even relatively recently, scholars have been known to hint darkly at 'the infiltration of the Roman population by foreigners' and to cast ex-slaves – particularly those who made money – as 'social climbers'. And we find repeated reference to 'undeserving' slaves, freed by their masters for 'trivial' reasons. Even Jane Gardner, in an otherwise excellent chapter on 'Slavery and Roman Law' in *The Cambridge World History of Slavery* can still refer to the 'abuse' of manumission (by the freeing of too many, or unworthy, slaves). There is a strange illogicality here: if slavery is always a terrible injustice (as our own morality insists), then it follows that granting freedom – for whatever reason, and whatever numbers – must be a good thing. Manumission, in those terms, cannot be 'abused'; such phrases sit very uneasily alongside the homilies about human rights that usually accompany any discussion of ancient slaves.

Of course, in treating Roman freedmen in this way, modern writers are partly (consciously or, more often, unconsciously) reflecting the prejudices of their ancient predecessors and sources. Historians in the Roman world certainly saw moral and political dangers in freeing too many slaves – most notoriously, Dionysius of Halicarnassus, whose history of Rome, written at the end of the first century BC, includes a rant about the slave criminals and prostitutes who used their ill-gotten gains to purchase freedom from their masters. And the most lurid caricature of a vulgar freedman comes from Petronius' novel, the

Satyrica, featuring the extravagant dinner party of the *libertus* Trimalchio – with its ludicrous luxury, its parodically expensive food, and hilarious discussion of proposals for a freedman's elaborate tomb to rival that of Eurysaces. Never mind that this is an elite skit, written by a one-time friend of the Emperor Nero about a member of the aspirant underclass; that hasn't stopped generations of modern historians writing as if Trimalchio was a 'typical' Roman freedman. In fact, in the eyes of many, the baker's monument provides nice confirmation of just how true to life Petronius' Trimalchio was.

But an extra problem for modern historians is that we have no familiar category that helps us make sense of the Roman *libertus*. We think we know about slavery; but the ex-slave is much harder. In a desperate search for a useful equivalent, we tend to reach for the caricature of the arriviste, the stereotype of the 'man on the make', with more money than taste. The truth is, needless to say, that most ex-slaves in Rome didn't have enough money to be tasteless.

It is, of course, that unfamiliarity – in particular the unique rules and conventions that produced so many ex-slaves – that makes Roman slavery so interesting. The basic point is that almost all slave-owning societies have had some mechanism for giving some slaves their freedom, but none – so far as we can tell – ever freed slaves in such large numbers as Rome. More than that, the Romans gave ex-slaves almost all the rights and privileges of Roman citizenship. In ancient Athens, a freed slave became at best a 'resident alien'; in Rome any slave freed, according to certain legal rules, by a Roman citizen, himself became a Roman citizen, with only a few restrictions (ex-slaves could not serve in the army, for example, or hold political office); and no restrictions at all applied to the second generation. The poet Horace is just one notable example of a son of an ex-slave who lived close to the top of the Roman pecking order. On one reckoning, most domestic slaves in Roman towns would have died as free citizens (though almost certainly far fewer agricultural or industrial slaves would have been freed).

Why Roman masters, and mistresses, released so much of their human property remains disputed: sometimes affection for their domestic household (and a good number of slave women were freed in order to marry their masters); sometimes a sense of economic self-interest (it is, after all, expensive to keep an elderly slave past their prime); sometimes perhaps because manumission was a useful carrot to ensure a slave's good behaviour; or it was simply 'what Romans did'. But, however it is to be explained, it was probably not true to say (in Orlando Patterson's famous phrase) that slavery in urban Rome was 'social death' – for many, if not most, Roman slaves, like Horace's father, it was a finite condition, a phase of 'temporary social paralysis'.

Mouritsen reminds us that the reality of Roman slavery and freedom was much more complicated, and uncertain, than we often like to admit. What is more, our whole understanding of Roman *liberti* is based on all kinds of perilous calculations and 'guesstimates' – many of which turn out to have a major impact on how we imagine Roman society as a whole, far beyond the issue of slavery itself. One key question is not simply how many slaves were freed, but what proportion of the ordinary free population of the city of Rome were ex-slaves or the descendants of ex-slaves. If we were to take the evidence of surviving tombstones at face value (and most are much simpler and much less loquacious than the baker's tomb), the vast majority of the free inhabitants of the metropolis were of slave origin. Leaving aside a few aristocratic commemorations and those of slaves themselves, roughly three-quarters of the people recorded on epitaphs from Rome are almost certainly ex-slaves, and most of the rest are probably their direct descendants.

The problem here is clear – and irresolvable. Should we really imagine (as some people do) that the population of the imperial capital was overwhelmingly made up of *liberti* and those of 'libertine' origin? Or are ex-slaves for some reason over-represented in the surviving evidence? Perhaps, for example, their newly acquired status made them particularly keen to commemorate themselves. Whichever way you jump, these thousands of relatively humble epitaphs are a world away from the stereotype of the vulgar, rich arriviste symbolised by Trimalchio.

But, in fact, the more you look at it, the more the clear binary distinction between the slave and the officially freed *libertus*, complete with his Roman citizenship, breaks down. Increasingly, from the first century BC on, there were stringent rules governing the formal practice of manumission: no one under twenty could free a slave; no slave could be freed before the age of thirty; there were limits to the numbers of slaves that could be freed by a dead master's will; in addition, most manumission was supposed to take place in front of a serving Roman magistrate. What is clear is that large numbers of slaves must have been freed against those stipulations. We see, for example, plenty of ex-slaves in epitaphs under the age of thirty, and although some people clearly could track down a convenient Roman magistrate (some surviving wax tablets from Herculaneum document a number who did), that cannot possibly have been feasible for all.

In practice, some were probably treated as if they were 'properly' freed, even when they were not. But others must have fallen into a halfway category (known technically as 'Junian Latin'), which gave them freedom, but not Roman citizenship – although they could later work up to citizenship by fulfilling certain additional criteria, such as having a surviving child. Quite how many people were in each of these categories is impossible to say (though some historians now suspect that the Junian Latins were far more numerous than we ever imagined). The important thing here is the complicated patchwork of statuses through which individuals might pass – from slaves, or even slaves of slaves (*vicarii* in Latin) to formally freed, citizen *liberti*. And it was not only upward social mobility. One Roman law ruled that a free woman having an affair with a slave, with the consent of his owner, was 'reduced' to the status of ex-slave; if she was acting without the owner's consent, she became his slave.

Mouritsen is an excellent guide to the tricky social history and economics of Roman freedmen, as well as their continuing links with their former masters or mistresses. He is less adept in discussing the literary and cultural impact of the ex-slave. His attempts to read Horace's views on *liberti* are rather plodding; and the fact that the assassins of Caesar could represent themselves as manumitting the state by his murder (the distinctive hat worn by newly freed slaves is featured on the assassins' coinage, p. 98) surely tells us more about the way Romans could conceptualise the whole notion of the freedman than Mouritsen's brief mention allows. But the most important achievement of Mouritsen's *Freedman* is to make it absolutely clear that it would be impossible to understand Roman slavery without taking ex-slavery into account too.

So it is a pity that, overall, the first volume of the *World History of Slavery* devotes so little space to *liberti* (a vast category which thus falls into limbo, unless – as I very much doubt – a *Cambridge World History of Freedmen* is planned). In many ways this is an absolutely excellent volume, including twenty-two authoritative essays on different aspects of ancient slavery by some of the international leaders in the field:

from Paul Cartledge nicely summing up the Spartan helots to Keith Bradley discussing the various forms of Roman slave resistance to their masters (much more often petty pilfering and insolence than full-scale rebellion or even running away). All the same, I missed any explicit, extended discussion of Roman manumission and its implications.

To be sure, it creeps in at the edges in relation to particular problems and questions, notably in Walter Scheidel's fine chapter on Roman slave supply. This has recently become a fiercely contested topic. If, as is estimated, the Roman Empire as a whole needed to find between 250,000 and 400,000 new slaves per year, simply to keep the slave population steady, where on earth did they come from, once Rome's major wars of conquest were over, and prisoners of war had dried up? Almost certainly there would have been a variety of different sources: the home-grown children of existing slaves (*vernae*), the slave trade which presumably engaged in people-trafficking beyond the boundaries of empire, the 'rescuing' of babies who had been exposed by their parents. But the proportions are crucial here, and make a huge difference to our view of Roman society more generally (if babies plucked from dung heaps were a significant element in the equation, it must be telling us something about the prevalence of child-exposure).

And rates of manumission – as well as estimates of the average age at which slaves were freed – are absolutely central to this debate. For these factors help to determine the number of slaves that would have to have been replaced (the more freed, the more needed); and they also help to fix the number of babies a female slave could have produced, as *vernae* for the household, before she was freed (the later her manumission, the more potential babies, the greater her contribution to slave supply). One thing that Roman slave women would not have gone without – however unwilling they, no doubt, often were – was an active sex life.

But the Roman 'culture of manumission' has even wider implications for how slavery was understood by the Romans themselves. The simple fact that slavery was for so many a temporary condition rather than a life sentence must have had an enormous impact on the way slavery was theorised at Rome (on this Mouritsen is absolutely correct to say that Varro never used the term 'speaking tool' or *instrumentum vocale* specifically to denote the slave, although that common myth still persists, even in the *World History* – Varro put free labour in that category too). And the simple fact that very many, perhaps the majority, of the free population of the metropolis were ex-slaves or closely related to them must have made a difference to the way that slaves were perceived by the ordinary man and woman in the street there.

In short, Roman slavery must have been a very different thing from slavery in the classical Greek city, where the barriers between slave and free were much more rigorously policed. Yet it is classical Greece (and its native theorists, such as Aristotle) that has tended to drive our approaches to 'ancient slavery'.

And as for Eurysaces? He does get a brief mention in the *World History's* very useful chapter by Michele George on 'Slavery and Roman Material Culture'; but it is as much for the slaves he himself owned, and who (as we see on the sculpted friezes of his tomb) toiled away making the bread in his bakery. I suspect that he would be rather disappointed that neither he himself, nor the *libertus* in general, figured larger in the book.

Review of Henrik Mouritsen, *The Freedman in the Roman World* (Cambridge University Press, 2011); Keith Bradley and Paul Cartledge (eds.), *The Cambridge World History of Slavery, Volume One: The Ancient Mediterranean World* (Cambridge University Press, 2011)

20

FORTUNE-TELLING,
BAD BREATH
AND STRESS

Is my wife having a baby? Am I going to see a death? Will I become a councillor? Am I going to be sold? Am I about to be caught as an adulterer? These are just a few of the ninety-two questions listed in one of the most intriguing works of classical literature to have survived: the *Oracles of Astrampsychus*, a book which offers cleverly randomised answers to many of ancient life's most troubling problems and uncertainties. The method is relatively straightforward, but with just enough obfuscation to make for convincing fortune-telling ('easy to use but difficult to fathom' as one modern commentator nicely put it). Each question is numbered. When you have found the one that most closely matches your own dilemma, you think of a number between one and ten and add it to the number of your question. You then go to a 'table of correspondences' which converts that total into yet another number, which directs you in turn to one of a series of 103 lists of possible answers, arranged in groups of ten, or 'decades' (to make things more confusing there are actually more lists of answers than the system, with its ninety-two questions, requires or could ever use). Finally, go back to the number between one and ten that you first thought of, and that indicates which answer in the decade applies to you.

Confused? Try a concrete example. Suppose that I want to know if I am about to be caught as an adulterer, which is question 100. I think of another number – let's say five, giving a total of 105. The table of correspondences converts this to the number 28. I then go to the twenty-eighth decade, and pick out the fifth answer, which brings good news: 'You won't be caught as an adulterer' (and in some versions adds the extra reassurance: 'Don't worry'). If I had chosen the number six, the same procedure would have offered me only a temporary reprieve: 'You won't be caught as an adulterer for the time being'. Number seven would have brought bad news of a different kind: 'You're not an adulterer, but your wife loves another man'.

The introduction to this little book of oracles – it amounts to some thirty pages in modern editions – claims that its author was a fourth-century-BC Egyptian magician, Astrampsychus, who used a system first invented by the famous philosopher-cum-mathematician Pythagoras. Not only that: by way of an advertisement, it also claims that the book had been the *vade mecum* of Alexander the Great, who relied on it to decide matters of world governance, 'and you also will have unwavering renown among all people if you use it too'. In fact, however wayward Alexander's decision-making processes may have been, they could not have depended on this system of oracles, which was almost certainly nothing to do with any fourth-century magician or with Pythagoras, but was a product of the Roman Empire of the second or third centuries AD. Our best guess is that the book was not so much an early self-help manual but part of the equipment of professional, or semi-professional, fortune-tellers – who would probably have invested the mechanical process of consultation with some impressive ad-lib mystery and mumbo-jumbo.

However this oracle book was actually used, it seems to give us a rare glimpse into the day-to-day anxieties of the ordinary inhabitants of the Roman Empire. For (never mind the publicity yarn about Alexander the Great) this is not elite literature, or certainly not literature aimed exclusively at the elite; in fact, the question about 'being sold' implies that slaves were among the intended clientele. It looks as if we have here a long list of the kinds of problems that made ordinary Roman men (and they do seem to be exclusively male questions) anxious enough to resort to fortune-tellers.

Some of these are the perennial issues of sex, illness and success ('Will I split up from my girlfriend?' 'Will the one who is sick survive?' 'Will I be prosperous?'). But other questions reflect much more specifically Greco-Roman concerns about life's fortunes and misfortunes. Alongside worries about the wife's pregnancy, we find questions about whether or not to rear the expected offspring: a vivid reminder that infanticide was one orthodox method of family planning in the ancient world, as well as being a convenient way of disposing of those who emerged from the womb weak, sickly or deformed. Debt and inheritance also bulk large among the topics of concern, accounting for at least twelve of the ninety-two questions ('Will I pay back what I owe?' 'Will I inherit from a friend?'). So do the dangers of travel ('Will I sail safely?') and the potential menace of the legal system ('Am I safe from prosecution?' 'Will I be safe if informed against?'). Even illness may be thought to be the result of crime or malevolence, as the question 'Have I been poisoned?' shows.

Jerry Toner, in *Popular Culture in Ancient Rome*, is excellent at squeezing the social and cultural implications out of this material. As well as reflecting on the perilous, debt-ridden, short and painful human lives that the oracle book reveals, he notes some surprising absences. There is nothing here (poisoning apart) to suggest a fear of violent crime, despite the fact that we often imagine that the Roman Empire was full of highwaymen, pirates and muggers. Nor is there anything on the institution of patronage. Modern historians have written volumes on the dependence of the poor on their elite patrons – for everything from jobs, to loans or food. Toner speculates that the intended users of these oracles were so far down the Roman social hierarchy that they were below the reach of the patronage system (which only extended so far as 'the respectable poor'). Maybe. Or maybe the whole system of patronage was far less important in the life of the non-elite than the Roman elite writers, on whom we mostly rely, liked to imagine. Or, at least, maybe it was far less important in whatever corner of the Roman Empire this strange little book originated.

Pushing the evidence a little further, Toner suggests that we might see in these oracles a rudimentary system of risk assessment. He reckons, for example, that the answers on the fate of a newborn baby (where one in ten suggests that the baby will 'not be reared' – that is, exposed or killed – and two out of ten suggest that it will die anyway) more or less match up to the social and biological reality of infant survival. Referring to other similar sets of oracles, recorded in ancient inscriptions found in cities in modern Turkey, he points out that 18 per cent of oracular responses warn that a business venture will fail

– roughly the same rate of failure implied by the rate of interest that was regularly charged on so-called 'maritime loans' (for shipping and trading expeditions). On Toner's view, in other words, the oracular responses reflected real-life risks and probabilities.

I am not so sure. On that principle, there was an eight-out-of-ten chance that a consulter of these oracles would become a local councillor. That would mean either that those who used these oracles were higher up the social hierarchy than Toner (and most other historians) would like to imagine, or that those who asked that particular question ('Will I become a councillor?') were a self-selected group, or that fortune-telling trades in over-optimism. Conversely, it seems sometimes to trade in gloom. Five out of ten oracular answers to the question 'Have I been poisoned?' suggest the answer 'Yes'.

Popular Culture in Ancient Rome is, overall, a spirited, engaging and politically committed introduction to the culture of the 'non-elite' in the Roman Empire. Toner notes in his introduction that his mother, to whom the book is dedicated, was a 'college servant' in Cambridge; and the leading idea of the book – that there is a popular culture in the ancient world to be discovered beyond the elite literature that is the mainstay of modern 'Classics' – is driven by a political as well as a historical agenda.

Toner's achievement is to open up the world of the Roman tavern, rather than the senate house; the world of the garret rather than the villa. Drawing on material out of the mainstream of classical literature, from the *Oracles of Astrampsychus* to the one surviving Roman joke book (the *Philogelos* or *Laughter-Lover*) or the book of dream interpretation by Artemidorus, he vividly conjures up a vision of Rome very different from the shiny marble of the usual image: it is a world of filth and stench (for Toner, Rome was basically a dung heap), of popular pleasures, carnival and the lower bodily stratum, of resistance, as well as submission, to the power of the elite. The only misjudged chapter is one on mental health, with its superficial modernising ideas about the stress levels that affected the Roman poor. Despite Toner's denial that he is trying 'to give retrospective diagnoses of the dead', we are left with the strong impression that he thinks St Anthony of Egypt was a schizophrenic, and that rank-and-file Roman soldiers were likely to be victims of combat stress and PTSD.

The big question, though, is whether the Rome that Toner conjures up for us is as 'popular' as he suggests. Is this dirty, smelly, dangerous world the world of the peasants and the poor, or is it also the world of the elite? Maybe, whatever his political agenda, Toner has succeeded best not simply in taking us into the real life of the disadvantaged, but in showing us another side of the culture of the elite too. For it is still unclear how far the texts that we now choose to designate as 'sub-elite' or 'non-elite' (because that is where they fit on our hierarchy) were really 'popular' in the ancient world. There are more hints than Toner admits in the *Oracles of Astrampsychus* that, alongside the slaves and the poor, the intended customers may have included those who were relatively upmarket. 'Will I become a councillor?' (which could equally well be translated 'Will I become a senator?') is not the only question to hint at privileged consumers. An early Christian edition of the text includes the question 'Will I become a bishop?', with five out of ten answers indicating 'yes' (albeit one, with a realistic view of the problems of power in the early Church, prophesying 'You'll become a bishop soon and you'll be sorry'). Much the same is true of the Roman joke book. We could not disprove any claim that the *Philogelos* was a record of the kind of popular banter you would have heard at the ancient parish-pump or barber's shop, but the compilation of jokes, as we have it, is more likely to be a desk-job encyclopedia by some relatively well-heeled Roman academic (p. 56).

Those dilemmas point at an even more fundamental issue in the cultural history of Rome. For it is almost impossible to identify – even if, like Toner, you are looking hard for them – clearly divergent strands of elite and popular taste. Rome was not a culture, such as ours, where status is paraded and distinguished by aesthetic choices (there is no sign in antiquity of any such markers of class as the Aga). Quite the contrary. So far as we can tell, cultural and aesthetic choices at Rome were broadly the same right across the spectrum of wealth and privilege: the only difference lay in what you could afford to pay for. This is strikingly clear at Pompeii, where the decoration of all the houses – both large and small, elite and non-elite – follows the same broad pattern, with roughly the same preferences in themes and designs. The richer houses are distinguished only by having more extensive painted decoration and by painting of greater skill: the more you paid, the better you got. Whether there was such a thing as 'popular culture' (as distinct from dirt, poverty and hunger) is a trickier issue than Toner sometimes acknowledges.

In *Resurrecting Pompeii*, Estelle Lazer takes a different approach to the lives and lifestyles of 'ordinary Romans' with her meticulous analysis of the human bones of the victims, rich and poor, of the eruption of Vesuvius in 79 AD. It is an eye-opening book in many ways, not least for its description of the conditions in which she worked on these bones in modern Pompeii – about as far from the glamour of Indiana-Jones-style archaeology as it is possible to imagine. Apart from some celebrity skeletons and plaster casts of dead bodies on display to the public, most of the human remains that survived the Allied bombing raids on the site during the Second World War were piled up in two main stores, each in an ancient bath building not normally accessible to ordinary visitors. Lazer spent most of her research time, months on end over seven years, in these depots – ill-lit (she worked for part of the time with a handheld bicycle light) and infested by wildlife. The identifying labels once attached to the bones had long ago been eaten by rodents; many of the skulls had provided convenient nesting boxes for the local birds (covering the bones and what Lazer calls the key 'skeletal landmarks' with bird lime); in one store a 'cottage industry' had been established, which used the human thigh bones to make hinges to restore the ancient furniture on the site. 'This has contributed', as Lazer writes, with deadpan understatement, 'a novel source of sample bias to the femur collection.'

From this very difficult material Lazer has drawn some very careful conclusions about the victims of the eruption and the population of Pompeii (and to a lesser extent Herculaneum) more generally. She has no time at all for the more sensational conclusions that have been based on the study of some ancient bones, and is particularly critical of the analysis of more than 300 skeletons that were found in the early 1980s in a series of so-called 'boat sheds' along the seafront at Herculaneum. The study of this material was financed by *National Geographic*, and the magazine got the vivid, personal details about the dead that it had paid for: one, with a skeleton that suggested highly developed muscles, must have been a slave; another, who happened to be carrying a sword and dagger, was called a 'soldier'; another was identified as a helmsman simply because it was found near a boat.

Lazer not only points out how flimsy these identifications are (the boat turned out to be in a completely different archaeological layer from the 'helmsman', and the so-called 'soldier' also carried a bag of carpentry tools); she also underlines how tricky and contested the conclusions drawn from ancient skeletal material almost always are, no matter who is paying and with what sensationalist aims. Determining the sex of pre-adult skeletons is always a guessing game. There has been no reliable DNA sequence obtained from any of the human remains at Pompeii or Herculaneum. Most striking of all, two different studies of the bodies in the boat sheds have produced estimates of the average height of the victims that differ by a couple of inches. There is clearly something more involved here than getting out a ruler and just measuring the skeletons.

Despite (or maybe because of) her caution in drawing ambitious conclusions from the bones, Lazer has a great deal to say about the population of Pompeii – beyond the well-known fact, now repeatedly demonstrated from the analysis of hundreds of teeth and jaws, that the levels of oral hygiene in the Roman world were truly dreadful. (When the Roman poet Martial attacked some of his contemporaries for their bad breath, it was probably not poetic fantasy.) One important observation relates to the demographic profile of the victims. It is often said that those left behind in the city, as Vesuvius rumbled and eventually exploded, must have been the weaker section of the population: the very young, the very old, the disabled, or those in some other way incapacitated. In carefully going through the stored bones, Lazer has found no indication of any such bias: the surviving human remains seem to represent a typical distribution of age and sex that you would expect in a Roman town.

Even more important for our understanding of Roman society in general is the relative homogeneity of human remains. Pompeii was a port town, and to all outside appearances decidedly multicultural – from the famous temple of the Egyptian goddess Isis to the Indian ivory statuette found in one of the houses. Yet the telltale visible characteristics of the skeletons (for example, double-rooted canine teeth, or particularly distinctive formations of the tibia) suggest to Lazer a relatively homogeneous population, 'either as a result of shared genes or a common environment during the years of growth and development'. More than that, the telltale characteristics of the skeletons at Herculaneum appear to be consistently and significantly different. This would imply that – whatever their multicultural trappings – these small towns around the Bay of Naples were more like inbred Fen villages than the homes of a mobile population, as we often assume.

Resurrecting Pompeii is a remarkable (if not always elegantly written, or meticulously edited) book, partly because Lazer is so careful never to go beyond what her most exacting standards of proof will allow. She also consistently writes with respect for the material she is dealing with, never seeming to forget that her material is all that is left of the human victims of a terrible natural disaster, albeit 2,000 years ago. The eruption of Vesuvius was, of course, an ancient tragedy of rare proportions. But in the calculations of the victims, in their decision whether or not to run for it or to stay put, it must remind us of the dilemmas of those who consulted the *Oracles of Astrampsychus*. As Toner suggests, the fact that seven out of ten answers to the question 'Am I going to see a death' say 'yes' tells us something of the realities of ancient life, for everyone.

Review of Jerry Toner, *Popular Culture in Ancient Rome* (Polity Press, 2009); Estelle Lazer, *Resurrecting Pompeii* (Routledge, 2009)

21

KEEPING THE
ARMIES OUT
OF ROME

As a warrior state, ancient Rome was wisely and deliberately cautious about the presence of serving soldiers in the capital city itself. Roman armies conquered vast tracts of territory, from Scotland to the Sahara, and as far as Iraq in the East. It has been estimated that during the Republic, at least, a larger percentage of the Roman citizens was actively engaged in warfare than was ever the case in any other pre-industrial empire. The links between public prestige and military success were so strong that even the scholarly old Emperor Claudius was reduced to invading Britain to establish his credentials for the throne. Yet the city itself, within its sacred boundary or *pomerium*, was a strictly demilitarised zone: no soldiers under arms, nor even serving generals, were allowed in. True, under the one-man-rule of the Empire, there was a small special militia stationed in the city: the Praetorian Guard, whose job it was to protect (or sometimes assassinate) the ruling emperor. And there were occasional outbreaks of civil war in which Roman armies ran amok in the historic centre; in the so-called 'Year of the Four Emperors' (69 AD), for example, when rival claimants and their troops battled for the throne, fighting and associated arson destroyed even the Temple of Jupiter Optimus Maximus on the Capitoline Hill. All the same, Rome did not indulge in the kind of military march pasts and display of deadly hardware that is a feature of many modern states. There was not even a Roman equivalent of the anodyne pomp of Trooping the Colour or Remembrance Sunday. The only time that regular soldiers legitimately entered the city was to celebrate a triumph: the parade of booty and enemy prisoners that marked Rome's greatest victories (and, almost by definition, the end of a campaign). Though more frequent in the Republic, from the first century AD a triumph was a roughly once-in-twenty-years event. This is not to suggest that visitors to ancient Rome would have missed the militaristic ethos of the society they were entering. It would have been impossible for anyone with their eyes open to have mistaken Rome for some proto-pacifist state (if any such ever existed). As the essays in *Representations of War in Ancient Rome* underline, instead of soldiers in flesh and blood, the place was full of images and memorials of fighting and conquest. The speaking platform in the Forum, known as the 'rostra', was named after the beaks or rams (*rostra*) of the captured enemy ships, which were displayed on it. Spoils and enemy weapons were fixed to the outside of the houses of successful generals, as permanent reminders of their victories. It was said that once fixed these were never removed – unlikely in practice, but the ideal is significant enough. Statues of emperors often depicted them dressed for battle or in the act of conquering the enemy. The main thing missing from the famous equestrian statue of Marcus Aurelius that used to stand in the centre of Michelangelo's piazza on the Capitoline (now in sheltered stabling within the nearby museum) is the figure of the prostrate barbarian over whom the emperor was originally shown trampling. And all this is in addition to those detailed representations of military campaigns that still wind around the columns of Trajan and Marcus Aurelius: visual accounts of Trajan's successful onslaught on the Dacians in the early second century AD, and of Marcus's massacres of assorted German tribes about half a century later. The functions of this profusion of images of war are fairly clear, in broad terms. It was a far safer option to parade military power in marble or bronze than to take the risks that came with the presence in the capital of armed troops, however impressive or useful they might have been. The Romans' emphatic split between the demilitarised centre and the zone of military activity which was by definition outside Rome itself (a split nicely reflected in the standard Latin phrase for 'at home and abroad', *domi militiaeque*) by and large served their homeland security well. The bouts of civil war waged in the capital itself may have been very bloody and memorable, but, from the reign of Augustus on, they were relatively infrequent. Yet there were other factors at play too. These images had a crucial role in linking the increasingly distant theatres of war with the world of the metropolis. Well before the first century BC, the extent of Rome's territory meant that the vast majority of military campaigns took place well out of the view of the city's population. Already in the mid-second century, Polybius – the Greek historian of Rome's rise to power, who was a long-term resident-cum-hostage in the city – claimed that the purpose of a triumphal parade was to bring before the eyes of the Roman people at home the deeds of their generals overseas (triumphs displayed paintings of the conflict, as well as the loot). The sculptures on, say, the columns of Trajan and Marcus Aurelius did something similar: they gave to the people in the city, few of whom by the imperial period had ever witnessed a military operation, a vision of themselves as part of an imperialist enterprise. In that sense, it is perhaps not unlike the function of the shipping forecast on British public radio: few of us actually need to know the strength of wind at South Utsire, but it is important that we should remember that we live on an island and are at the mercy of the waves. There was also a point in these monuments of war for the individual Roman general. As Tonio Hölscher argues in an astute chapter in *Representations of War,* one of the biggest challenges for the Roman elite was to convert military victory far away into bankable political capital at home. The mechanism of that conversion was very often building and other forms of visual display in the city. From the fourth century BC, successful generals channelled the profits of their spoils into temples – thank-offerings to the gods, which would also act as permanent reminders of their own achievements. Later, cash would be channelled into monuments even more directly associated with public entertainment. The Colosseum originally displayed inscriptions (or so the latest reconstruction of the text would have us believe) declaring that it had been built with the spoils that came from the Emperor Vespasian's victory over the Jews (p. 158).

Even before the age of the emperors, Pompey the Great's military profits went to building the first ever permanent theatre in the city of Rome, crowned by a temple of Venus Victrix (Venus 'Giver of Victory') and linked to porticoes and parklands where the art works he had looted were displayed. As if to emphasise the connection between this vast architectural development and Pompey's military success, the shows which inaugurated the theatre almost certainly mimicked the triumphal parade which he had choreographed some years earlier. The inaugural play, on the subject of Agamemnon's return from Troy, most likely featured wagon-loads of Pompey's spoils which had already been trundled through the streets in triumph. We can only wonder how many people interpreted the implied parallel between Pompey and the cuckold (and murdered) Agamemnon as a rather black omen. So far, so good. But scratch the surface of this approach, and the problems become a little trickier. For a start, what in Rome is to count as part of 'the art of war'? The contributors to *Representations of War* seem to have in mind a capacious definition: of course including the images that depict successful Roman campaigns and the temples and monuments built explicitly out of the spoils; but also, among other things, the 'original' Greek art that ended up in Rome as a result of the conquest of Greece, as well as the hyper-realistic ('veristic') style of Roman portraiture, warts and all, which evoked the qualities of good generalship and military distinction. An ingenious but not entirely convincing chapter by Laura Klar, for example, argues that the distinctive form of the stage facade, or *scaenae frons*, in the Roman theatre (tall, and in contrast to the Greek equivalent, articulated with columns and niches) can be explained by its derivation from the temporary theatrical displays of victorious generals – the niches originally designed to show off the precious statues that were regularly a large part of the booty of conquest. Maybe. But on this view all Roman art risks coming under the rubric of 'the art of war', if for no other reason than the fact that, directly or indirectly, the profits of military victory paid for it. By that token, all Athenian art of the fifth century BC would also be defined as 'the art of war', not to mention a good deal of the artistic tradition of Western Europe.

There are more specific difficulties too – notably about the significance and documentary realism of some of the most famous monuments. Do they, or do they not, give an accurate impression of Roman conduct in battle? It is clear enough that a statue of a mounted emperor trampling a barbarian underfoot is more plausibly seen as an iconic representation of autocratic imperial power than as a snapshot of the emperor's behaviour. But the detailed visual narratives of the columns of Trajan and Marcus are not so easy to categorise. It has long been recognised that they each portray a very different style of warfare. Trajan's column downplays the

10. The Roman soldier steals the enemy's child? Or is it all a game? A seventeenth-century engraving of a scene from the column of Marcus Aurelius (late second century AD).

atrocious side of military conflict. With a few exceptions (including a puzzling scene in which a group of women appear to attack naked captives with flaming torches), the war against the Dacians proceeds with a ruthless dignity – more or less abiding by the ancient equivalent of the Geneva Convention. Marcus's column offers a much nastier vision, often centred on the mistreatment of women in the war zone, who are assaulted, dragged off by their hair, stabbed and killed. One notorious scene seems to show a soldier tearing a young child from the arms of its mother: a 'war crime' in the eyes of several modern commentators, and a stark Roman reminder of the horrors of conflict (though intriguingly it was read as a playful 'joke' – light relief among the battle lines – by one, not very playful, nineteenth-century student of the monument). Why the difference between the columns? Some have argued that the reasons are essentially stylistic. The column of Trajan, they insist, still falls, just, within the period of high classicism, with all its rhetoric of restraint; fifty or so years later, that of Marcus already shows signs of the emotional intensity of the post-classical or early medieval world. Others have proposed a real difference between the two campaigns. Paul Zanker, for example, puts the sharply contrasting treatment of the women down to the different aims of the wars: Trajan was conquering Dacia to turn it into a regular province ('peaceful coexistence' being the ultimate aim); Marcus was quashing an invasion of barbarians, to whom no quarter was to be given. In *Representations of War* Sheila Dillon, rightly in my view, feels uneasy with the realist explanation; both wars were probably equally violent. She tries instead to focus on the message to the Roman viewer. Trajan was fighting in a period when memories of 'The Year of the Four Emperors' (Chapter 17) and of the armies' atrocities during it were still raw; the aim of the images of the disciplined army, engaged in its wholesome activities of wood-clearing, bridge-building, sacrifice and the like, was to underscore the discipline and moderation of the Trajanic regime more generally. The violence, particularly against women, portrayed on the other column, was intended to mobilise a different image of male Roman imperial power, and to reassure the Roman viewer that, with the massacre of the German women and children, their 'victory would extend into the next generation'. This is convincing – up to a point. But, how far it, or any other of the more ambitious interpretations of the columns, stands up against the fact that these visual narratives were virtually invisible from the ground, I am not sure.

Representations of War is an engaging, well-illustrated and timely collection of essays. Almost inevitably it has much to contribute to the study of ancient warfare itself, as well as to the study of its artistic (and literary) representations. The final essay in the volume, a sharp contribution by William Harris on the 'Narrative Literature of Roman Courage', poses hard questions about Roman military behaviour as well as about its literary versions. Why were the Romans so committed to war? How did they promote the required courage – or, to put it more simply, how did they stop the 'poor bloody infantry' running away? What were the psychological roots to such unremitting militarism? Most of the other contributors touch on these questions too, even if fleetingly. The Romans do not come well out of their answers. It is here that the book is at its weakest. Roman armies appear alternately, and somewhat self-contradictorily, as 'frenzied' mobs driven by bloodlust, and brutally efficient, well-trained war machines (frenzy and efficiency are not usually partners in crime). At the same time, Roman conduct is supposed to plumb even lower depths of cruelty than is the norm for antiquity. 'Greeks might kill the adult male population and sell the women and children into slavery. But this was not always the case', observes Katherine Welch in her introduction – congratulating the Greeks, while implying, quite wrongly, that Romans always did indulge in such atrocities.

11. The Dying Gaul: a Roman version of an earlier Greek
sculpture, offering a view of a noble – but dying – barbarian.

Even more to the point, Roman culture in general is painted as if
it were univocally and enthusiastically supportive of a narrow military
ethos and of the political capital it might bring. There is hardly a
mention of the subversive voices of the Latin poets who challenged that
military ideal; and only brief reference to Tacitus' devastating criticism
of some of the worst excesses of Roman butchery. There is nothing
at all on those works of art, which also might offer a discordant view.
I am not thinking here so much of Augustus' famous 'Altar of Peace'
(for which 'Altar of Successful Pacification' might be a better title). But
the famous statue of the 'Dying Gaul' (probably once on display in the
pleasure gardens of Julius Caesar himself) wonderfully encapsulates
the noble death of a barbarian, and hints at an admiring view of Rome's
enemies closer to Tacitus and the poets than to the authors of this book.
In the end, the Romans were less monochrome, and more interesting,
than *Representations of War* allows. If the contributors had reflected harder
on the Romans' own doubts, subversions and self-criticism they would
have done the Romans more justice, and made an even better book.

Review of Sheila Dillon and Katherine E. Welch (eds.), *Representations of War
in Ancient Rome* (Cambridge University Press, 2006)

22

LIFE AND DEATH IN ROMAN BRITAIN

Hadrian's Wall must have been a decidedly undesirable posting for a soldier in the Roman army. Many a British schoolchild has reflected on just how undesirable it was, with the help of W. H. Auden's engaging piece of doggerel, 'Roman Wall Blues':

Over the heather the wet wind blows
I've lice in my tunic and a cold in my nose.
The rain comes pattering out of the sky
I'm a Wall soldier; I don't know why.
The mist sweeps over the hard grey stone
My girl's in Tungria; I sleep alone …

And so it goes on, for a few more verses, in much the same vein.

What neither the children nor, I suspect, most of their teachers have often realised is that this poem – as its title hints – was originally a song, with music by Benjamin Britten (the score, once believed lost, has recently been re-discovered – showing that Britten could be very 'Blues-y' indeed). It was written to be part of a radio documentary for the Home Service broadcast in 1937, on the ancient and modern history of the Wall. In fact, this Reithian background probably explains some of the poem's coyness: when Auden goes on to characterise an irritating Christian mess-mate as being against 'kissing' ('There'd be no kissing if he had his wish'), it's hard not to imagine that Auden had something a bit more raunchy in mind.

Auden's script of the whole programme survives intact. It is an imaginative interweaving of two stories. The first features a motley family of tourists making a visit to the fort at Housesteads: the kids are enthralled by their guidebook's account of the building of the Wall; Dad refuses to be impressed ('I'm glad they put up notices to tell you what's what. It looks to me more like a housing estate after the builder's gone broke'). The second story, told in song and spoken dialogue, is that of the Roman garrison, with their discomforts and troubles, lice and all. It ends on an unsettling note, as Auden poses the question that dogs so many histories of Roman Britain: whose side are we on in this conflict between invader and native? Auden's answer is bleak and even-handed. There is little to choose between Romans and Britons and not much moral difference between (Roman) imperialism and (native) barbarity: 'That man is born a savage, there needs no other proof than the Roman Wall. It characterizes both nations as robbers and murderers'. The very last line of the script must have struck home in the late 1930s: 'Whoever deprives an unoffending man of his right, is a barbarian'.

The fact that Auden's lyrics are less well known now than they were twenty or thirty years ago has little to do with changing tastes in poetry, and not much to do with any decline of Classics from the school syllabus (the Romans in Britain still have a secure place in Key Stage 2 of the National Curriculum). It has more to do with the fact that teachers can now offer their pupils authentic Roman voices from the Wall and dispense with Auden's ventriloquism. These voices come from the famous documents that since the 1970s have been unearthed at the fort of Vindolanda. Never mind the fact that Vindolanda is actually a mile south of the Wall, or that the overwhelming majority of the preserved texts date from a period before it was even built. The documents discovered there, written on small sheets of wood – letters, complaints, lists and accounts – bring us much closer to real Roman soldiers than Auden ever could. How far they have captured the scholarly and popular imagination is shown by a television vote on Britain's 'Top Ten Treasures' in 2003. BBC viewers put them second only to the finds from Sutton Hoo.

Out of the hundreds of texts so far discovered, the popular favourite is a letter from the wife of one officer to another, inviting her to a birthday celebration ('I give you a warm invitation to make sure that you come to us, to make the day more enjoyable for me by your arrival'). This has been a godsend to teachers looking for a female angle in the generally blokeish world of Roman military history. It has also launched a load of nonsense about just how like us the Romans were (they even had birthday parties ...). More interesting are the apparently more austere documents. A 'Strength Report', for example, of the cohort garrisoning Vindolanda at the end of the first century AD gives the lie to our usual image of cohesive, individual units of the Roman army, based all together at a single camp. Out of the 750 soldiers who made up this cohort, more than half were absent from base: including over 300 at the neighbouring fort at Corbridge, a handful on some business in Gaul, eleven in York 'to collect the pay'. When you subtract the 15 sick, the six wounded and the ten squaddies with an eye infection, only 265 at Vindolanda were 'fit for active service'. Other documents in the collection give the Roman view of the military capabilities of the 'bloody Brits' (*Brittunculi*), list the impressive quantity of poultry consumed in the officers' mess, request that hunting nets be sent, or record the dispatch of new underwear.

David Mattingly's *An Imperial Possession: Britain in the Roman Empire* is by no means the first history of Roman Britain to make use of these documents. But it is the first major historical synthesis to integrate the implications of the Vindolanda texts into its whole interpretation of the province. Thanks to these texts, Mattingly's views about the character of the military zone are much more nuanced than that of most of his predecessors. He paints a picture of a 'community of soldiers' in Britain (about 55,000 in all in the second century AD) that is unlike our usual vision of an army in a war zone. It was all much more 'family friendly' than we would expect (other finds at Vindolanda include a good number of children's shoes), with closer social and domestic links to the communities outside the garrison walls. 'The old belief', he stresses, 'in a rigid demarcation between soldiers inside and civilians outside seems much less acceptable.'

As part of this approach he boldly – and possibly unwisely – takes the number of prostitutes supplied by the twentieth-century Japanese army command to their troops (a ration of one per forty soldiers) and adds a total of 1,375 prostitutes to the population of the Roman province.

Mattingly seems to have two aims for his book: that it should both be a work of reference and make a radical contribution to our understanding of Britain under Roman rule. In some respects that combination works well. He avoids the relentless narrative history that so many textbooks offer ('Chapter 22: The Third-Century Crisis'), giving instead a brisk chronological account followed by a series of thematic chapters on different aspects of the subject, from the uncertain success of Romano-British towns, through conflicts of religion, to the economy of the countryside. There is some excellent analysis here, and a refreshing fearlessness in admitting the fragility of much of our archaeological evidence. He is more open than many, for example, to some healthy scepticism about the history and function of the Roman 'palace' at Fishbourne, which is usually assumed without much argument to be the residence of the British king, and Roman ally, Togidubnus. And Mattingly very properly refuses to be drawn to identify the cathedral of the fourth-century AD bishopric of London: one favourite candidate, he points out, could be an entirely secular building. (Not that his scepticism always goes far enough for my taste. He blithely repeats the current fantasy that the undistinguished scraps of curved metalwork discovered in a Late Iron Age tomb at Lexden near Colchester were parts of a Roman magistrate's official chair – and so are good evidence for close diplomatic contact between the Iron Age princelings and the Roman authorities in the pre-invasion period.)

That said, some of Mattingly's reference sections do make dreary reading. I challenge anyone but a narrow specialist to derive much pleasure from the region-by-region survey of rural settlement patterns. And the complete absence of illustrations (presumably an editorial decision for this new series of the Penguin History of Britain) will repeatedly leave anyone not already familiar with the material evidence quite baffled. Many of the arguments about the culture of Roman Britain are necessarily founded on the character of pottery, mosaics, coins or sculpture. Is this 'bad art' or is it intentionally 'Celtic'? How far does this pre-Roman British coin type derive from Roman or Greek models? It is almost impossible to understand these issues, let alone evaluate them, without the image in front of you.

Yet the problems run deeper than the style of presentation. One of Mattingly's major goals is to liberate the study of Roman Britain from the old question of 'Romanisation'. Since the work of Francis Haverfield in the early twentieth century, and his pioneering study in 1915, *The Romanization of Roman Britain*, the big issue in Romano-British studies has always centred on problems of cultural contact and change.

How Roman did the province of Britain ever become? What were the main vehicles of acculturation? How far down the social hierarchy did Roman culture reach?

Mattingly bravely dubs this a 'defective paradigm', dependent on a simplistic and monovalent view of both Roman and native culture. He aims to replace it with a view of Roman Britain based on the idea of (as he calls it, following various post-colonial studies) 'discrepant experience'. He emphasises, in other words, that different groups within the native Britons had different forms of contact with, and responses to, the occupying power of Rome. So, for example, the urban elite engaged with Rome and Roman culture to a very different degree from the rural peasants.

Mattingly must be right about this. The problem is not his interpretation of the ancient evidence but the judgement he passes on his scholarly predecessors and colleagues. If Romano-British studies did still adopt the kind of undifferentiated model of Roman and British culture that he claims, if they still posited a simple form of cultural transition between the 'native' and the 'classical', it would indeed be a subject ripe for revolution. But, in fact, Mattingly is pushing at an open door. Although his colleagues by and large do still find the idea of 'Romanisation' a useful idea to work with (or debate), they are already using the basic idea of 'discrepant experience'. Archaeologists such as Jane Webster or Martin Millett do not for a moment imagine that a single model of cultural change fits all. To imply that they do, is almost insulting much important recent work in the field.

Another problem is Mattingly's uneasy relationship with the Roman literary evidence for the province of Britain. Like most archaeologically inclined historians, he takes a good deal of care, and many pages, to distance himself from what Romans themselves, such as Tacitus or Julius Caesar, wrote about the place. In fact, he sharply reprimands most ancient writers for their woeful historical and political inadequacies: they were not 'critical researchers of their material'; they were writing for an aristocratic readership; they were relying on elite stereotypes of barbarity, and seeking, in provincial histories, 'confirmation of their own innate superiority and the backwardness of others'; and much of what they say is not confirmed by the science of archaeology anyway.

It is easy enough to see where these arguments are coming from. In part, they are a healthy reaction to a previous generation of Romano-British historians who slavishly followed whatever any ancient source chose to tell them, however improbable. But this gloomy pessimism about the ancient literary texts is also to miss the point. True, they offer a biased, elitist, culturally loaded version of the history of Britain. But try telling scholars who work on other pre-industrial empires that in the case of this most remote of ancient Roman provinces we have not only an autobiographical account by one of the first invaders (that is, Caesar), but also a biography of one of the first governors written by his son-in-law (that is, Tacitus' *Agricola*). Their response would surely be to suggest we analyse them with all the care and sophistication these complex texts deserve, not dismiss them with a gamma minus for political correctness.

Besides, even the most stringent archaeologists are too seduced by the nuggets of 'information' in these texts to pass them over entirely, especially when they fit neatly with their own position. So, after reprimanding Caesar and Tacitus for their blinkered, elitist perspective, Mattingly happily trots out, as if it were fact, Cassius Dio's claim that one of the causes of the revolt of Boudicca was big business: namely the multi-millionaire philosopher Seneca, who suddenly called in the lavish loans that he had made to the unsuspecting Britons and left them desperate for cash (p. 152). Dio, of course, was living a century and a half after the events he described, and relying on information gleaned from who knows where, reliable or not; but it is too tempting a defamation of a Roman bigwig for Mattingly to discard, despite all the warning notes he sounds about the dangers of believing what ancient writers have to say.

It is too tempting because, for Mattingly, the Romans by and large were, and are, the enemy. Again this is an understandable response to some of his predecessors, who often revealed 'a nostalgic association with the colonizers', and welcomed the benefits of civilisation, from baths to brooches, that the Romans brought to the spiky-haired, unwashed natives. It is in this spirit, as he points out, that a statue of Agricola stands in 'pride of place over the entrance to Manchester Town Hall', as if he were an honorary Mancunian blessing the civic virtues on display in the Council Chamber. (Thomas Thornycroft's statue of Boadicea on the Embankment in London may, however, tell a rather more complicated story, associating nineteenth-century values with a rebel British queen.)

Mattingly rejects any cosy picture of cultural progress, emphasising instead that 'Roman Britain' was a period of military occupation and foreign domination. For him, the Romans were a group of obsessive militarists: 'Their whole society became structured around the idea of war' (well, not absolutely all of it); they had a keen eye for economic profit; and they inflicted untold damage on the civilian population of these islands. Of course, he is right to remind us of the violence that underpinned all ancient imperial expansion (it is easy to forget that ancient wars had casualties, too). But it is not clear exactly what we should do with that realisation. Mattingly's own next step is to attempt to assemble some data about the scale of destruction. He estimates, for example, that in the period of conquest (43–83 AD), between 100,000 and 250,000 people were killed, out of a total population of some two million. Sounds bad. But where on earth do those figures come from? There is no good evidence whatsoever for either.

But in the end the problem is not one of mere numbers, inflated or otherwise. It is that, for all his detailed discussion, his up-to-the-minute information and his sometimes sophisticated sections of analysis, Mattingly is still in danger of replacing one oversimplified model with another (for 'Romans were good', read 'Romans were bad'). The point is that there are no heroes in this story and no innocents. The prospect of living under Boudicca is no more appealing than that of living under her adversary, Suetonius Paulinus (who was, by all accounts, brutal even by Roman standards). And that, of course, is what Auden saw so clearly and encapsulated so much more neatly in his 1937 documentary. Both nations were murderers and robbers. The poor squaddies on the Wall were victims as much as they were victors.

Review of David Mattingly, *An Imperial Possession: Britain in the Roman Empire, 54 BC–AD 409* (Allen Lane, 2006)

23

SOUTH SHIELDS
ARAMAIC

A series of school textbooks used in the late Roman Empire bears
an uncanny resemblance to modern children's 'easy readers'. In
simple scenes and dialogues, they carefully describe a Roman child's
daily activities: he gets up, washes and dresses, goes to school,
meets his friends, has his lunch, enjoys a party and goes to bed.
Through a nicely judged repertoire of domestic vocabulary, the reader
explores an instantly recognisable world of parents and siblings,
playmates and relatives, family routine and schoolroom discipline.
But the similarity is, of course, deceptive. Almost every sentence
captures the characteristic hierarchies, cruelties and social inequalities of ancient Rome. Slavery bulks large even in this juvenile world: it
is the imperative rather than the present indicative that is the child's
favourite verbal form ('Get up slave, see if it's light. Open the door,
open the window ... Give me my stuff, pass my shoes, fold up my clean
clothes ... Give me my cloak and mantle'). And in a gesture that would
have been dramatically out of place in the world of Janet and John, the
boy rounds off a long list of those he must greet on his return from
school with a reference to the family eunuch.

Yet no less striking is the simple fact that these texts were bilingual,
written in matching Latin and Greek versions. The function of this
dualism has been much debated. Some modern critics have seen the
books as elementary guides to Greek for ancient learners already fluent
in Latin; others have suggested that, even if Greek teaching came to

be their eventual purpose, the first editions were produced for Greek speakers wanting to master Latin. In fact both these explanations fly in the face of what is clearly stated in the texts themselves. For they claim to be aimed at the simultaneous learning of both languages. If that sounds to us like a pedagogical nightmare, for the teacher as well as for the pupil, it is roughly what was advocated by the most famous educational theorist of the Roman world. Quintilian, in his treatise on the *Education of the Orator* (written at the end of the first century AD), urged that a child's formal instruction in Latin and Greek should go more or less hand in hand (for equal attention to both languages will ensure that neither 'gets in the way of the other'). The Roman Empire was a polyglot world. Its linguistic varieties comprised not just the Latin and Greek of these textbooks, but a host of different languages, alphabets, syllabaries and scripts – from Celtic to Egyptian, Aramaic to Etruscan; and there were yet more pidgins, regional dialects and local accents. The traditional view that the vast territory of the empire was divided into two neat linguistic halves (a Greek-speaking East and a Latin-speaking West) bridged by an elite minority of Roman bilinguals, such as Quintilian's ideal pupil, hardly matches the realities of language use on the ground. At the very least, it is a misleading oversimplification, even if it is derived in part from one powerful strand of Roman imperial ideology that was happy to turn a blind eye, and a deaf ear, to any languages other than 'the two'; *utraque lingua* ('both languages') was a standard Roman shorthand, as if nothing other than Latin and Greek counted, or even existed.

In fact, there are plenty of hints, even in elite Roman writers, of a much richer linguistic landscape than that. The poet Ovid is probably the most famous and most reluctant ancient polyglot of all. Fallen foul of the Emperor Augustus and living in exile at Tomi on the Black Sea, he was forced, or so he writes (in Latin), to learn the local Getic; he even claims to have written a poem in that outlandish, barbarous tongue – albeit in the safely familiar framework of Latin metre (*nostris modis*). Other occasions and contexts brought different languages to the attention of Roman writers. Tacitus, for example, tells of a peasant in first-century AD Spain, who was accused of murdering a Roman official, refusing to respond to cross-questioning in any language other than his native Hispanic. Two centuries earlier, Plautus had brought a Punic-speaking character onto the Roman stage in his play *Little Carthaginian*; while the Roman Senate is supposed to have commissioned (or dragooned) a 'committee of experts in Punic' to translate into Latin a classic, twenty-eight-volume Carthaginian treatise on agriculture.

It hardly needs arguing that below the level of the literate elite, the range of languages in use must have been yet wider. Although we cannot be sure exactly what combination of language, signing, desperate improvisation and sheer greed allowed trade to take place across the frontiers of the Roman Empire, we can be absolutely confident that such exchange was not regularly conducted in Ciceronian Latin. In the Museum of London, the taped background noise that introduces visitors to the Roman galleries is a blurred cacophony of dog Latin, mixed with a now incomprehensible variety of 'barbarian' accents and tongues. It is about as accurate an approximation to the street voices of a Roman provincial port as you could get.

J. N. Adams's *Bilingualism and the Latin Language* is a marvellously informative study of the contacts between Latin and other languages in the Roman world, exploring the linguistic diversity of the empire on a scale, and at a depth, that no one has done before. By 'bilingualism' Adams does not mean that rare phenomenon of equal fluency in two languages (the common modern understanding of the word 'bilingual'), but more or less any kind of active competence or ability to perform in a second language – from (in our terms) 'holiday French' through to the 'native-like control' of a child brought up to speak two languages from birth. Into his net he draws not only that relatively familiar group of elite Romans well-versed in Greek, but Greeks who picked up Latin, Romans who could get by in Carthaginian ('holiday Punic'?), soldiers in the army managing both in Latin and their own vernacular, Gaulish potters working partly in Latin for Roman bosses, Italian traders on the Greek island of Delos operating in different contexts in different languages, and a whole variety more. The study goes far beyond the details of language to raise some of the most important questions in our understanding of the Roman empire and of the culture of Roman imperialism. How far, or how fast, did Latin eradicate the other native languages of the Roman empire? How does a polyglot army function effectively? To what extent is multilingualism built into the judicial and administrative processes of imperial government?

Adams is rightly aware of the difficulty of using the evidence of ancient literary sources in tracking down the day-to-day practice of second-language acquisition and use. Roman writers almost always had another axe to grind when they were discussing the vernaculars of the empire. However evocative Ovid's accounts of his struggles with Getic may be, they are not reliable guides to his linguistic experiences in Tomi. For Ovid, the opposition between Latin and Getic is a way of talking about the plight of an exile, and the loss of linguistic – and so of social, political and cultural – identity that comes with banishment from Rome. (Even Adams seems rather too trusting when he concludes that Ovid may, if nothing else, throw light on Roman attitudes to 'the possibility of second-language learning'.) Likewise Tacitus rarely mentions a native language without it being a vehicle for some cynical observation on the nature of Roman power and its corruption. The classic case of this is the famous passage in the *Agricola* (the biography of Tacitus' father-in-law and governor of Britain) when he concludes that the keen adoption of Latin by erstwhile Celtic-speakers in the province was another facet of their enslavement.

So Adams relies heavily on the evidence of inscriptions and papyri. Not exclusively. One substantial chapter focuses on the use of Greek phrases or sentences in Cicero's, predominantly Latin, letters; it asks in what circumstances and for what reasons Cicero adopts this form of 'code-switching', as the linguistic jargon terms it. (The answer is a complex mixture of – among other factors – self-display, accommodation to the different degrees of 'Greekness' of his correspondents, and the psychological state of Cicero himself; strikingly, he rarely uses Greek 'at a time of crisis'.) But non-literary documents produced by much more ordinary people – though not so 'ordinary' that they were illiterate, as the majority of the population of the empire must have been – have a larger place in Adams's work. These include potters' lists of kiln production, graffiti scratched on the tourist monuments of Roman Egypt, soldiers' tombstones, papyri documenting the procedure of courts or the activities of entrepreneurs.

He squeezes these difficult data very hard, looking for grammatical traces that might indicate a writer operating in a second language or, in bilingual texts, for hints of which language was the dominant one and the linguistic competence of the intended audience. It is a fascinating search, if extremely technical.This is not a book for the Latin-less reader; and a basic command of ancient Greek (plus Etruscan, Punic and Aramaic) would help too.

A particularly appealing example, and one that captures some of the complexities Adams is handling, is the 'Roman' tombstone put up in modern South Shields by a man from Palmyra, Barates,

12. The tomb of Regina, an ex-slave, erected in Britain by her
partner Barates. The inscription is in Latin and Aramaic.

to commemorate his British wife (and ex-slave), Regina. It carries a
sculpture of the dead woman in a strongly Palmyrene style. (Adams,
with his rigorously linguistic focus, has nothing to say of this visual
idiom.) The text itself is in both Latin and Palmyrene Aramaic – though,
as there could never have been a substantial Palmyrene population in
South Shields (no Palmyrene army unit was stationed on Hadrian's
Wall), the function of the Aramaic text must have been more a proc-
lamation of ethnic identity than any practical attempt to communicate
with an Aramaic readership.

The Latin text is longer than the Palmyrene and includes extra
information on the dead woman's age (30) and her tribe (the Catuvel-
launi). But it is also written – in the eyes of Adams and other editors (I
was not so sure) – in much more erratic lettering than the Palmyrene
version, suggesting a stone-cutter more at home in Aramaic than
Latin, or at least happier carving from right to left rather than left to
right. At the same time, to add to the puzzle, the unorthodox case
endings of some of the Latin words are reminiscent of Greek usage.

Adams speculates that Barates was a Palmyrene trader – if he was not identical with '... rathes' (the first part of his name is lost), a Palmyrene standard-bearer, whose tombstone is at Corbridge. And he plausibly suggests that he was a first-language speaker of Aramaic, bilingual in Greek, whose Latin was influenced by familiar Greek grammatical forms. Even so, not all the questions raised by the text are answered. What was the relationship between the carver of the memorial and Barates, its commissioner? Were they one and the same? Or were they both Palmyrenes living in Roman South Shields? And why does the Aramaic text omit the vital piece of information that Regina was the wife of Barates, referring to her only as his ex-slave?

Bilingualism and the Latin Language repeatedly touches on major issues of Roman cultural history. At one point, Adams states that 'this book is overwhelmingly about identity'. And so indeed it is; though any student of Roman cultural identity would be faced with a good deal of work in processing the information Adams presents. The work would, however, be well worth the effort, for there is material here that promises to shed light on a whole range of Roman cultural and political practices, far beyond the specialist concerns of language. Take, for example, Roman engagement with the historical topography of their province of Egypt. How did they understand, and relate to, the physical reminders of previous rulers and civilisations that were an even bigger mark on Egyptian landscape 2,000 years ago than they are today? In one chapter, Adams looks at the language of the graffiti carved onto various Egyptian monuments by Roman soldiers and tourists. He uncovers a striking discrepancy. On the famous Colossus of Memnon (the huge 'singing statue' visited by, among others, the Emperor Hadrian) Roman inscriptions are predominantly in Latin. At another major Roman 'pilgrimage' site, the underground tombs of the pharaohs at Thebes (the so-called 'syringes'), Greek appears to be the language of choice – even with those classes of visitor (such as Roman prefects) who aggressively signed the Colossus in Latin. The difference of language strongly hints at a different significance for these Egyptian antiquities in the Roman cultural imagination: the Colossus prompting an assertion of Roman identity from its visitors, the syringes eliciting a response in the more 'native' Greek.

Yet wider implications emerge from Adams's treatment of language use in the Roman army. He effectively demolishes the view that throughout the empire Latin was the 'official' language of the army, at least in any simple sense. He shows that Greek could be used for all kinds of 'official' purposes, and recognises that the junior ranks in many of the provincially recruited units may have had very limited competence in the Latin of their officers, communicating easily only in their own vernacular. Where does this leave our vision of the structure, organisation and cohesion of the Roman army? Somewhat closer to the linguistic and cultural disarray of a modern premiership football team than to the image of lookalike, monoglot soldiers familiar from film, fiction and school textbooks.

It is, however, the implications of Adams's work for our understanding of the whole basis of Roman provincial administration that are the most important, unsettling and potentially controversial. Adams makes it clear that Romans could take learning Greek in their stride, but finds little evidence that they had the same attitude to mastering the other vernacular languages in the Western part of the empire. True, at a relatively early date, you can find Romans who apparently know some Etruscan or Punic: besides the committee given the unenviable task of translating twenty-eight volumes of Punic thoughts on agriculture, Livy tells the story of a Roman consul's brother being sent on a reconnaissance mission into Etruscan territory in the early fourth century BC because he was fluent in the language (he was supposed to have been educated in the Etruscan town of Caere and to have learnt it there). But, in time, the evidence that Adams assembles increasingly suggests that, while speakers of the various vernaculars mastered Latin, Romans did not return the compliment.

Caesar, for example, in Gaul used 'locals who had learnt some Latin', and on one occasion a Gallic chieftain, to interpret between his invading forces and the native population. And, although there are interpreters documented as serving with the Roman army, there is no conclusive evidence that any of them were Latin-speakers by birth. In short, as Adams sums it up, 'the onus was on locals to learn Latin ... as their masters treated vernacular languages as if they did not exist'. The picture this presents of Roman administration in the West is a difficult one. At their most extreme, the implications of Adams's position would cast the Romans as a linguistically emasculated and vulnerable occupying power, dangerously dependent at that crucial interface between ruler and subject on the interpretative skills of the subject. If true, this is a completely different model of the linguistics of imperial rule from that adopted in the British Empire. Leonard Woolf, for example, was not untypical when he went out as an administrator to Ceylon already having mastered Tamil, and prepared to add a few more Eastern languages to his repertoire.

Of course, the distinction in the Roman world between bona fide 'Romans' and their subjects became increasingly blurred through the first centuries AD. The fact that Roman citizens (and so imperial administrators) were often themselves from provincial and probably multilingual backgrounds must have served to muddy the apparently sharp linguistic divide between ruler and ruled. Julius Classicianus, for example, the man appointed as procurator of Britain in the wake of the Boudiccan rebellion, was (despite his fine-sounding Latin name) of Gallic origin and may well have had some language to match.

But, at the same time, I suspect (as Adams himself at one point allows) that many more Romans acquired some competence in native vernaculars than the surviving evidence ever indicates. Governors arriving for a short spell of duty may have had little opportunity or inclination to learn more than a few phrases of politesse, if that. Those officials based in the provinces or on frontiers for longer could hardly have avoided some competence in the native languages. After all, many of them, we know (like Barates the Palmyrene), took local wives, girlfriends, or prostitutes; they presumably did not have sex only in Latin. It is hardly surprising that this level of bilingualism makes no mark even in the ephemeral documents, the hurried scrawlings, or the crudely inscribed tombstones, that Adams emphasises. It is not just that we are dealing here with part of the submerged illiterate majority of the ancient world; but many of these native languages would have had no written form at all and *could* not have made it to the written record.

Such reflections only add to the rich picture of linguistic diversity that Adams paints. *Bilingualism and the Latin Language* is an extraordinarily impressive book and a masterful collection of material. It presents a Roman Empire that is culturally more complex and frankly stranger than we often imagine; and, perhaps even more important, it demonstrates just how central the study of language is to any proper understanding of the ancient world.

Review of J. N. Adams, *Bilingualism and the Latin Language* (Cambridge University Press, 2003)

Section Five

ARTS & CULTURE; TOURISTS & SCHOLARS

The modern history of Classics has been a prominent theme through this book from its first chapter (on the prehistoric palace at Knossos and Sir Arthur Evans, its excavator and reconstructor). This final section focuses directly on the scholars who have interpreted the classical world for us, the artists and drama-tists who have recreated it, and the early travellers and tourists who (as they saw it from a Northern European perspective) 'explored' the Mediterranean lands of the Greeks and Romans.

The first two chapters concentrate on how ancient literature and art have been used and re-used. Chapter 24 celebrates the revival of Greek drama in the twentieth century; though it also warns against rosy-tinted views of the modern influence of ancient Greece. It is true that Athenian tragedy has sometimes been re-performed to powerful effect in support of all kinds of noble liberal causes, from women's suffrage to the anti-apartheid struggle. But we must not forget that it has been a favourite art form of totalitarian regimes too. Bobby Kennedy may have quoted Aeschylus in his famous speech after the assassination of Martin Luther King: 'Even in our sleep, pain which cannot forget falls drop by drop upon the heart …'. But, as we discover, that same phrase has had some much less savoury re-appropriations too.

Chapter 25 looks at the most influential piece of ancient sculpture ever discovered: the so-called 'Laocoon'. Dug up in Rome in 1506, it captures in marble the story from Virgil's Aeneid *of a Trojan priest and his sons, throttled to death by snakes (Fig. 15). It has prompted more discussion than any work of* art ever – from debates on how it should be restored (the priest's right arm has kept restorers busy for centuries) to more theoretical questions of our response to it (how can we enjoy looking at a sculpture that depicts such a ghastly death?). But it has had an intriguing afterlife too: it was, for example, familiar enough to Karl Marx that he could make it a symbol of the evils of capitalism.

The next two chapters turn to travel, and to how tourists (especially the British) have experienced the classical world on the ground. What was a visit to Greece or Italy like in the nineteenth century – loaded down, if you followed the instructions of your guidebook, with mosquito nets, pith helmets and saddles? How were you supposed to regard the 'natives'? At Pompeii, as Chapter 27 explains, early visitors were not only encouraged to reflect on human mortality, they were also advised to be on their guard against tricks, scams and over-charging restaurants. But in Greece (the focus of Chapter 26) there tended to be a much more romantic, or patronising, attitude to the locals – as if the modern Greek peasant had hardly changed since the days of Homer. It's an illusion of 'continuity' that we still haven't quite shaken off.

Travel is also the theme of Chapter 28, but in a metaphorical sense. James Frazer's founding text of anthropology, The Golden Bough, is full of far-flung examples of 'savage' practices drawn from every corner of the British empire. But in fact he had never been further than Greece and, as he himself insisted, had never met a 'savage'! Frazer was, of course, by training a clas-sicist, and the model of 'exploration' that underlies The Golden Bough was drawn directly from classical literature (from the 'Golden Bough' in the Aeneid that allows Aeneas safe passage to the underworld). After Frazer comes a far less desk-bound scholar, R. G. Collingwood. Though he is now most famous as a philosopher and author of The Idea of History, Chapter 29 brings his other, largely forgotten, interest back into view. For Collingwood also was a classicist, in particular an expert in the Latin inscriptions of Roman Britain. He spent his summers traipsing around the country – tracking down, deciphering and recording epitaphs, graffiti, religious dedications and milestones, the inscribed traces of the Romans in Britain.

Chapter 30 takes a wider sweep, by thinking about that motley group of people who have (sometimes implausibly, to be honest) counted as 'British clas-sicists' – from Elizabeth I to A. E. Housman and Arnaldo Momigliano. But it also reflects on how we choose to remember scholars, and why we can be almost wilfully reluctant to face up to their faults and failings. Taking as the prime example the brilliant and terrifying Oxford Latinist, Eduard Fraenkel (teacher of Iris Murdoch and Mary Warnock among many others), I ask what belongs (or doesn't) in a history of classical scholars and scholarship.

The focus of the final chapter is the place where many people first begin their encounter with Classics: that fictional Gaulish village, still standing out against the Romans, which is home to the plucky Astérix and his friends. What, I wonder, makes Astérix so popular across Europe? And what does he have to tell us about our own myths of Rome?

24

ONLY AESCHYLUS WILL DO?

On 4 April, 1968, the evening after the assassination of Martin Luther King, Bobby Kennedy addressed an angry crowd in the black ghetto of Indianapolis. In the middle of his speech, he famously quoted some lines from a chorus of Aeschylus' *Agamemnon*: 'Even in our sleep, pain which cannot forget falls drop by drop upon the heart, until, in our own despair, against our will, comes wisdom through the awful grace of God'.

It was a powerful performance, but nonetheless a slightly stumbling use of a classical text. 'My favourite poem', he began, 'My favourite poet', he corrected himself, 'was Aeschylus …'. And the quotation itself is the victim of some (maybe constructive) misremembering. What Kennedy had in mind was Edith Hamilton's 1930s translation of the play, but where he spoke poignantly of 'our own despair', Hamilton had actually written 'in our despite' – an archaising and accurate translation of Aeschylus' original, with a significantly different sense. Edith Hall is politely silent about Kennedy's inaccuracy. In her splendid, punchy essay in *Dionysus Since 69*, she takes his speech as one of the key examples of modern political engagement with the plays of Aeschylus. At this moment, 'one of the darkest in modern history', she writes, 'only Aeschylus would do'. She is mostly concerned, though, with more recent cases where the capacity of Aeschylean drama for 'saying the unsayable' has been deployed in political debate – whether for rethinking the horrors of military conflict from the Balkans to the

Gulf or (as in Tony Harrison's *Prometheus*) for addressing the 'enemy within', in the shape of poverty and class.

Particularly memorable is her discussion of Peter Sellars' 1993 adaptation of *The Persians*. The original play took as its theme the defeat of the Persian fleet by the Athenians at the Battle of Salamis in 480 BC, and is remarkable, as Hall notes, 'because its cast consists exclusively of Persians, the invaders of Athens and their much-hated enemies'. Sellars transferred the setting to the first Gulf War, with Xerxes and his fellow Persians reinterpreted as the Iraqi enemies of the United States. The behaviour of Saddam Hussein was given no more sympathy than Aeschylus gave to Xerxes, but highlighting the suffering of the Iraqi victims of the war and, even more, having the actors 'say the unsayable' ('I curse the name of America ... They are terrorists, you see') amounted to an extraordinary assault on the audience. During the play's run in Los Angeles, about a hundred people, out of an audience of 750 or so, walked out on every single night. But the ghost of Bobby Kennedy haunts this collection of essays beyond his famous quotation of Aeschylus. For Kennedy himself was assassinated on 5 June, 1968, just the day before the opening of the play *Dionysus in 69*, which lies behind the book's title. That radical version of Euripides' *Bacchae* by Richard Schechner, first staged in the Performing Garage, New York – complete with improvisation, nudity, birthing rituals and an audience perched on or under ladders, mingling perforce with the actors – is often identified as the turning point in modern productions of Greek tragedy. It marks the start of ancient drama's extraordinary recent renascence ('more Greek tragedy has been performed in the past thirty years than at any point in history since Greco-Roman antiquity', observes Hall) and of its powerful engagement with the struggles and discontents of the late twentieth century, worldwide. The coincidence of this production with Kennedy's death is itself revealing: the theatrical revolution went hand in hand with a real-life, political tragedy that saw the last hope for a liberal, anti-war America shattered.

In *Dionysus Since 69*, Froma Zeitlin offers a refreshingly hardheaded analysis of that now almost mythical show. Reflecting on her own vivid memories of being in the audience, she endorses its landmark status in the history of theatre. Schechner took an ancient tragedy that had not been performed commercially in the USA throughout the whole of the earlier twentieth century and showed just how eloquently its

themes – of 'violence, madness, ecstasy, release of libidinal energy …
transgression of taboos and freedom of moral choice' – could speak to
1960s New York. At the same time, she avoids the trap of judging its
innovations wholly successful. One striking attempt at cast-audience
interaction – 'The Total Caress' – went particularly (and amusingly)
awry. This took place towards the end of the play, 'when Pentheus
and Dionysus had briefly retired from the scene for a homoerotic
encounter'. The idea was that the other actors should circulate among
the spectators and engage them in what was euphemistically called
'sensory-exploration dialogues', modelled, as Zeitlin puts it, on the
'peacefully sensual behaviour of the bacchants in Euripides'. These
encounters took a predictable turn. So Schechner substituted a much
more stylised interlude, inadvertently revealing in the process the
controlling zeal that lurks behind much apparently improvisatory
theatre. The Total Caress had been 'dangerous and self-defeating', he
said. 'The theatrical event became less and less controlled by the Group.'
The productions discussed in *Dionysus Since 69* spread far beyond the
avant-garde performance spaces of New York City, from Ireland (in
Oliver Taplin's elegant appreciation of *The Cure at Troy* by Seamus
Heaney, a version of Sophocles' *Philoctetes*) to Africa and the Caribbean.
Between them, the contributors have unearthed an extraordinary
cornucopia of the famous, not so famous and sometimes frankly weird
modern versions of ancient tragedy. Helene Foley, for example, has
great fun with John Fisher's 1996 camp parody, *Medea, the Musical*
– a play within a play, about the troubles of a theatre director who
attempts to relaunch the story (and overturn its sexual politics) with
a gay Jason. This is picked up by Peter Brown, whose intriguing survey,
'Greek Tragedy in the Opera House and Concert Hall' identifies as
many as a hundred new musical versions of Greek tragedy performed
in the past thirty-five years, by composers from India, China, Lebanon
and Morocco, as well as more predictably from Western Europe and the
USA. Fisher's gay parody is here seen next to such diverse offerings as
a Creole *Medea* from New Orleans, abandoned by her white sea-captain,
and Tony Harrison's *Medea: a sex-war opera*, eventually performed as a
play after its composer had died without finishing the score.

By the end of the book, the reader will realise that almost every
worthy political cause of the past three decades – women's rights,
AIDS awareness, the anti-apartheid movement, the Peace Process
(from Northern Ireland to Palestine), gay pride, CND, not to mention

various struggles against dictatorship, imperialism, or the Thatcher Government – has found support through (and has in turn inspired) new performances of Greek tragedy; and that almost every horror of that period, notably the wars in the Balkans and the Gulf, has been analysed and deplored using Greek tragic idiom (for the destruction of Troy, read Kosovo, Baghdad, or where you will). This is very much part of the collection's considerable appeal – and, at the same time, its nagging problem.

All the contributors seem to share a number of assumptions about the recent history of Greek drama: that the past thirty years have seen a more intense cultural interest in Greek tragedy than any time since antiquity itself; that these modern performances have been more politicised than ever before; that Greek tragedy is a uniquely powerful medium for the discussion of the most intense and complex human problems; and that this power has recently been harnessed by the forces for good in the world in their struggles against the forces of oppression (by the representatives of peace against military might, by women against misogyny, sexual liberation against repression, and so on). Some of this is fair enough. It is no doubt true that, in terms of the sheer number of productions, there has been an unparalleled interest in ancient drama over the past few decades – though it is also worth remembering that one of the hallmarks of Classics as a discipline has always been the capacity of each succeeding generation to congratulate itself on its own fresh rediscovery of classical antiquity, while simultaneously lamenting the decline of classical learning. The critics of the 1880s, after all, were saying much the same about the mania for Greek plays in their own day. But some of the other assumptions are more tendentious. *Dionysus Since 69* might have been an even better book if it had given space to some of that debate, or had found a place for a contributor or two who was not singing from exactly the same hymn sheet.

Is it really the case, for example, that Greek tragedy has a unique power to 'say the unsayable', as the contributors repeatedly suggest? When Hall writes of Bobby Kennedy's speech that 'only Aeschylus would do', why does she think that a carefully chosen quote from Shakespeare, say, would have done Kennedy's job any less well? It would have been useful, in fact, to see some discussion of how the fate of the Bard (who has his own honourable record as a vehicle for political dissent all over the world) differs from that of Greek tragedy.

It would even have been useful to get a glimpse of some opposition to the current theatrical enthusiasm for all things Hellenic. What of the argument, for example, that ancient tragedy is more the problem than the solution, and that part of the reason why Western culture deals so ineffectively with the horrors of war, or the inequalities of gender, is that it cannot think through these issues outside the frame established in Athens more than two millennia ago? And what of the argument, rather briefly skated over by Lorna Hardwick in her essay on post-colonialism, that performances of the *Bacchae* in Cameroon or *Antigone* in South Africa – far from being politically empowering interventions – in fact represent the ultimate victory of the colonial power. Native culture may throw out its political overlords, but it is still left performing their damned plays.

The engaging enthusiasm of most of the contributors to *Dionysus Since 69* for Greek tragedy on the late twentieth-century stage has also induced a collective amnesia about the political commitment of many earlier revivals of ancient drama. There is no recollection in this volume of the performances of Gilbert Murray's translation of *The Trojan Women* during the First World War (including a tour of the USA sponsored by the Women's Peace Party) or in support of Murray's favourite cause, the League of Nations, in Oxford in 1919. Nor is there any word of the performances of Euripides' *Ion* in the 1830s which were a thinly veiled manifesto against slavery, nor of the battles against theatrical censorship in late Victorian and Edwardian England, largely fought around performances of Sophocles' *Oedipus the King*. Most readers will come away with the misleading impression that the politicisation of ancient drama was an invention of the past few decades, and with a far too rigid sense of what Hall terms the '1968–69 watershed'.

Even more misleading is the blind eye consistently turned in *Dionysus Since 69* to the less comfortable political appropriations of Greek tragedy. True, there is a whole litany of good causes – from universal suffrage to striking miners – that ancient drama has been called upon to support. But the fact is that its use in support of some of the worst causes in the modern world has an almost equally impressive history. Hitler's 1936 Olympics, for example, were accompanied by an extremely loaded production of Aeschylus' *Oresteia*, interpreted as a story of the triumph of Aryanism. Mussolini was a keen supporter and sponsor of the long-standing festival of ancient drama at Syracuse in Sicily. And – much as *The Merchant of Venice* was performed in the Third Reich as a weapon both for and against anti-Semitism – Anouilh's *Antigone* was lapped up in wartime France by the Resistance and occupying powers alike.

The oddest political turn, however, is the subsequent fate of Kennedy's famous passage of Aeschylus, a fate which sits awkwardly next to its hallowed status in the annals of liberal America and in the mythology of the civil rights movement. As the Canadian classicist Christopher Morrissey has recently observed, exactly the same passage was appropriated by Richard Nixon as one of his own favourite quotations. Not only, then, was it used as a memorial of the death of Martin Luther King; it was the phrase that Henry Kissinger claims buzzed through his own head as he shared Nixon's last night in the White House with him. Only Aeschylus would do, presumably.

Review of Edith Hall, Fiona Macintosh and Amanda Wrigley (eds.), *Dionysus since 69: Greek tragedy at the dawn of the third millennium* (Oxford University Press, 2004)

25

ARMS AND THE MAN

A famous drawing by J. H. Fuseli shows an artist, 'overwhelmed', as the title has it, 'by the grandeur of ancient ruins', sitting and weeping next to a colossal Roman sculpted foot (in fact, a foot – now in the Conservatori Museum in Rome – that once belonged to a statue of the Emperor Constantine). Fuseli's point is not just that ancient art can still drive a man of sensibility to tears. He is also, rightly, emphasising that most of the masterpieces of Greek and Roman sculpture rediscovered since the Renaissance emerged from the ground in a sadly ruined state: headless corpses, dismembered torsos, tragically amputated limbs. His artist is weeping for what has been lost, as much as he is overwhelmed by antiquity's continuing grandeur.

The fact that so much classical sculpture on show in the major museums of the world is, nonetheless, in apparently pristine condition is largely due to the efforts of Fuseli's colleagues and predecessors, from Michelangelo to Thorvaldsen. As soon as a ruined masterpiece was unearthed in sixteenth- and seventeenth-century Rome, the leading sculptors of the day would instantly be on the scene. A series of well-rehearsed refusals to tamper with the surviving fragments of antique genius was usually their first reaction. But such scruples did not stand in their way for long; for these artists were soon busy equipping the new discovery with all the things it needed (from – literally – heads to toes) to make it look the part, as a perfect classical statue should. There are few exceptions to the general rule that any ancient sculpture apparently still endowed with its unbroken outstretched fingers (or

13. Fuseli ponders on the impact of classical antiquity.

raised arm, or, in most cases, nose) has actually been the beneficiary of some such modern makeover.

Unsurprisingly, given the artists involved, some of these interventions have become highlights of the popular repertoire of classical sculpture. It was, for example, the addition of Bernini's luscious mattress that elevated the awkward 'Hermaphrodite' in the Louvre to stardom. And Bernini again gave us the winning face of Eros, who peeps out from behind the legs of the sullen Ludovisi 'Ares' (a sneaking reminder of the god of war's adultery with Eros' mother, Aphrodite). In other cases, an attractive Renaissance restoration provided a serious rival to the later serendipitous – often, it must be admitted, suspiciously serendipitous – discovery of a statue's 'real' missing part. When, some years after the recovery of the bulk of the sculpture, the 'original' legs of the Farnese 'Hercules' were said to have turned up, most people still preferred the ones that Michelangelo's pupil, Guglielmo della Porta, had designed. It was a long time before those Renaissance additions were removed to make way for the 'originals' – and, even then, della Porta's versions continued to be displayed next to the statue itself (as they are, once more, in the Naples museum today). Recent scholarship has taken these restorations very seriously. Despite a few fits of purism in the twentieth century (such as the

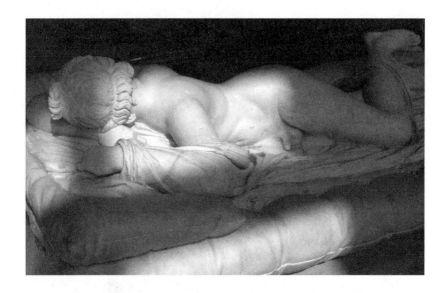

14. The hermaphrodite springs a surprise. From one side (below) it appears to be a sleeping woman; from the other side (above) we see the complications.

notorious stripping of Thorvaldsen's elegant neoclassical restorations from the most famous group of Greek sculpture in the
Munich Glyptothek, or the Louvre's decision to remove their
'Dying Seneca' from his gory red, Renaissance bath and stand him
on a concrete block), art historians and museum curators have
generally come to see the interventions of Bernini and his like as an
important part of the ongoing, creative history of classical sculpture;
not accurate maybe, but well worth studying in their own right.
That creative history was, in fact, celebrated in a splendid exhibition at
the Louvre, *D'apres l'Antique* – which featured not only a dazzling array
of contemporary artists' re-workings of classical themes (including
modern art photographs of Fuseli's foot, and no fewer than five of
Salvador Dali's full-size variations on the 'Venus de Milo'), but also a
well-chosen series of earlier restorations, replicas and reinventions of
Greek and Roman sculpture.

The superbly illustrated catalogue makes an excellent introduction
to the aims and methods of Renaissance restorers as well as to the often
unexpected *Nachleben* of some of the most famous pieces of ancient
statuary (in the last fifty years, the 'Venus de Milo', for example, has been
used to advertise fast cars, gas cookers, Levi jeans, mineral water and
support hosiery!). Restoration, of course, still goes on. We may think
we have learned to admire ancient sculpture in its fragmentary state –
but only up to a point. The 'Venus de Milo', tantalisingly unrestored,
minus her arms, is one thing; the vast sculpture groups discovered in the
1950s in a cave near the village of Sperlonga, south of Rome, smashed
into several thousand small pieces, are quite another. And inevitably
the re-created masterpieces now on show in the Sperlonga museum
contain as much plaster and resin as they do original marble; they are no
less creative reinventions than any of the ambitious projects by Bernini
or Thorvaldsen. The puzzle is not that these restorations took place
(who, after all, would bother to visit Sperlonga to see a pile of marble
chippings?); but rather that art historians, increasingly interested
in the principles and practice of Renaissance intervention in ancient
sculpture, have by and large turned a trusting blind eye to the activities
of contemporary restorers – as if the 'science' of restoration was now
above suspicion, unlike the creative fictions of the previous regime.
The classic case of this blindness is the Vatican Museums' restored
'Laocoon' group. Laocoon was that doomed priest of Troy, who, in
Virgil's *Aeneid*, failed to persuade his countrymen of the dangers of

15. The Trojan priest Laocoon is strangled to death by
snakes. Here we see the 'old' version of the restoration
with the arm of Laocoon stretched out, upright.

wooden horses and 'Greeks bearing gifts' and ended up throttled to
death, along with his two sons, by serpents sent by his divine enemy
Athena or Minerva.

The flamboyant marble version in the Vatican, showing father
and boys hopelessly grappling with the menacing snakes, became
from the moment of its rediscovery in Rome in 1506 one of the best-
known and most influential works of art ever, ancient or modern. It
prompted some of the most important debates at the very origin of
the modern discipline of art history (notably between Winckelmann
and Lessing). It was soon established as an enduring household image
across Europe and later America: for Karl Marx, it provided a symbol
of the evils of capitalism; for Dickens a picture of Scrooge wrestling
with his stockings; for generations of cartoonists, an instantly recognisable schema for all kinds of political trouble (Nixon strangled by his
tapes, or plucky 'Mac' in 1960 ensnared in 'the European problem').
It remains at the top of the academic agenda, and is the subject of two

books, each by a leading figure in classical art history: *My Laocoön* by Richard Brilliant and *Laocoonte: Fama e stile* by Salvatore Settis.

The statue of 'Laocoon' appeared, in 1506, with an excellent literary pedigree. As both Brilliant and Settis emphasise, much of its immediate impact came from its obvious links with the *Aeneid* and with the description of a statue in Pliny the Elder's encyclopedic *Natural History*. Pliny had written of a 'Laocoon in the palace of the Emperor Titus ... (showing) Laocoon, his children and the wonderful clasping coils of snakes carved from a single block ... by Hagesander, Polydorus and Athenodorus, all from Rhodes'. The match with the statue that Pliny had seen and described was almost too good to be true. That said, the 'Laocoon', as it had been discovered, was far from complete. It was missing not just the usual extremities and the odd bits of snake; but each of the figures had lost their right arms. A huge debate followed (orchestrated by Michelangelo and Raphael among others) as to how those arms were to be restored – and particularly the arm of the central figure of Laocoon himself: bent back or extended straight up? By the 1530s, they had agreed that it should stretch up in the air; and each of the (many) succeeding restorations kept to this model, restoring the sons to match. This became the canonical image of the sculpture.

So far, nothing out of the ordinary. But, in the twentieth century, the story took a surprising twist. For, in 1906, Ludwig Pollak, a German archaeologist-cum-dealer, wandering around a mason's yard in Rome, spotted a fragment of a bent marble arm, with bulging muscles similar in style to the 'Laocoon'. He presented it to the Vatican Museums where it stayed in the stores until the 1950s – when the museum authorities decided that it actually belonged to the original 'Laocoon' itself, dismantled the statue, removed the traditional restorations and inserted the Pollak arm. There are, in fact, very strong arguments against this: the new arm does not directly join with the father's broken shoulder (a wedge of plaster has had to be inserted); it appears to be on a smaller scale and in a slightly differently coloured marble; Pollak himself believed only that it came from a statue like the 'Laocoon'; not to mention the fact that the circumstances of its discovery are vague at best, at worst suspicious – no more or less believable than the stories of 'serendipitous' finds of missing parts in the Renaissance. Not surprisingly the new restoration as a whole has not caught the popular imagination. (Cartoonists wanting an instantly recognisable

'Laocoon' still thrust his arm straight up.) For some reason, however, professional art historians have almost universally taken it on trust; loath, it seems, to subject the work of modern museum restorers to the same kind of hardheaded analysis as is given to that of leading Renaissance sculptors.

Brilliant and Settis are no exception: both explicitly endorse the 'new' 'Laocoon' in broad terms, though Brilliant would opt for a slightly more radical rearrangement of the three figures; and they apparently see no need to produce any particular argument in favour of the authenticity of the Pollak arm. In each case, this is a rare lapse. For both *My Laocoön* and *Laocoonte*, in their different intellectual styles (Brilliant working at the intersection of art history, philosophy of art and aesthetics; Settis in an Italian tradition of classics and cultural history), offer consistently perceptive analyses not just of the sculpture in its ancient context, but also of 'Laocoon' as an object of intense debate and controversy over the past 500 years. Brilliant, especially, approaches it as a paradigm object, raising central issues of art history and theory: identification, imitation, iconography, dating and response. The sculpture amounts to, in his words, 'a topos for the analysis of interpretation itself'.

It is an excellent subject for that project. Almost every aspect of the 'Laocoon' has been hotly contested at some point since its rediscovery. Even the apparently simple 'fact' that the sculpture described by Pliny is one and the same as the Vatican 'Laocoon' has not proved quite so simple. True, the subject matter matches (Laocoon, sons and writhing serpents); and the find spot, though vague in the Renaissance sources, could conceivably be compatible with a 'palace of Titus'. The problem is that Pliny claims his statue to be made out of one block of marble ('ex uno lapide'), while 'our' 'Laocoon' is certainly not. Almost since the moment of discovery, the possible explanations for this have been clear: either Pliny was wrong; or 'ex uno lapide' does not mean what we think it does; or the 'Laocoon' that Pliny saw was not ours, but some other version of this famous subject that no longer survives. Settis plunges in to argue (probably rightly) that, in Latin, 'ex uno lapide' is a well-known conceit, signalling a tour de force, and should not be taken literally. Brilliant stands back from the fray to reflect, more generally, on how the existence of such a text inevitably affects our understanding of a work of art.

Pliny's account also raises issues of dating and originality. He names three Rhodian artists – at first assumed to be the artists who sculpted 'our' statue at some disputed date, but obviously before Pliny wrote in the mid-first century AD. But what if, as many critics have since imagined, the Vatican 'Laocoon' is a 'copy' of some earlier Greek 'original'? In that case, were Pliny's sculptors responsible for the 'original' or the 'copy'? And how do we explain the fact that the same three names were found inscribed on the base of one of those piles of marble fragments at Sperlonga? And can we possibly feed in the tantalisingly coincidental fact that the Emperor Tiberius is known to have had a narrow escape when some cave in which he was dining at Sperlonga collapsed? Theories proliferate wildly, and dates at least three centuries apart have been seriously put forward for our 'Laocoon'. Most notorious of all, proposed in a whole stream of publications over the last thirty years, are the theories of Bernard Andreae, one time Director of the German Archaeological Institute in Rome and heavily involved in reassembling the fragments from Sperlonga into recognisable sculpture. On very little evidence indeed, Andreae claims the Vatican 'Laocoon' to be a copy of a bronze original, commissioned by the King of Pergamum in *c.*140 BC – aimed, he speculates, at harmonising Pergamene-Roman relations by an appeal to common Trojan origins. For him, Pliny's three Rhodians were the copyists, working on their marble version during the reign of Tiberius, at the same time as they were decorating the Sperlonga cave (now confidently identified as the site of the ill-fated dinner party), as an imperial commission, with sculptural themes 'pertinent to Tiberius' life story'.

Neither Brilliant nor Settis has much truck with any of this (it is perhaps double-edged when Brilliant calls Andreae 'the Winckelmann of the twentieth century'). And neither believes that searching for 'originals' and 'copies', in any simple sense, is a particularly useful procedure in the complex artistic world of the Roman Empire. Nonetheless, Settis plunges in again and argues directly against Andreae. A good proportion of his own text consists in an attempt to prove that our 'Laocoon' is an 'original' work of the late first century BC. Brilliant once more stays aloof, offering no preferred date of his own. In many ways this is the single most striking achievement of *My Laocoön*: to show the reader, by example, that fixing the date of a Roman sculpture is not the most important, or even a necessary, art-historical question.

There remains in the end, however, a sense that both Brilliant and Settis have pulled punches they might have delivered. Their shared commitment to the history of responses to 'Laocoon' leads them to take seriously a number of positions (Andreae's included) which in other contexts would have deserved polite ridicule. The truth is that a good proportion of recent writing on this sculpture should be pilloried as much as it is analysed. If anyone wishes to see the force of a clever satire on these contributions, they should consult an article in the periodical *Antike Welt*, where Tonio Hölscher returns to the 'Laocoon', with a whole series of political readings that outstrip even Andreae (Suppose we see 'Laocoon' and his sons standing for Augustus, with his failed heirs Gaius and Lucius? Is the elder boy in the statue (Gaius?) an older version of the Cupid that crawls up Augustus' leg in the Prima Porta statue? And so on.) Attentive readers, however, will not have worried. Alerted by the flagrantly 'old' restoration of 'Laocoon' that illustrates the article, they will soon have spotted that the first letter of each paragraph forms an entirely appropriate acrostic (in German): 'Praise be to nonsense.'

Review of *D'après l'Antique: Paris, musée du Louvre,16 octobre 2000–15 janvier 2001* (Réunion de musées nationaux, 2000); Richard Brilliant, *My Laocoön: Alternative claims in the interpretation of artworks* (University of California Press, 2000); Salvatore Settis, *Laocoonte, Fama e stile* (Donzelli, 1999)

26

DON'T FORGET YOUR
PITH HELMET

'In the language and manners of every Greek sailor and peasant the classical scholar will constantly recognize phrases and customs familiar to him in the literature of Ancient Hellas.' So the anxious tourist was reassured in the preface to the 1854 edition of Murray's *Handbook for Travellers in Greece*. The message was simple: on a Greek boat you will find yourself back with Odysseus ('the nautical contrivances and tactics of the ancients may be observed in daily use … the Greek seas are still as fickle as ever'); in a country cottage you will find yourself entertained by someone who could pass for Homer's swineherd Eumaeus. 'Even the ferocious attacks of vermin, which soon find out an Englishman, are exactly described in the graphic accounts given by Aristophanes of similar sufferings in Greek houses of old.'

Recapturing this world of antiquity was not, of course, without its hazards and difficulties, and the *Handbook* tried to demonstrate its own indispensability with some very lurid warnings about what could happen to the traveller who ventured to Greece unprepared. Health, indeed survival, was top of the agenda. 'The abundance of fruit is a temptation to foreigners,' it warned, 'but nothing is more pernicious, or more likely to lead to fatal consequences.' Protection against the Aristophanic vermin could be achieved only by means of a cheap but enormously complicated mosquito net whose daily assembling must have defeated all but the most obsessive and dexterous: 'I have found that the best mode of entering it is to keep the opening in the middle of the mattress, and, standing in it, draw the bag entrance over my head.' The problems of travel came a close second. Was it worth taking an English saddle? On balance yes, since they were so much more comfortable, but they did tend to injure the backs of the animals, given 'the wretched condition' of Greek horses. English servants, on the other hand, were better left at home, or if not at home, then in Corfu: 'They are usually but little disposed to adapt themselves to strange customs, have no facility in acquiring foreign languages, and' – revealing the characteristic blindness of the elite to the habitual discomforts of the working class – 'are more annoyed by hardships and rough living than their masters.' It was far more 'agreeable and advantageous' to hire a local, so long as no antiquarian knowledge was expected, let alone trusted if offered. For that, (hand)books were the thing.

It is hard to imagine that this advice was followed to the letter, any more than are the alarming prohibitions on sunbathing in the *Handbook*'s modern equivalents. The role of these guides is as much to construct an image of ideal travel (and with it a frisson of danger allayed) as it is to direct or constrain the traveller's actions. All the same, however practical their advice was or was meant to be, the successive editions of Murray's *Handbook for Travellers in Greece* (published with the authority of their publishing house; the authors and editors are indicated by initials only) clearly document the changing attitudes to the country as a destination for British tourists, from the first edition in 1840, just after the Greek War of Independence, into the twentieth century. In this period the country was redefined in the British imagination from an arena of dangerous exploration to a plausible destination for the upper-middle-class traveller and tourist. Exactly how far the various editions of the *Handbook* document 'real' changes in Greece itself is harder to say. In part, they certainly do. Successive editions list, for example, an ever-increasing number of upmarket hotels ('at least as good as those in the large towns of Italy'), and this presumably represents a change in the amenities available for travellers as well as in the economic life of Greece. But it is not always so clear. When the 1884 edition notes the presence of a dancing teacher in Athens, is that because such a facility had not existed before? Is it because tourists now had different expectations of what they might get out of Athens? Or is it because the *Handbook* (which had swelled to two volumes in 1884) was becoming ever keener on the idea of complete and comprehensive information, whether useful or not?

By and large, however, the inclusion of the dancing teacher fits with the increasingly domesticated – or, at least, more manageably foreign – image of Greece that developed as this series went on. Where the first edition of 1840 thundered that 'a tent is the first requisite' for travel in Greece, the revised edition of 1854 more moderately held that 'a tent, though requisite in many parts of Asia, is unnecessary and unusual in Greece.' By 1884, 'tents are a useless encumbrance'. So too, in later volumes, other erstwhile essentials of civilised travel in the wild are dismissed: a canteen, a carpet and the elaborate mosquito net (replaced by 1884 with, at most, a light wire mask). Only occasionally do the recommendations appear to point in the other direction. The earlier editions advised that a good straw hat was sufficient to keep off the sun, but in 1884 the traveller was told that nothing less than a pith-helmet would do ('indispensable after the end of April', the 1896 edition added).

Through all these changes and redefinitions, one thing remains more or less constant: the idea that modern Greece and the modern Greeks preserved something of the spirit and customs of the ancient world. It had been a cliché of many earlier travellers' accounts of Greece in the eighteenth and early nineteenth centuries that – impressive though the archaeological remains were – the inhabitants were a pale and disappointing shadow of their ancient ancestors. If they had gone to the country expecting to meet 'the descendants of Miltiades and Cimon', travellers found instead brigands, cheats and hucksters; and the women, as Valérie de Gasparin was sadly forced to acknowledge, bore precious little resemblance to the Venus de Milo. Partly in reaction to this, the guides of the later nineteenth century taught their readers to look elsewhere for the inheritance of antiquity. If you scratched the surface of day-to-day peasant life, if you listened harder to the language that was spoken, all kinds of resonances with the classical world would strike you. Sailors used the techniques described in Homer and farmers the methods recommended by Hesiod; and with enough imagination the superstitions that flourished in the Greek countryside could be traced back to pagan ideas and practice.

These questions of continuity obviously intersect with the academic war over Greek ethnicity that has been waged on and off, sometimes viciously, for two hundred years or so. Is the modern population of Greece the direct descendant of the ancient? Or is it a Slavic newcomer, as J. P. Fallmerayer in the nineteenth century or

Romilly Jenkins in the twentieth notoriously had it? The level to which this controversy has occasionally descended can be seen from a marginal comment scrawled by a racist reader in a copy of the first (1966) edition of Patrick Leigh Fermor's *Roumeli: Travels in Northern Greece* held by the Cambridge University Library. Where Leigh Fermor refers to the modern Greek language as being the 'undisputed heir of ancient Greek', the anonymous scribbler has added: 'Nonsense. It is the barbarous pidgin of the Albano-Slavs who defile the land of their occupation with the deformity of their "dago" bodies and the squalor of their politics'. But ideas of continuity also raise more general, and no less important, issues about how we perceive similarities between modern practice and its ancient predecessors, how travellers and tourists project primitivism and historical continuity onto the countries they visit, and how tourist destinations and their populations anywhere in the world invest in and encourage those projections (think, for example, of the Beefeaters or Anne Hathaway's cottage) as well as exploiting them for their own ends. What we are dealing with, in other words, is one aspect of the power struggle – or at least the complex negotiation – between visitor and visited.

This is clear enough in what now seems the quaintly old-fashioned advice given to travellers of a century or so ago. We find it harder to see how it works in contemporary tourism and the writing associated with it, from the cheapest guidebooks to travel literature of higher pretensions. Here, the legendary Greek hospitality – with its roots that supposedly go back to the Homeric world – provides a revealing and complicated case.

'The Greeks' reputation for hospitality is not a myth', the recent *Lonely Planet* guide trumpets, before going on to detail (in an account that closely echoes the earlier *Blue Guide*) 'hospitable' practices. You are likely to be 'invited into a stranger's home for coffee, a meal or even to spend the night'; it will be bad manners to refuse what is offered, or to attempt to pay for it, or to refuse to answer the personal questions that are put to you. Indeed, through the websites of Greek holiday bloggers, vignettes of just such occasions are sprinkled: photos of the old man (with his donkey), who took the whole family off to his house and plied them with endless coffee, delicious local hooch and loads of fruit for the kids. It is easy to forget that the Greeks are not, and could not possibly be, on any objective calibration, more hospitable than any other people in the world. Rather, we have chosen to interpret their version of social interaction as hospitality in its purest form.

We have done so, partly, to allow ourselves to behave when in Greece in ways we would not at home (isn't going into a stranger's house for the night precisely what we warn our children not to do?); and, partly, to enable the process of domestication that I referred to earlier. It takes only a moment to see the alternative narratives that could be constructed out of these 'hospitable' encounters: the 'delicious local hooch' is 'undrinkable spirit'; the fruit is bitter and unripe; and the temple ruins you really wanted to visit are a good hour away down a dirt track that it is now too late to travel; still less are you likely to make it safely back to where you are staying by nightfall. Under the slogan of 'hospitality' we translate potentially alarming cultural difference into a primitive (indeed Homeric) virtue that we can admire and, at the same time, faintly patronise. Successive editions of the *Handbook*, on the other hand, took a suspicious view of such invitations and firmly warned the reader against accepting free beds in Greek villages even when pressingly offered – largely on the (equally Homeric) principle that there is no such thing as a free gift.

How all this appears from the point of view of the old man with the donkey is harder, for me at least, to guess. You don't need to look very hard at Greek tourist brochures and posters to see that, in what is now an inextricable circle of supply and demand, the country's tourist industry sells itself in terms of the folksy primitivism implied by these stories of Homeric hospitality – recession or no recession. It is a paradox we have come to take for granted that a modern European nation chooses to project on its postcards images of wrinkled, toothless peasants or – in a more Wild West version of primitivism – road signs splattered with bullet holes.

By and large, however, British observers remain blind to the ways that these stereotypes are part of a more intricate game of power between tourist and 'native'. When, in the late nineteenth century, the classicist Jane Harrison's request to be taken to the temple of Bassae was refused by her young guide on the grounds that evil spirits resided there, she was both annoyed and overjoyed: annoyed that she would have to find another way of reaching the temple; overjoyed that she had found evidence of primitive religious beliefs. It never seems to have struck her that the boy might have been buying her off with exactly the kind of excuse he knew she would love to hear. Nor does it usually strike us that when we are being waylaid with the undrinkable spirit and unripe fruit, we are actually being hoist with the petard of our own fixation with primitive hospitality; the joke, in other words, is on us.

At first sight, Patrick Leigh Fermor's celebrated accounts of his wanderings in Greece before and after the Second World War play up to all the assumptions and myths of twentieth-century romantic Hellenism. *Roumeli* and *Mani: Travels in the Southern Peloponnese*, include admiring tales of the thuggish banditry in the Mani (the middle prong of the Southern Peloponnese). These laddish tales rub shoulders with intricate and outdated disquisitions on arcane parts of Byzantine history and culture, as well as the predictable insistence on the continuity of Greek customs and ideas since the age of Homer. In one especially enthusiastic set piece about his entertainment in the Deep Mani, he writes:

> Many things in Greece have remained unchanged since the time of the *Odyssey* and perhaps the most striking of these is the hospitality shown to strangers ... No better description exists of a stranger's sojourn at a Greek herdsman's fold than that of Odysseus when he stepped disguised into the hut of the swineherd Eumaeus in Ithaca. There is still the same unquestioning acceptance, the attention to a stranger's needs before even finding out his name: the daughter of the house pouring water over his hands and offering him a clean towel, the table laid first and then brought in, the solicitous plying of wine and food.

All of which should be enough to provoke a cynic to cast almost any form of social exchange in Homeric terms. ('At the average British dinner party, the visitors come offering gifts, the most precious of these – i.e. the most expensive bottles – are stored away for use at another time. Meanwhile the daughter of the house offers to the guests small pieces of food, often olives, before retiring to her own chamber.') Significant similarities, after all, are *made* not found.

Leigh Fermor is still well known for his leading part in the 1944 kidnap of General Kreipe, the German commander on Crete (and among classicists, at least, for his recital of Horace's Soracte Ode along with his captive when they woke the next morning in a cave in the Cretan hills – the upmarket equivalent of singing 'Silent Night' across the trenches). Whatever the consequences of the kidnap for the Cretan civilian population or for the progress of the war, the story has a blokeish tone which tinges some of his travel writing, too. Leigh Fermor was accompanied on many of his journeys after the war by his partner, and later wife, Joan; but she very rarely gets a look in, and when she does it's usually in a decidedly passive role (much as Murray's *Handbook* advises only a very subsidiary part in Greek travel for 'ladies'). This absence is exacerbated in the recent reprints, which have retained John Craxton's characteristic cover designs, but omitted the arresting black and white photographs taken by Joan that were included in the first editions.

Despite all this, *Mani* and *Roumeli* remain extraordinarily engaging books. This is partly thanks to Leigh Fermor's ability to turn an insight into a telling phrase ('There are towns in transition which have lost touch with the difference between nice and nasty' is a quip that could be applied to a thousand places between Shrewsbury and Heraklion); and partly thanks to his capacity to weave a compelling story out of sometimes unpromising material. One of the best tales of all is the hilarious digression in *Roumeli* on the attempted recovery of a pair of Byron's slippers from a man in Missolonghi, on behalf of Byron's very odd great-granddaughter Lady Wentworth. Along with other excerpts from his books and pieces of journalism (including his own account of the Kreipe affair), this story is collected in *Words of Mercury*, which provides a good taster of what Leigh Fermor's writing has to offer.

That is more than just a good eye for an aphorism or a story, more than a gift for elegant belles-lettres. When you see through all the nonsense about Hellenic continuity, there is, underneath, a much more nuanced account of the ambivalences of modern Greece, its people and its myths (its own myths about itself and us, as much as our myths about it). For example, a telling postscript to the story of Byron's slippers, not included in the excerpt in *Words of Mercury*, recounts in less than a page the story of the posthumous career of Rupert Brooke on the island of Skyros, with its different sort of primitivism. Brooke had never set foot on Skyros; he was merely buried there. But this did not prevent 'O Broukis' being conscripted into the island's cultural history and landscape. 'He used,' as one shepherd put it, 'to wander about the woods in silence, the very picture of an old-fashioned

English gentleman ... Tall, dignified, flowing hair, burning eyes and a long white beard.'

Predictably enough, Leigh Fermor is disdainful of modern mass tourism in Greece. After conjuring up a picture in *Roumeli* of the modern Athenian taverna ('Docile flocks converge on them, herded by button-eyed guides ... all Manchester, all Lyons, all Cologne and half the Middle-West at heel'), he looks to the future: 'In dark moments I see bay after lonely bay and island after island as they are today and as they may become ... The shore is enlivened with fifty jukeboxes and a thousand transistor wirelesses. Each house is now an artistic bar, a boutique or a curio shop; new hotels tower and concrete villas multiply.' What he failed to predict was that he might become an object of tourism himself. The *Lonely Planet* guide directs its readers to the village in the Mani where, it emphasises, Leigh Fermor (then ninety, he died in 2011) still lived for part of the year – and to the taverna run by his former housekeeper. A far cry – or perhaps not – from the Victorian *Handbook* guiding its readers on the search for the hut of Eumaeus and the ships of Odysseus.

Review of Patrick Leigh Fermor, *Roumeli: Travels in Northern Greece* (John Murray, 2004); Patrick Leigh Fermor *Mani: Travels in the Southern Peloponnese* (John Murray, 2004); Patrick Leigh Fermor, edited by Artemis Cooper, *Words of Mercury* (John Murray, 2004)

27

POMPEII FOR
THE TOURISTS

If you wanted to visit Pompeii in the mid-nineteenth century, you were best advised to take the train from Naples to the nearby station, and walk or ride to one of the main entrances to the site. That is certainly what Pope Pius IX did on 22 October, 1849, during his brief exile from revolutionary Rome. Pius arrived on the 8.30 train, accompanied by a posse of Swiss Guards, some Neapolitan dignitaries and his own personal chef. 'To save His Holiness from a long walk in the ruins', a cart was laid on – and, as its modern wheel gauge did not match the ancient, many of the famous Pompeian stepping stones across the streets had to be removed in his path, never to be replaced. The Pope toured the site, admired the House of the Faun (where the famous Alexander mosaic (Fig. 2), now in the Archaeological Museum in Naples, was still in place), and then watched an excavation in progress, which conveniently turned up some antiquities for him to take away.

Minus the cart, the vandalism and the over-sized escort, this was the standard pattern of visit followed by more ordinary tourists. The first edition of Murray's *Handbook for Travellers in Southern Italy*, published in 1853, recommended arriving by train, unless you were in a party of more than five when – ticket prices being what they were – a carriage all the way from Naples was cheaper (a piece of economic common sense that was obviously lost on the Pope). When you reached the station it strongly advised entering the site along the Street of Tombs, now the main tourist route out of the city to the Villa of the Mysteries, and walking through the ruins back to the Hotel Bellevue by the station, where you could get a late lunch from 'a very civil and obliging landlord'. The energetic could then either choose to visit the amphitheatre or take in Herculaneum on the way home. Though the Pope had made a special visit to this other buried city a few days after his Pompeii excursion (and picked up some more loot in the process), for most tourists Herculaneum, which had been one of the greatest European cultural attractions a century earlier, was now worth only a stop on the return journey if there was time. Pompeii was what you came to Naples to see.

Of course, the visitor's experience changed in many ways through the nineteenth century. By 1865 the site was charging an entrance fee, which covered the cost of a now compulsory guide or *cicerone*; while the Hotel Bellevue was under new management, had been renamed the Hotel Diomede and become a dangerous tourist trap (readers of 'Murray' were warned not to order a meal without coming to 'an agreement as to the charge beforehand with mine host'). But many essentials of the visit remained the same.

The entrance to the city via the Street of Tombs, which continued to be the recommended route until the 1870s, underlined the fact that for most nineteenth-century tourists a visit to Pompeii was a visit to the city of the dead. It was a funerary as much as an archaeological site, prompting reflections on the tragedy of the destruction and the fragility of the human condition at the same time as it, paradoxically, seemed to bring the ancient world to 'life'. Skeletons had always been high on the visitor's agenda. But the pathos of the Pompeii experience was even further intensified by the technique of making casts of the bodies of the victims, developed in the 1860s by Giuseppe Fiorelli (the erstwhile radical politician, who became one of the most influential directors in the history of the Pompeian excavations). Plaster poured into the cavities left by the decomposed flesh and clothing of the dead produced startling images of their physical features and the contortions of their last moments.

These casts are the subject of a fascinating chapter by Eugene Dwyer in *Antiquity Recovered*, a sumptuously illustrated collection of essays on the modern history of Pompeii and Herculaneum. Dwyer explains how the heavy clothing visible on the casts, the trousers apparently worn by both sexes and the scarved heads of the women – 'all'uso degli orientali', as one archaeologist put it – dispelled the popular image of

Roman dress as scanty, if not lasciviously revealing. (Others have since wondered if what people decide to wear in the middle of a volcanic eruption can really be taken as typical everyday clothing: maybe the headscarves were not so much 'oriental' as a practical device to keep ash out of the hair.) He also follows the history of several casts that became particularly famous symbols of the city and its destruction. These included one of the first group to be made by Fiorelli: a woman fallen on her back, straining upwards to breathe, her skirt gathered around her hips giving the probably misleading impression that she was pregnant. Some Victorian scholars took her to be a prostitute (she was carrying a small statuette of Cupid and a silver mirror); others saw her as a dutiful housewife (on the basis of a large iron key she was also carrying). Either way, this 'pregnant woman', as she was usually known, took a starring role in discussions of the site in the 1860s and early 1870s and is recorded in many early photographs – until she was upstaged by yet more evocative images of suffering, and her cast was mysteriously lost.

These dying figures continue to haunt the modern imagination. As Jennie Hirsh discusses in another essay in *Antiquity Recovered*, two such casts, clinging to each other even in death, take a cameo role in Rossellini's 1953 film, *Voyage to Italy* – serving as a sharp and upsetting reminder to two modern tourists to the site (Ingrid Bergman and George Sanders) of just how distant and empty their own marriage has become. And even the most stony-hearted or austerely academic visitor finds it hard not to be a little moved by the few casts still displayed in glass cases on the site – their death agonies, uncomfortably, on show for all to see.

In other respects, however, the experience of visiting this city of the dead today is very different indeed from a century and a half ago. To be sure, many of the tourist highlights remain the same, even though more than twice the area exposed in the 1850s has since been uncovered: besides the attraction of the casts, visitors still flock to the House of the Faun, the Temple of Isis and the Stabian Baths. But the crucial point is that the underlying purpose of the visit has narrowed. Modern visitors mostly come to see an ancient city, to 'step back in time' (albeit in the company of a couple of million others each year). Nineteenth-century visitors also came with those aims in mind; in fact, the idea that here for the very first time the daily life of the Romans was exposed to the modern gaze gave Pompeii its special edge for those early tourists. But they also came to see the processes by which

16. This nineteenth-century model of Pompeii shows the ruins of
the so-called *macellum* in the middle-distance – with its puzzling
circle of stones (statue bases, pergola supports?) in the centre.

the ancient past was revealed. They were interested in *what* we know
about the ancient city, but they were no less interested in *how*.

One aspect of this interest in process comes out in the eager
engagement of those nineteenth-century guidebooks with the doubts,
uncertainties and debates on the identity and function of the ancient
monuments on view. It was simply not obvious when they were first
excavated what many of these buildings were, or were for. A classic
case is the large structure, on the right-hand side of the Temple of
Jupiter in the main forum of Pompeii, presented to modern tourists
– uncontroversially – as a 'market', or *macellum*. It is now one of the
least prepossessing of ruins on the site, the brilliant wall paintings
enthusiastically hyped by many a Victorian traveller now faded beyond
recognition. But there were originally shop stalls down one side, a
butcher's counter at the rear and a fish-preparation area (to judge from
the large quantity of fish scales discovered) beneath a canopy in the
centre of the main courtyard – all operating under the divine protection of the deified emperors of Rome, whose shrine stood at the far
end of the building, next to the butcher. Or so we are confidently told.

The nineteenth-century visitor, by contrast, was entertained with a range of conflicting interpretations. It might have been, so some of the best authorities then thought, a shrine of the twelve gods or Pantheon (on the assumption that the twelve supports now believed to have held up a central canopy were in fact twelve statue bases). Or it might have been a large cult area for the worship of Augustus, with 'cells' for the priests of the imperial cult in what have been more recently identified as shops. Or, if you were Sir William Gell, whose *Pompeiana*, the best-selling handbook to the site of the first half of the century, lay behind Bulwer-Lytton's even better-selling *Last Days of Pompeii* (1834), it was a nice 'caff' with a shrine attached (in other words a city-centre coffee house or restaurant, the so-called shops being nothing of the sort, but the ancient equivalent of private dining booths – and that butcher's counter being, actually, the fixed couches of a *triclinium* or dining room). True, sometimes more recent study or excavation has solved the puzzles that preoccupied previous generations. But often, as with this *macellum*, a convenient if dubious modern orthodoxy has simply taken the place of nineteenth-century debate and discussion.

These different priorities are also seen in the tradition of staged excavations of the kind which were laid on for the Pope in 1849, and had been the stock-in-trade of the Pompeian tourist industry since the eighteenth century – when any visiting dignitary was fair game for treasure, painting or (best of all) a skeleton to be dug up, apparently unexpectedly, in front of his very nose. We tend now to laugh at the crudeness of these charades and the gullibility of the audience (could visiting royalty have been so naive as to imagine that such wondrous discoveries just happened to be made at the very moment of their own arrival?). But, as often, the tricks of the tourist trade reveal the hopes and aspirations of the visitors as much as they expose the guile of the locals. Here the visitors wanted to witness not just the finds themselves, but the processes of excavation that brought the past to light.

Instructive, too, are the rhetorical conventions of the nineteenth-century guidebooks themselves, and of other popular accounts. For, in their description of the monuments, these not only included the ancient history of each one, but also carefully and systematically noted the date and circumstance of their modern rediscovery. It is as if those early visitors were supposed to keep two chronologies running in their heads at the same time: on the one hand, the chronology of the ancient city itself and its development; on the other, the history of Pompeii's gradual re-emergence into the modern world.

Pompeii Awakened by Judith Harris and *Antiquity Recovered* both in their different ways try to recapture something of that stereoscopic vision, seeing the story of the re-excavation of the buried cities as crucial to our understanding of the sites as we visit them today. Both offer colourful and sometimes acute insights into the modern history of Pompeii and Herculaneum, from the first explorations under the idiosyncratic Bourbon kings (and their often formidable queens) and the archaeologically energetic Napoleonic regime, up to the two most distinguished directors of the more recent excavations. The first of these is Fiorelli, who not only invented the technique of corpse-casting, but also divided Pompeii into the archaeological 'regions' and 'blocks' (*regiones* and *insulae*) by which it is still known, policed and surveyed. The second is Amedeo Maiuri, who survived Fascism and its fall to head the site from 1924 to 1962, who excavated more of Pompeii than anyone before or since – and who notoriously subsidised the work in the 1950s by offering the volcanic rubble from the excavations to the builders of the Naples–Salerno *autostrada* in return for workmen and digging equipment.

Histories of archaeology can be rather smug in tone, in a 'look how much better we are than our predecessors' kind of way. Even the excellent *Antiquity Recovered* is not entirely free from this vice. In an otherwise interesting essay on the paintings from the 'Porticus' in Herculaneum, Tina Najberg so often berates the poor old Bourbon excavators for ignoring the demands of 'contextual' archaeology and for ripping out the best paintings from the site and taking them back to their museum, that I found myself leaning to the Bourbon side. After all, if the paintings in the *macellum* had been hauled off to the museum when they were first unearthed in all their brilliance, we would still be able to make out what they showed.

For the most part, though, *Antiquity Recovered* hardly puts a foot wrong. It includes some marvellous case studies of the modern history of Pompeii by some of the best scholars working in the field. I particularly enjoyed James Porter's reflections on the Villa of the Papyri at Herculaneum and his debunking of so many of the myths which have fuelled the campaign for its re-excavation (that, for example, it was owned by Piso, a relation of Julius Caesar and patron of the philosopher Philodemus, or that its 'Latin Library' may await our discovery). Likewise Chloe Chard's excellent essay on the significance of early tourists' picnicking habits and their descriptions of conspicuous consumption on site (if the Pope dragged his private chef along to Pompeii, he can hardly have eaten more lavishly than at Anna Jameson's 1822 'Picnic party of pleasure, à l'Anglaise' which included oysters, 'London bottled porter, and half a dozen different kinds of wine'). And Lee Behlman's nice contribution on the myth of the Roman guard, whose skeleton was supposed to have been found at the Herculaneum Gate, where he had died at his post as the ash fell, doggedly 'Faithful unto Death' as the title of Edward Poynter's heroising painting of the scene put it.

But if there is a single contribution which demonstrates that the 'reception' of Pompeii and the history of its excavations is not an optional extra but an essential part of the modern archaeological understanding of the site, it is Bettina Bergmann's chapter on the famous 'Dionysiac' frieze from the Villa of the Mysteries. Lavishly published by Maiuri in 1931, in a state-sponsored (i.e. Fascist) volume, with state-of-the-art colour photography, these paintings – often taken to depict a marriage, or a mystic initiation complete with flagellation and revelation of the phallus – are now so closely associated with Maiuri's name that many people imagine that he was the original excavator. In fact, the Villa had been uncovered in 1909 in what is euphemistically dubbed a 'private' excavation by a local hotel owner, Aurelio Item – hence the first name of the site, 'Villa Item', not 'Villa of the Mysteries'. And it had been published and discussed three times, with rather dreary black-and-white photographs, before Maiuri got his hands on it. In the course of a wide-ranging study of the frieze, which extends to its later appropriations in media as diverse as psychoanalysis and HBO's *Rome*, Bergmann poses one crucial question. How close were Maiuri's images of the frieze to what was originally excavated? Or, for that matter, how accurate a reflection of what was found in 1909 is what we now see on the site? Many visitors may realise that the roof of the room concerned and the upper walls are modern restoration (although my own observation suggests that a good number believe that the whole room, roof and all, is a miraculous piece of preservation from antiquity). Most tourists – and indeed most academic visitors – assume that the paintings, at least, are presented more or less as they came out of the ground. Are they right? Are we looking at the 'freshness and vividness of the originals', as archaeologists have claimed?

Through searching out old photographs and with some careful work in the Pompeii archives, Bergmann shows how much a modern construction these most famous and 'best preserved' of all Roman paintings are. In the period between their first discovery and the Maiuri publication, they were left deteriorating for a few years, unprotected but for some cloth hangings; they were pilfered and reassembled (some pieces were found in Item's hotel); they were removed from the wall and remounted (on what was effectively new masonry); and they were repeatedly coated with a solution of wax and benzine (hence their shiny 'fresh' tones). And that is just what we can document. Bergmann honestly concludes that we will never now be able to reconstruct the Roman appearance of the Dionysiac frieze – though we can be certain that it was significantly different from what we now see. I for one will never look at this frieze in quite the same way again.

Review of Judith Harris, *Pompeii Awakened: A story of rediscovery* (I. B. Tauris, 2007); Victoria C. Gardner Coates and Jon L. Seydl (eds.), *Antiquity Recovered:The legacy of Pompeii and Herculaneum* (Getty Publications, 2007)

28

THE GOLDEN BOUGH

'He has changed the world – not as Mussolini has changed it, with coloured shirts and castor oil; not as Lenin has changed it, boldly emptying out the baby of the humanities with the filthy bath of Tsarism; nor as Hitler, with the fanfaronade of physical force. He has changed it by altering the chemical composition of the cultural air that all men breathe.'

The cultural revolutionary celebrated here (unlikely as it must now seem) is Sir James Frazer, extravagantly written up over half a page in the *News Chronicle* of 27 January 1937. The article – under the title 'He *discovered* why you believe what you do' – certainly does not stint its praises of the grand old man, then in his eighties. Later on in the piece Frazer is portrayed as a hero-explorer of time and space, 'at home in the Polynesia of a thousand years BC or the frozen north before even the Vikings had touched its shore'. And he ends up compared (to his own advantage, once more) with one of the most romantic of British heroes: 'this quiet sedentary student has a mind similar to the body of Sir Francis Drake, ranging distant countries and bringing back their treasures for his own kind.'

It would be convenient to dismiss this nonsense as the outpourings of a pre-war hack, with an unabashed talent for hyperbole and a peculiar passion for *The Golden Bough*. But the uncomfortable truth is that this is just one example (and not even a particularly extreme one) of the widespread idealisation of Frazer in the 1920s and 1930s. The press throughout the Empire – from the *Huddersfield Examiner* to the *Melbourne Age* – colluded in turning into a contemporary hero an obsessive, retiring Victorian academic.

Part of Frazer's appeal was precisely his shy donnish character – the stereotype of the unworldly professor, devoted to learning at all hours of the day and night. 'To Sir James Frazer,' ran one report (based on an interview with 'a close friend') 'work is a rite. During his life as a scholar he has worked 14 to 16 hours a day, seven days a week, and the same on holidays.' No admission here of the tedium of such a regime; nothing but admiration for the strange paradox that Frazer's writings explored the farthest-flung regions of the world, while Frazer himself rarely left his study. 'Authority on savages – but he has never seen one', declared (approvingly, it seems) the headlines of several articles; and they went on to reassure their readers that Sir James 'is fond of saying that he has never seen a savage in his life; his books are the outcome of research into original scientific work.' This was, in fact, exactly what Frazer did say to the gossip columnist of the *Sunday Chronicle* in conversation at a literary lunch in August 1937. The ignorant columnist had naively assumed that the anthropologist must have 'pottered intellectually around Polynesia, New Guinea, the Great Barrier Reef and a few other places where our aboriginal brothers and sisters reside'– but was assured by Frazer that he 'had never been further than Greece'.

All the trivia of Frazer's life became good copy for any journalist. While the readers of *Les Nouvelles Littéraires* were let in on the secret that 'Sir James vendrait son âme pour des fruits confits' ('Sir James would sell his soul for candied fruits'), the British public lapped up anecdotes about his ludicrously high-minded devotion to scholarship. These had greatest appeal when they showed him fearlessly neglecting all thought of his own comfort, even his own safety, in pursuit of just a few more precious moments at his books: he barely looked up, so it was reported, when a German aeroplane circled overhead; when he had singed off half his beard and his eyebrows in an exploding meths stove, he quickly reassured his wife that he was all right and got straight back to his books. The latter incident ended up as a cartoon (one of Lady Frazer's treasured possessions) showing a group of 'savages' dancing round a blazing cauldron in which Frazer sat calmly reading a book on folklore.

There was more to this heroisation than newspaper gossip. Frazer himself, however unwillingly, became implicated in acting out the public role of intellectual hero. In a strange reversal of the image (and reality) of the retiring scholar, he came to play the lead part in a range of incongruous ceremonies. These were not merely the traditional public occasions which a distinguished academic, a knight and a member of the Order of Merit might normally be expected to attend. Frazer also found himself wheeled out to meet (and impress) an odd assortment of visiting dignitaries. One of these – in perhaps the most bizarre of the encounters on record – was the young Jesse Owens, passing through England on his return from the 1936 Berlin Olympics. Against all the odds, the meeting seems to have been at least a partial success. Owens claimed to have been 'thrilled' at talking to the famous scholar who knew more about the ancient Olympic Games than any other living soul. What Frazer himself made of the occasion we do not know.

The regular highlight of Frazer's public year was his birthday – marked in the last decade of his life (he died in 1941 at the age of 87) by a series of theatrical parties, orchestrated by Lady Frazer and, of course, admiringly reported through the British press. The most lavish of these was his 83rd, in 1937. More than two hundred guests met in London to do homage to Frazer, who obligingly stood under a 'golden bough' – a branch of mistletoe which had been specially imported from Norway for the occasion. The spectacles laid on included a vast cake with 83 candles, the performance of an operetta based on a play by none other than Lady Frazer (called, appropriately enough, *The Singing Wood*) and a display of indoor fireworks. Frazer himself, according to the reports, claimed to have been 'particularly charmed' by the fireworks – but, as he was by this date completely blind, one suspects a certain irony in the remark, perhaps even an unease with the whole occasion. If that is correct, it is an unease that he rarely let show. It is true that a few press reports picked up his general preference for a good day's work in the comfort of his study over such forced jollifications. But, by and large, he seems to have acquiesced in these public displays, offering appreciative quotations and posing for photographs in the long-suffering manner of royalty.

This cult of 'Frazer the man' in the years before the Second World War was matched by an almost equal craze for *The Golden Bough* itself. Admittedly some critics, even in the popular press, were beginning to sense that Frazer's approach was a bit 'Victorian'. One writer in the *Sydney Morning Herald*, for example, contrasted Frazer's 'pity' for the poor savage – because he is so ignorant of the 'blessings of civilisation' – with the attitude of the radical young anthropologist of the new generation, who 'usually *envies* the savage for exactly the same reason'. Such qualms, however, did not do much to dampen enthusiasm for Frazer's brand of anthropology. The abridged edition of *The Golden Bough* sold more than 33,000 copies in the first ten years (between 1922 and 1933). And, as the 1930s came to an end, the London literary columnists constantly recommended the book as a good companion for the long nights of the war to come – an idea supported by Mrs Neville Chamberlain herself, who, according to the *Evening News*, used to take *The Golden Bough* with her on most of her travels. This success was not even an exclusively British phenomenon. In New York in 1940 *The Golden Bough* ran neck and neck with *Mein Kampf* as bestselling reprint of the year.

It is not easy to understand this extraordinary enthusiasm for Frazer and *The Golden Bough*. There were other books of anthropology which included almost as much exotic information and were a considerably easier, and shorter, read. But – except perhaps for the works of Margaret Mead – none reached the Frazerian level of popularity. There were also literally hundreds of dons in Oxford, Cambridge and elsewhere whose weird and eccentric habits could have provided columns of copy for a journalist in search of an easy story. But it was Frazer who found his way onto the pages of the popular press. Why?

Robert Fraser (no relation, different spelling) has not set out directly to answer that question, but his book does serve to highlight the problems of Frazer's success. *The Making of 'The Golden Bough'* is a work of intellectual history. As his subtitle (*The Origin and Growth of an Argument*) makes clear, Fraser is concerned with *The Golden Bough*'s theoretical implications and the background from which it came. He explores in detail Frazer's debt to the Scottish intellectual tradition (particularly Hume) and his formative relations with Robertson Smith, a colleague at Cambridge whose *Religion of the Semites* was published just a year before *The Golden Bough*. And – the qualifying test, it seems, for all bona fide students of Frazer's vast output – he traces the changes and developments in the argument of *The Golden Bough* over its various editions, from the mere two volumes of 1890 through to the 12-volume third edition (1906–15) and the abridgement of 1922.

Fraser has a light touch with some uncompromisingly heavy material. Occasionally there is an irritating, drama-documentary feel to the book. (Is there any evidence for Robertson Smith's breathless dash across the college to tell the understandably hesitant young

Frazer to 'Get going, man!' with his article on 'Priapus' for the *Encyclopaedia Britannica*?) And occasionally the wry humour makes some quite simple points almost incomprehensible. ('Ominous noises emanating from the Hôtel Printemps' refers, as far as I can tell, to Frazer's new ideas for the third edition of *The Golden Bough*, developed while staying at a *pensione* in Rome!) As a work of intellectual history, however, *The Making of 'The Golden Bough'* is for the most part a job well done, and a useful supplement to Robert Ackerman's excellent, but more strictly biographical, study of Frazer.

The underlying problem is that it is not at the level of 'high culture' that *The Golden Bough* most demands an explanation. The strictly academic claims of Frazer's book, its distinction between magic and religion, its theory of sacrifice, its development of Humean philosophy, may all in some ways have encouraged its wide popular standing – but, surely, not to any significant extent. Most of the readers of the *News Chronicle* or the *Staffordshire Sentinel* who avidly devoured all eulogies of the great man had not the slightest interest in the similarity between Frazer's theories of sympathetic magic and Hume's principles of resemblance and contiguity. They may well not even have heard of Hume, let alone Robertson Smith. Their passion for Frazer and his work must have had other causes. Those causes are not explained by any of the recent studies of *The Golden Bough* (Fraser's included), which often express slightly baffled admiration at the size of the sales figures, but neglect the popular cult of Frazer and the rich material that documents it.

One of the most important aspects of *The Golden Bough*'s popular appeal was the theme of exploration and travel. The book does not, of course, document an actual voyage: in fact, as the press accounts constantly stressed, Frazer had never visited most of the countries or witnessed the customs and rituals he described. Nevertheless, eulogy after eulogy portrayed him as the hero-explorer, the new Sir Francis Drake. And Frazer himself in his introduction wrote of *The Golden Bough* as a 'voyage' – the author as helmsman, setting sail with 'the wind in our shrouds'. What kind of travel was Frazer suggesting? Not, certainly, the once daring, now commonplace travel around the Mediterranean. After all, in the first chapter of the book, it was the coast of Italy that was conjured up as the relatively safe starting point of the whole adventure. Frazer's voyage took the reader to places much further away in time and space, to the lands of all things strange, where the bizarre customs of primitive Britain (corn-dollies, maypoles and so on) stood side by side with the eccentric habits of the aboriginal populations of the Empire. Part 'reality', part 'metaphor', this was a journey to the Other, to the Foreign, to all that was different from the increasingly urban, industrial life of early twentieth-century southern England.

It was in some respects an alarming journey: on the one hand, there were the strange and violent customs of the 'savages'; on the other, the unsettling sense that Britain, too, had once had its fair share of 'irrationality'. But whatever the frisson of danger, at least the reader returned home safely in the end (i.e. landed up in Italy again). That is, of course, exactly what the title of the book – *The Golden Bough* – tells us. The academic reader, to be sure, would eventually realise that it related (in a rather complex, even perverse way) to Frazer's introductory analysis of the peculiar Roman cult in the sacred grove of Diana at Nemi – the famous grove whose 'priest-king' held office only until murdered at the hands of a rival claimant. But it was also a reference to Virgil's 'Golden Bough', that magical branch which, on the instructions of the Sybil, Aeneas plucked to ensure himself a safe journey into the Underworld, and a safe passage back out. The title, in other words, proclaimed its purpose: like Aeneas's bough, it took its readers on a strange voyage into a terrifying foreign world, and then brought them back once more to safety.

This image of Frazer's 'voyage' was developed in an unexpected way in a popular novel published in 1890 and based explicitly on *The Golden Bough* (whose first edition had appeared only months before). Grant Allen's *The Great Taboo* turned Frazer's metaphorical journey into a literal tale of travel and adventure. It is the story of a young English couple, Felix Thurstan and Miss Muriel Ellis, washed overboard from a steamer in the South Seas and cast up on an island called Boupari, where the religious habits of the natives are a close replica of those described by Frazer. There are some ludicrous moments in the tale: Felix (by now desperately in love with Muriel) being forced to kill the cannibalistic god-king and assume the role of deity himself; the horrible secrets of the island's religious customs divulged to our heroes through the mouth of an aged talking parrot. But in the end the happy pair reach England again – and, of course, marry. The final scene sees them trying to deal with Muriel's crusty old aunt, who objects to the fact that they spent so many months on the island together, but unmarried. 'Taboos,' as the concluding remark of the novel goes, 'are much the same in England as in Boupari'.

This is not a great novel; it is a crude and simplified retelling of *The Golden Bough*. But partly for that reason it is important for our understanding of the immediate popular reception of Frazer's work. Felix and Muriel, in their dreadful melodrama, act out the experience of every reader of *The Golden Bough* – embarking on a journey into a frightening and unknown world, then returning safely to familiar civilisation, but now with a heightened awareness of the taboos and constraints of their own culture. In *The Great Taboo, The Golden Bough* shows its true colours as a voyage of exploration.

There were, of course, other factors behind the pre-war success of *The Golden Bough*. The sheer bulk of the third edition, a monument to encyclopedic knowledge, gave it instant authority – and its 400-page index turned it into an easy reference work for the whole of world culture. At the same time the book's incorporation and explanation of the customs of the native populations of the British Empire gave it a link with contemporary political reality. Some critics interpreted this link in very practical terms – one remarked that 'many mistakes would have been avoided in the government of backward and primitive peoples if more attention had been paid to the knowledge which Sir James has revealed of habits, customs and traditional beliefs.' And Frazer himself was said to have hoped that his books would 'be of help to those whose task it is to govern primitive peoples'. More important, though, was Frazer's symbolic service to the cause of Empire. *The Golden Bough* represented the imperial subjects to their masters, legitimising British imperialism by turning the natives into convenient supporting evidence in a grand scholarly project. This was political domination neatly converted into academic prose.

Why *The Golden Bough* still remains popular today is more of a mystery. The 1922 abridgement has never been out of print; and the publishers reissued a reprint of the twelve-volume edition for the centenary of the first edition – presumably in the hope of some commercial success. It would be naive to suppose that Frazer's theories and arguments had much to do with his popularity. Admittedly (to judge from its presence in occult bookshops and the lurid cover of the paperback edition), there may be some link between Frazer's theories of death and rebirth and modern esoteric religion. But even the most enthusiastic follower of the occult would find it hard to see the relevance of Frazer's outdated ethnography to their interests. And to the average reader, lacking that incentive to persevere, *The Golden Bough* must seem a long-winded, impenetrable text, made all the more baffling by its insistent comparisons between one now unfamiliar world and another.

The book remains important to us not because it is any longer avidly read, but because it was once read (with pleasure, or sometimes distaste) by writers who do still matter to us – by Eliot, Joyce, Malinowski, Lawrence, Leach, Yeats. We see the book through their eyes, irrevocably distanced from any sense of direct excitement at Frazer's text. Reminiscing in 1925 on her own generation's first encounter with Frazerian anthropology, Jane Harrison, the Cambridge classicist and specialist in Greek religion, wrote: 'at the mere sound of the magical words "Golden Bough" we heard and understood.'

The magic is no longer quite the same.

Review of Robert Fraser, *The Making of 'The Golden Bough': The Origin and Growth of an Argument* (Macmillan, 1990)

29

PHILOSOPHY MEETS
ARCHAEOLOGY

In February 1938, R. G. Collingwood, then Waynflete Professor of Metaphysical Philosophy at Oxford and aged only 48, suffered a small stroke. It was the first of a series, each one more serious than the last, that would kill him within five years. The usual treatment in the 1930s was less effective than modern medical intervention but rather more enjoyable. His doctors recommended a prolonged period of leave from his job, lengthy walks and sea cruises. He was also encouraged to continue writing: even if teaching was deemed bad for the blood vessels, research was supposed to be good for them.

Signing off from Oxford for a year, he immediately bought a small yacht in which he planned to sail, single-handed, across the Channel and around Europe (hardly a leisured cruise perhaps, but relying on the same basic principle that sea air was restorative). Disaster struck. Just a few days into the voyage, he was rescued from a terrible storm by the Deal lifeboat and towed to shore. He set off again but soon suffered another stroke, which he seems to have weathered by anchoring the yacht far out to sea and lying in his bunk until the headache eased and his normal movement returned. By the time he reached dry land again, he had already started writing his autobiography.

After a few months convalescing in his family home in the Lake District, he had finished the autobiography: an outspoken, sometimes boastful little volume, which ended with an unguarded attack on some of the Oxford philosophers 'of my youth' as 'propagandists of a coming

Fascism'. The University Press had to overcome a few qualms, and insisted on some revisions, before publishing it the following year. In the meantime, Collingwood had embarked on another journey, this time on a Dutch vessel bound for the Far East. It was onboard this ship, where the captain rigged up an open-air study for him on the bridge, that he began his *Essay on Metaphysics*, finishing the first draft in a hotel in Jakarta. On the way home, he edited out some of the most offensive passages of the autobiography, while also writing substantial chunks of what he called his 'masterpiece': a book that was to be known as *The Principles of History*.

He stayed in Oxford barely a couple of months after his return. According to his own scarcely credible story, he was accosted by an unknown American student outside Thornton's bookshop on Broad Street and invited to sail with him and his student crew to Greece. He agreed; they left in June and Collingwood came back only shortly before war was declared. In 1940, his account of the journey, *The First Mate's Log*, appeared from OUP.

This frenetic activity was not typical of Collingwood's life up to that point. True, he was always an insomniac workaholic, but he had lived undemonstratively, and at a decidedly more gentlemanly, donnish pace. If his career had been at all unusual, it was because of his two parallel, but at first sight quite distinct, research and teaching interests: on the one hand, philosophy; on the other, Roman history and archaeology – especially the archaeology of Roman Britain. In fact, before he was elected to the Waynflete chair in 1935, he had held a curious hybrid post, as university lecturer in philosophy and Roman history. Much of his time was spent working on his own peculiar brand of idealist philosophy – increasingly old-fashioned as it must have seemed by the mid-1930s to those who were starting to listen to A. J. Ayer and J. L. Austin. The summers he devoted to digging, and to transcribing, recording and drawing Roman inscriptions (from tombstones to milestones), in preparation for a complete collection of the *Roman Inscriptions of Britain* – a project on which he worked for almost all his academic life. Before 1938, he had published some important studies in Romano-British archaeology and had made one or two notable contributions to academic philosophy. But as Stefan Collini observes in his chapter on Collingwood in *Absent Minds*, if he had died in 1938 from his first stroke, his work would probably have earned 'only a small footnote in the more conscientious surveys of 20th-century

British philosophy and academic scholarship' (and, one might add, he would have been thought rather lucky to win the Waynflete chair). It is the work that appeared after the stroke that made his name.

In fact, the pace of his activity – in both his personal and his professional life – increased yet further when in 1941 he became convinced, rightly, that he had very little time left to live. In January he finally resigned from his university chair. Then, with the recklessness of the dying, he divorced his wife and married his mistress, Kate, a former student turned actress, twenty years younger than himself (Fred Inglis in his biography of Collingwood reasonably wonders whether all his foreign travel in the late 1930s was driven less by a spirit of adventure and a confidence in the healthy properties of sea air, more by a desire to escape from his complicated domestic affairs). Kate gave birth to their child in December 1941, and Collingwood died in the Lake District in early 1943, increasingly paralysed by further severe strokes. But that was not before he had finished another book, *The New Leviathan; or Man, Society, Civilisation and Barbarism*, which appeared in 1942. As the title more than hints, it was an uncompromising, sometimes truculent attempt to muster Hobbesian political philosophy in the fight against Fascism – 'his contribution to the war', as Inglis sees it. It also included some frankly 'batty' attacks, as even his admirers concede, on some of his increasingly favoured targets – among them, the educational system whose great beneficiary he had been. Late Collingwood was a passionate advocate of home-schooling, and believed that one of Plato's biggest crimes was to have 'planted on the European world the crazy idea that education ought to be professionalized'.

Apart from the *Autobiography*, with its sometimes tactless, sometimes engaging assertions of the relevance of philosophy to modern politics, his most influential works weren't published in these final few years but later, after his death, and in some cases long after. His most famous book of all, *The Idea of History*, with its now familiar attacks on what he called the 'scissors and paste' method of historical inquiry, and its defence of history as always a 'history of the mind', was published in 1946, compiled posthumously from various surviving manuscript sources by his ex-pupil and literary executor, Malcolm Knox. It has only recently become clear quite how partial Knox's compilation was – omitting, for example, or toning down much of Collingwood's critique of Hegel.

There was even more to come over the next half-century. His most lasting contribution to Romano-British studies was the 800-page compendium of the *Roman Inscriptions of Britain*. This project had been inaugurated by Francis Haverfield (p. 203) before the First World War. After the first chosen editor fell in action in the Dardanelles in 1915 Collingwood was selected as his successor and worked on the book, on and off, mostly during the summer vacations, until 1941 – when he passed the material over to his junior editor, R. P. Wright. It finally appeared in 1965, with Collingwood and Wright as joint authors (the latter admitting, plaintively or accusingly, in the preface that 'the writing of the text took longer than I had been led to expect'). Thirty years after that, *The Principles of History*, the 'masterpiece' that Collingwood started on the trip to the Far East but never finished, finally saw the light of day. It had been believed lost, possibly destroyed after Knox had gutted it in preparing *The Idea*. But in 1995 two sharp-eyed archivists found the manuscript, hidden away at OUP. It was published in 1999, more than fifty years after his death.

Inglis's *History Man* is an enthusiastic appreciation. Unusually for the biography of an academic, it is particularly revealing about Collingwood's childhood in the Lake District, where his father, W. G. Collingwood, was secretary to the elderly Ruskin, where the sons and grandsons of William Wordsworth were still prominent in the local community, and where Arthur Ransome was a frequent visitor to the Collingwood family home. Inglis, in fact, hazards a guess that R.G. was the inspiration for the elder brother, John Walker, in Ransome's *We Didn't Mean to Go to Sea*. True or not, it reminds us that when Collingwood set out, single-handed, on his ill-fated voyage into the English Channel in 1938, he had a lifetime of risky sailing experiences behind him. Inglis is rather less surefooted on Collingwood's life and experiences at Oxford, and trots out many popular clichés about the eccentrically conservative world of the ancient universities between the wars, from the *Brideshead* circle of the upper-class undergraduates to the buttoned-up, waspish and for the most part bachelor dons. It is impossible not to suspect that Collingwood was getting rather more out of the intellectual air of 1920s and 1930s Oxford than Inglis is prepared to concede. As well as the revolutions in philosophy that were underway, it was the time that Roman history was being rethought (and re-politicised) by Ronald Syme, whose famous *Roman Revolution* appeared in 1939.

For all the engaging enthusiasm of the book, two important

questions about Collingwood's achievements and his academic profile remain only half convincingly answered. First, how important is *The Idea of History*, the posthumous book which remains his most famous work? Second, what was the connection, if any, between the two academic sides of his career, the Romano-British archaeology and the philosophy? What, in other words, does the *Roman Inscriptions of Britain* have to do with *The Idea of History*, let alone the *Essay on Metaphysics*?

The Idea of History has had some very distinguished supporters. By his own account, it was the book that inspired Quentin Skinner at the start of his own historical career – and Skinner of course went on to give his own distinctive spin to Collingwood's slogan about all history being a 'history of the mind'. And, if only in the absence of much competition (it is a classic, as Collini has observed, 'in a field not over-supplied with classics written in English'), it used to be the theoretical standby of undergraduates reading history at university, or of sixth-formers wanting to do so. It still appears on general bibliographies and is warmly recommended to their pupils by ambitious schoolteachers (though when, a few years ago, I asked a group of about 50 third-year students studying History in Cambridge whether any of them had read it, not a single one put up their hand). The problem in judging it now is that its big claims seem fairly uncontentious. In part, no doubt, that is a tribute to the book's popular success. But in part also those claims were never particularly original in the first place, and were expounded in such a way that it would be difficult to disagree. After all, who could possibly claim, in Collingwood's terms, to prefer 'scissors and paste' history to the 'question and answer' style of history that he advocated? Could anyone object to the idea that part of the point of studying history was to help us see (as Inglis puts it) 'how we might think and feel otherwise than as we do'?

Re-reading *The Idea of History* after some thirty years or so, I found myself less impressed than I had been as a student, or at least more counter-suggestible. His image of the mindless, unquestioning narration of 'scissors and paste' history, and of generations of historians being content merely to stick one source after another, now seems very largely a self-serving myth. It did not require the birth of narratology or the return to fashion of 'grand narrative', to realise that historical narration is always selective and always posing questions about the evidence. No history – not even the most austere chronicle

– has ever been as unquestioning as Collingwood paints his imaginary methodological enemy. Maybe also his 'question and answer' method is not as self-evidently productive as he claimed, and certainly not in that practical branch of history known as archaeology. In the *Autobiography* he is vitriolic about those antiquarians, following in the tradition of Pitt-Rivers, who excavated sites out of mere curiosity (the excavations at the Roman town of Silchester were his particular target). The best archaeologists, by contrast, 'never dug a trench without knowing exactly what information they were looking for'. But this is to ignore the equally important fact that some questions blind the investigator to the wider potential, to the surprises, of their material. Some of the best history, no less than the best archaeology, is curiosity-driven and opportunistic – rather than outcome-driven, as Collingwood and his unlikely descendants in the Arts and Humanities Research Council and other government funding bodies like to imagine.

What finally are we to make of the relationship between the two sides of Collingwood's academic career, the philosophy and archaeology-cum-history? Collingwood himself recognised the problem, with his constant calls for a 'rapprochement' between the two. Where he explicitly ranks his different activities, he puts the philosophy first, characterising the archaeological activity more as a practical application of his ideas about the philosophy of history. After all, despite his hybrid lectureship, he went on to become the Waynflete Professor of Metaphysical Philosophy, not the Camden Professor of Roman History. Most studies of his career have followed this ranking, giving much more weight to his philosophical activity and sometimes relegating the archaeology to a summer hobby. But this must partly be because the writers in question have been philosophers and cultural historians, whose grip on the ancient world and on Collingwood's importance in the study of antiquity has been fragile to say the least. Inglis is a particularly woeful culprit here. He does not seem aware of the importance of the *Roman Inscriptions of Britain*; he confuses Virgil's *Eclogues* with his *Georgics*; he imagines that *Res Gestae* (the Latin for 'achievements') has something to do with 'gesture'; and he claims that Alcinous, after whom the boat on which Collingwood sailed to the Far East was named, was the 'mother of Ulysses' lover Nausicaa' (wrong on two counts: Alcinous was Nausicaa's father and she and Ulysses were not lovers, at least not in Homer's version). Even Collini manages to stumble over the title of the journal in which many of

Collingwood's major archaeological articles appeared: it was (and still is) the *Journal of Roman Studies*, not the *Journal of Roman History*.

As so often, things look rather different if you approach them from a classical standpoint. Collingwood himself may have chosen not to reflect on the influence of his formal education; he became more concerned to attack the whole history of professional pedagogy as far back as Plato. But it is surely crucial that he was a product of the old Oxford 'Greats' (that is, Classics) course, which focused the last two and a half years of a student's work on the parallel study of ancient history on the one hand, and ancient and modern philosophy on the other. Most students were much better at one side than the other, and most stories tell of the desperate attempts by would-be ancient historians to cram enough Plato, Descartes and Hume to get their high-flying pass in the final exams (or alternatively of desperate attempts by would-be philosophers to remember enough of the Peloponnesian War or Agricola's campaigns in Britain to do the same). In the context of Greats, Collingwood was not a maverick with two incompatible interests. Given the educational aims of the course, he was a rare success, even if something of a quirky overachiever; his combination of interests was exactly what Greats was designed to promote.

To put that another way, Collingwood was not simply – as Inglis and others would imply – a philosopher with an archaeological hobby. We might better see him as an unusually successful product of a distinctive Oxford version of Classics that is now no more (Greats was 'reformed' decades ago). It should come as no surprise that the last voyage he made, with that group of students, was a trip to Greece, and that he went – as he put it in *The First Mate's Log* – 'not so much a tourist as a pilgrim' to Delphi, where Socrates had travelled two and a half thousand years earlier. 'If a man looks to Socrates as his prophet,' he wrote, 'the journey to Delphi is the journey to his Mecca.' That is the credo of a Greats-man.

Review of Fred Inglis, *History Man: The Life of R.G. Collingwood* (Princeton University Press, 2009)

30

WHAT GETS
LEFT OUT

Eduard Fraenkel was one of the most renowned classical scholars of the twentieth century: refugee to England from Nazi persecution; Corpus Professor of Latin at Oxford from 1935 to 1953; radical reinterpreter of the Roman comedy of Plautus, who showed that it was much more than second-hand pastiche of lost Greek plays; pioneer in new methods of classical teaching (notably the German-style 'seminar', rather than the traditional lecture or tutorial); and – to judge from the accounts of several of his women students – a serial groper. Isobel Henderson, Tutor at Somerville, used to warn her students in advance that, although they would learn a lot, they would probably be 'pawed about a bit'. At least the Somervillians knew what to expect. According to her own memoirs, Mary Warnock, a student at Lady Margaret Hall, was not so prepared. Fraenkel picked her up from one of his famous seminars in the early 1940s and promptly arranged private after-dinner tutorials. These combined some heady and inspiring discussions of Latin and Greek with 'kisses and increasingly constant fumblings with ... (my) underclothes'. Warnock dreamt up a clever wheeze to continue with the teaching but to avoid the 'pawing'. She invited her friend Imogen, who was over from Cambridge, to their sessions. But Fraenkel was ahead of the game. Imogen, he pointed out, needed to pay more close attention to Pindar, whereas Mary should be concentrating on early Latin and the *Agamemnon*. And so he managed to end up with two evenings a week of this kind of sport, one with his 'black sheep' and one with his 'white' (as he himself dubbed them, on the basis of their hair colour). Time was only called when a less compliant student from LMH shopped him to her tutor, and the tutorials were stopped. Any academic woman older than her mid forties is likely to have an ambivalent reaction to this. On the one hand, it is impossible not to feel outrage at a straightforward case of persistent sexual harassment and the abuse of (male) power. On the other hand, if we're honest, it is also hard to repress a bit of wistful nostalgia for that academic era before about 1980 when the erotic dimension of pedagogy – which had flourished, after all, since Plato – was firmly stamped out. Warnock herself shares that ambivalence, weighing the damage done (to Fraenkel's wife no less than to some of his 'girls') against the inspirational teaching which came with, and was inextricable from, the 'pawing'. In more than one newspaper interview she has singled Fraenkel out as the best teacher she ever had. However we choose to dispense or suspend moral judgement, this story of middle-aged donnish fumblings raises important issues in the writing of biography. What gets included, what excluded from the retrospective accounts of famous lives? What principles of censorship are at work behind the authorised versions of these lives, particularly as they are transmitted in biographical dictionaries and other such works of reference? And how far does this matter? Fraenkel's case is paradigmatic and one of the most revealing. It will come as little surprise that none of the standard English accounts of Fraenkel's life mentions his wandering hand or what went on in his tutorials with women. The closest we get is a single sentence in Nicholas Horsfall's account in Briggs and Calder's *Biographical Encyclopaedia* of famous classicists: 'He did enjoy, warmly, but most decorously, female beauty'. Most 'decorously'? Either this is staggering naivety on the part of Horsfall, or it is a guarded hint to those already in the know (in other words, most of the Oxford Classics establishment). Or, more likely, it is a pre-emptive defence against anyone who should risk leaking more widely what was already common knowledge in a restricted circle. To be fair to Horsfall, his version of Fraenkel is, overall, carefully judged and one of the most illuminating. His is the only major account, for example, to give due mention to Fraenkel's most striking physical characteristic: his withered right hand. By contrast Gordon Williams's long memoir in the *Proceedings of the British Academy*, marking Fraenkel's death in 1970, deals with the childhood illness that led to the disability but later devotes a whole paragraph to describing its subject ('short', 'magnificent forehead', 'fine eyes' and so on) without reference to the withered hand. It is as if a veil must be drawn post mortem over physical frailty as well as over sexual exploits.

The authorised version of Fraenkel's life now uniformly concentrates on his capacity for immense hard work and superhumanly long days. 'He was at his desk not later than 8.30 each morning', explains Williams. 'He worked until dinner, and, unless a guest claimed his attention, he would return to work till 10.30 or so. He then walked home to talk to Ruth (his wife).' The kind of guests that were 'claiming his attention', in Warnock's era at least, surely partly undermine the straightforward image of the workaholic professor, his eyes glued to his books. The other aspect of Fraenkel which completes the standard picture is his suicide, just a few hours after the death of Ruth. 'Fraenkel chose not to survive her and died at his home', as Hugh Lloyd-Jones elegantly puts it in the old (and new) *DNB*, or, in Horsfall's more extravagant words, 'We revere his suicide, for love'. It would be foolish to imagine that love for one's wife is necessarily incompatible with 'pawing' one's female students. But Fraenkel's uxoriousness does look rather different in the light of the experiences of Warnock (who refers directly to Ruth's unhappiness at Fraenkel's 'predilections'). At the very least, the authorised version of his career and character fails to do justice to what was obviously a much more complicated and interesting reality. Rather like tourist guide-books that continue to extol the peaceful little fishing village, when it has long since been bisected by a six-lane highway, these biographical accounts operate at one stage removed from the messy reality of life as lived. The least satisfactory and the most reticent of such versions of Fraenkel is published in the new three-volume *Dictionary of British Classicists* which draws together biographical essays by some 200 contributors on more than 700 classicists, from Edwin Abbott Abbott (sic), a nineteenth-century headmaster committed to the idea that learning Latin should be fun, to Gunther Zuntz, also a refugee from Nazi Germany, who taught for many years at the University of Manchester. The main qualifications for inclusion (apart from working in Britain, not necessarily being British by birth) is to have been active in classical learning or teaching by about AD 1500 and to have been dead by 2000; the ancient historian Nicholas Hammond and W. S. Barrett, editor of Euripides' *Hippolytos*, both somehow scrape under the wire, although neither died until 2001.

The essay on Fraenkel austerely refrains from mentioning almost any aspect of his 'private' life. There is not a single reference to Ruth, let alone to the suicide (which has been a crucial element in his posthumous reputation) or to the hands, withered or wandering. At the same time, it rarely succeeds in being anything but unnuanced hagiography. Fraenkel's deeply unsatisfactory book on the rhythm of Latin prose (which even Gordon Williams was happy to call 'a disaster') is here praised as a 'systematic treatment of this difficult and controversial subject'.

Fraenkel's famous seminars are lauded, while he himself is hailed as 'a distinguished and influential teacher'. Up to a point this is undoubtedly true, as Warnock and many other students still testify. But inevitably there was another side. Lloyd-Jones candidly admits that 'as a teacher he had certain defects. He was not quick on the up-take, and could seldom elicit suggestions from his hearers; he tended to extremes of praise or blame, and many of his pupils found him frightening'. Or, as Williams reports, one 'victim' once described his seminars as 'a circle of rabbits addressed by a stoat'. They were, in other words, as much an exercise in professorial power and domination as the radical pedagogical innovation that they are here taken to be. Inevitably, with over 200 contributors, the quality of the other entries in the *Dictionary* varies enormously. Some of the weaker ones are little more than paraphrases of the entry for their subject in the old *DNB*, down to very closely borrowed phrases. (Unsurprisingly several entries are the work of those who also wrote the essay in the new *DNB*, and there the overlap is even more substantial.) But there are faults of many other kinds. Objectivity has not been helped by commissioning, in at least three cases, children to write piously about their fathers (Classics does tend to run in families). And occasionally North American contributors demonstrate a less than sure touch with British institutions (in the essay on R. A. Neil, Cambridge classicist and orientalist and one-time boyfriend of Jane Ellen Harrison, the Scottish ecclesiastical term 'quoad sacra' is garbled into 'quondam sacra'). In general, the accounts tend to be franker and more open about human frailty when the subjects are long dead. We read, for example, of Richard Porson's (1759–1808) fondness for the bottle, but not of G. E. L. Owen's (Cambridge philosopher, 1922–1982).

The best entries are those (relatively few) where the writer is closely familiar with the academic work of their subject, is well informed about their personal circumstances, either directly or through a good long stint in the archives, and understands the social, cultural and academic context in which they worked. They alone escape the tralatician 'guidebook' style. M. L. West's accounts of historians of Greek music and Vivian Nutton's essays on historians of ancient medicine stand out. So too the series of articles by Christopher Stray which nicely captures the eccentricities of generations of Classics schoolmasters. Even more eccentric than most was Edmund Morshead, teacher at Winchester in the late nineteenth century: nicknamed 'Mush', he had his own private idiolect ('Mushri') that he shared with his pupils and he taught in a classroom known predictably enough as the 'Mushroom'. But Stray also repeatedly demonstrates these teachers' commitment to innovation and reform in the teaching of Classics and the curriculum more generally. The died-in-the-wool Mr Chips and the dreariness of the grammar grind is more our own modern myth than (at more radical schools, at least) the eighteenth-and nineteenth-century reality. Edwin Abbott Abbott, with his zeal for making Latin a pleasure, was not the exception. When he was not jabbering away in Mushri, Mush was publicly demanding that Classics teachers did not see scientists as the enemy, and pointing out that defences of Classics as a discipline could be as bigoted as the attacks upon it. Stray's essays work partly because they are amusing, without aggressively laughing at their subjects. So too, one of the most engaging entries in all three volumes: Malcolm Schofield's essay on Harry Sandbach (1903–1991), a Cambridge classicist best known for his work on Stoic philosophy and on Greek comedy. Schofield gently parodies the genre in which he is writing and so manages to tell us more about his subject than all those straight-faced accounts. Typical is the end of the article, a couple of deceptively simple sentences: 'Sandbach was a small, kindly man, incapable of a rash or wounding remark; not indeed prone to volunteer conversation at all, although delighted to participate on a minimalist basis once it was initiated. Otherwise one could enjoy a silence with him.' If only we could have had something as revealing as that for Fraenkel. In dictionaries of this kind there are always boundary disputes (British Monarchs – Lady Jane Grey in or out?). Here I missed several very obvious candidates who had failed to find a place. No Samuel Butler (author of *The Authoress of the Odyssey*), nor William Gell, who wrote the first English account of Pompeii. And the new *DNB* throws up scores of people designated as 'classical scholars', 'classical archaeologists', 'Latin' or 'Greek scholars' who do not make it into this Dictionary. The entries on women are rather few (under forty out of more than 700), largely an accurate indication of male dominance of the subject – but not entirely. Given a choice, I would have included Elizabeth Rawson, a major figure in Roman history who died in 1988, rather than Queen Elizabeth I. Rawson was presumably excluded by the rule that subjects should have 'been born by about 1920' – but it is an unhelpful omission. Equally unhelpful is the omission (for the same reason, I imagine) of Colin Macleod, pupil of Fraenkel and one of the most influential classical critics of the twentieth century, who committed suicide in 1981, and of the historian Martin Frederiksen, killed in a road accident in 1980. There is, however, as the mention of Elizabeth I hints, a bigger problem here about the definition of the whole project. Leaving aside the question of just how hubristic an undertaking a *Dictionary of British Classicists* is (or is it just the kind of thing disciplines do when they feel that they are in terminal decline?), it does make some sense for the period from the mid-nineteenth century on – when Classics first became a professional subject and an identifiable interest group. It was at this point that the term 'classicist' (or 'classic') was first used with anything like its modern professional meaning. Before then, when the teaching of Latin and, to a lesser extent Greek, dominated the school curriculum, it makes little sense to designate any elite male as a 'classicist' – or conversely you might argue that they all have a claim to be so called. So, predictably, the *Dictionary* has cherry-picked, including alongside Elizabeth I, Ben Jonson, Samuel Johnson, Johns Evelyn, Milton and Stuart Mill, and so on. But almost nothing is to be gained from seeing these next to the more recent professionals. There is, nevertheless, something to be gained from taking the opportunity that the *Dictionary* now offers to think about what, if anything, the professional classicists represented here share, and how this reflects on Classics as a discipline. The most striking aspect, for anyone reading from cover to cover, is the powerful and complicated relationship between British and German Classics. This is partly a consequence of the influx of refugees during the 1930s: the literary critics Fraenkel and Charles Brink, the historians Felix Jacoby and Stefan Weinstock, the archaeologist Paul Jacobsthal and many more. In fact the prominence of these refugees is nicely illustrated by one of the most genial anecdotes in the *Dictionary*. It concerns the internment camps where many of the refugees ended up (if only briefly). These were divided by nationality. In the Italian camp were just three professors (Arnaldo Momigliano, Lorenzo Minio-Paluello and Piero Sraffa) and a large number of waiters and chefs. The German camp was full of academics, many of them classicists. The English commander suggested to the three Italian professors that they might feel more at home in the German camp. The others were for moving, but Momigliano (according to Oswyn Murray) dissuaded them. 'It was better', he argued, 'to be three Italian professors in a camp full of waiters and chefs, than three Italian waiters in a camp full of German professors.' But it is not only a question of the physical presence of German scholars. From the early nineteenth century on, scholar after scholar is praised here by their biographer for being an important link in the chain that brought the distinctive traditions of German scholarship to these shores: Connop Thirlwall (1797–1875), for example, who 'helped to introduce the erudite German *Altertumswissenschaft* in Britain'; W. M. Lindsay (1858–1937), who carried the torch of German linguistic analysis, after two semesters studying at Leipzig; or Mrs Arthur Strong (1860–1943), who did the same for art-historical study, having studied in Munich with Adolf Furtwängler. No one, by contrast, is acclaimed for having introduced French or Italian traditions of scholarship to this country (although in different ways they are no less distinguished). A few are damned for not taking German scholarship seriously enough.

It is hard, however, to take this strong emphasis on repeated waves of influence from Berlin and Munich entirely literally. Some there certainly were. Yet if German intellectual imports had really been on the scale that these biographical essays together suggest, then Fraenkel would have found himself in a home from home when he arrived in Oxford in 1934. In fact, he did not – neither socially nor intellectually (as the controversy sparked by his election to the chair of Latin in 1935 makes entirely clear). Modern hagiographies may gloss over this, as over so much else. But part of the problem must have been, as the *Dictionary* inadvertently hints, an awkward clash between the 'myth' of German scholarship in the British imagination (plus its role as a symbolic badge of academic rigour) and the real thing in the shape of a bona fide German professor, with his new-fangled ideas about seminars. Any new biography of Fraenkel should certainly aim to expose, and engage with, some of the aspects that lie just beneath the surface of the image of the workaholic professor. It should also aim to set him and his refugee peers (many of whom, whatever we like to think, found acceptance here difficult) against the background of the complicated, heavily loaded, British fantasies about German classical scholarship.

Review of Robert B. Todd (ed.), *Dictionary of British Classicists* (Continuum, 2004)

31

ASTÉRIX AND
THE ROMANS

When René Goscinny, the creator of Astérix, died in 1977, it was, in the words of one French obituary, 'as if the Eiffel Tower had fallen down'. The cartoon adventures of the plucky little Gaul holding out against Roman conquest (with the help of a magic potion that could confer a few minutes' irresistible strength at a single gulp) were as much a defining part of French cultural identity as the most distinctive monument on the Paris skyline. A national survey in 1969 suggested that two-thirds of the population had read at least one of the *Astérix* books; and by the time of Goscinny's death total sales in France are said to have amounted to more than 55 million copies, putting Astérix substantially ahead of his main (Belgian) rival, Tintin. The first French space satellite, launched in 1965, was named in his honour (the US later matched this with spaceships called *Charlie Brown* and *Snoopy*). There was also, predictably, a more mundane range of Astérix spin-offs, from mustard to washing powder, that flooded the French market in the 1960s and 1970s. The story goes that Goscinny's partner, Albert Uderzo, once saw three advertisements side by side on a Métro station, for three completely different products each endorsed with equal enthusiasm by Astérix and his cartoon comrades. From then on, they put much tighter limits on the products they would allow their hero to advertise.

Goscinny was born in Paris in 1926, divided his childhood between France and Argentina, and learned the cartoon trade in New York, with the group of artists who went on to found *Mad* magazine. Returning to France in 1951, he teamed up with Uderzo – Goscinny wrote the words, Uderzo did the drawings. They had a dry run for *Astérix* with a short-lived cartoon called *Oumpah-pah*, featuring a Flatfoot Indian living in a remote village in the Wild West that was bravely holding out against the palefaces, but struck lucky when they launched their ancient Gaulish version of *Oumpah-pah* in 1959 in the first issue of the comic *Pilote* (which, like *Mad*, was aimed at adults rather than children). *Pilote* had the financial backing of Radio Luxembourg; and the instant success of the magazine and its cast of characters can hardly have been unconnected with the barrage of publicity provided by the radio station.

Their first fully-fledged book, *Astérix le Gaulois*, appeared in 1961; and at the time of his death, sixteen years later, Goscinny had just completed the script of the twenty-fourth, *Astérix chez les Belges* – a swashbuckling adventure with some remarkably stereotypical Belgians, large quantities of beer and brussels sprouts, plus the inevitable walk-on part for a pair of *Tintin* characters. This was almost the end of *Astérix*. Goscinny died before the book had been illustrated, and Uderzo was extremely reluctant to finish the job. But the publishers could not afford such sentiment and took him to court to try to force him to produce the drawings. They won the first round of the legal battle and Uderzo grudgingly turned his hand to the work. Ironically, the book had already been published when he got the judgment overturned on appeal. The last thirty years have seen Uderzo (now in his eighties) repeatedly retire, declaring the series over, only to come back a few years later with a new, solo-authored adventure. Meanwhile, he has been cashing in on the *phénomène Astérix* with an unusually tasteful theme park, Parc Astérix, just outside Paris, and a run of movies – including *Astérix et Obélix contre César* and *Astérix et Obélix: Mission Cléopatre* both starring Gérard Depardieu as an appropriately portly Gaul.

For fans of Astérix the big question is whether the books by Uderzo alone are any match for the 'classics' produced when the partnership was in its prime: *Astérix Gladiateur* (in which our hero enrols as a gladiator in order to rescue the village bard, captured by Caesar); *Astérix et Cléopatre* (the basis of the movie, in which Astérix and friends visit Egypt and find themselves in a hilarious parody of Mankiewicz's epic); *Astérix chez les Bretons* (in which a Gallic mission to take the magic potion to the struggling Britons ends up with Astérix teaching them how to brew tea). Before Goscinny's death Uderzo had never taken much part in the writing and to judge from *Astérix et Latraviata* (translated as *Asterix and the Actress*) the answer to the big question would be a disappointing no. The satire is stale. The storyline is over-complex and under-engaging. It starts with the (joint) birthdays of Astérix and his best friend Obélix, the menhir delivery-man; their mothers arrive full of ideas about getting their boys married off at last, while their fathers, too busy selling souvenirs in the local *oppidum* to join in the celebrations, send a splendid sword and helmet as a present; these turn out to be the stolen property of a Very Important Roman; the fathers end up in prison for the theft, while the Romans dispatch an actress, disguised as Obélix's heart-throb, Falbala ('Frippery' – the translators call her 'Panacea'), to try to wheedle the weapons back; inevitably, the real Falbala turns up and the obvious confusions follow. It reads rather like a bedroom farce sprinkled with some ponderous lessons in Roman history – one of the most densely packed speech bubbles in the whole *Astérix* series is here devoted to a breathless, and not entirely accurate, résumé of first-century BC Roman politics: 'Once upon a time Rome was governed by a triumvirate ... that means three consuls etc etc,' as Astérix explains to an understandably bemused Obélix.

Uderzo's form has not always been so poor. Some of his earlier efforts proved to be elegant sequels to the joint series, neatly in tune with the changing politics, and fashions in humour, of the 1980s and 1990s. *L'Odyssée d'Astérix* (*Asterix and the Black Gold*) sends the Gauls to the Middle East in search of a mysterious vital ingredient for the magic potion (petroleum, as it turns out) and brilliantly takes on the oil industry, pollution and the intricacies of Middle Eastern politics; on the way home with their precious cargo, a nasty mishap in the Channel produces the world's first oil-slicked seagull. A turn to the postmodern has become increasingly evident. 'I'm not enjoying this adventure very much,' Astérix complains to Obélix halfway through *Le Fils d'Astérix* (*Asterix and Son*). 'Oh it'll be all right!' Obélix says to calm him. 'It's sure to end with a banquet under the starry sky, same as usual.' He is referring to the distinctive last scene of every *Astérix* adventure – except, as the reader will discover, this one.

The even bigger question, though, is why these cartoon stories of ancient Gauls and their unfortunate Roman adversaries ever became so successful. Goscinny and Uderzo themselves always refused to show much interest in this. Confronted by interviewers suffering, as they saw it, from 'exegesis sickness', they would counter with a bluff, no-nonsense (and, I hope, ironic) lack of curiosity. People laugh at Astérix, Goscinny once pronounced, 'because he does funny things, and that's all. Our only ambition is to have fun.' On one occasion a desperate interviewer on Italian television suggested (not very subtly) that the appeal of Astérix's struggle against the Roman Empire was something to do with the 'little man refusing to be crushed by the oppressive weight of modern society'. Goscinny crisply replied that, as he didn't travel to work by the Métro, he didn't know about little men being crushed by anything.

Most critics, on the other hand, have thought that there was a good deal that needed explaining. Some, like the Italian interviewer, have dwelt on the appeal of the David-and-Goliath conflict between the Gauls and the Roman superpower. Or, at least, David and Goliath with a twist: Astérix doesn't beat brute force by superior cunning and intelligence – he does it thanks to his unexpected access to even bruter force than the enemy can deliver. In adventure after adventure, most of the Gauls' over-ingenious schemes misfire as badly as the best-laid Roman ones. The reassuring fantasy is that, thanks to the magic potion, Astérix and his friends can mess things up and still win out.

Others have made a lot of the cartoon's attraction for adults, as intended by the original *Pilote*. The books are littered with wry references to contemporary French culture and politics: Jacques Chirac's economic policy was thoroughly taken apart in *Obélix et compagnie*, with Chirac himself recognisably caricatured as a pretentious Roman economist; and the café in Marseille where Astérix and Obélix stop over in *Le Tour de Gaul* (*Asterix and the Banquet*) is, for those in the know, an exact copy of the one that features in the film of Pagnol's *Marius*. (Pagnol was apparently delighted: 'Now I know my work will be immortal.') There is also a whole series of clever parodies of classic works of art, even if these are not quite so thick on the ground as *Astérix*'s most intellectual fans would have us believe. By far the cleverest is the reworking of Géricault's *Raft of the Medusa* as a lifeboat for a ramshackle and disgruntled party of pirates in *Astérix légionnaire* ('Je suis medusé' – 'I'm medusa-ed/dumbfounded' – one of them shouts out for the benefit of those who've failed to spot the reference). This adult appeal is obviously a crucial factor in the books' sales, given that most child readers are dependent on adult purchasing power. As Olivier Todd once said, parents read *Tintin* after their children: they read *Astérix* before the children can get their hands on the books.

Another crucial factor must be the history that *Astérix* both recalls and satirises. Just as *1066 and All That* depends on our familiarity with the images and stories of British history that it parodies, so *Astérix* takes its French readers back to a moment they all know: when, according to the French school curriculum, French history starts. 'Nos ancêtres les Gaulois' is a slogan drummed into children by countless textbooks; and the key figure among these early ancestors is Vercingetorix, leader of the Gauls in a notable rebellion against Julius Caesar in the late 50s BC. Vercingetorix is written up in Caesar's own self-serving account of the Gallic War as a traitor and Gallic nationalist, who was resoundingly outmanoeuvred by Roman tactics at the Battle of Alesia; he surrendered to Caesar and was packed off to Rome, to be killed several years later as part of the celebrations of Caesar's triumph in 46 BC. In modern French culture Vercingetorix has become a national hero for both Left and Right. In the Second World War, for example, he did double duty as 'the first resistance fighter in our history' and as a symbol for Pétain and the Vichy Government of how to be noble, and nobly French, in defeat. The occasion on which, with all the dignity a failed rebel could muster, he laid his arms at Caesar's feet, has become a mythic image, one of the key moments in the history of the nation. It appears in the second frame of *Astérix le Gaulois*, where, in a characteristic twist, Vercingetorix manages to drop the bundle of weapons on Caesar's toe – so prompting not a victory speech, but a loud 'Ouch'. In fact, throughout the series Astérix himself can be seen as Vercingetorix's double, the fantasy of a Gallic nationalist who managed to escape Caesar's clutches.

But if Astérix is so deeply rooted in French popular culture, how do we explain his enormous success in the rest of the world? (So far as I know, *1066 and All That* has never touched much of a chord in France, Iceland or Japan.) Ambitious translation is part of the answer. The English translators of the whole series, Anthea Bell and Derek Hockridge, have approached the job in the most energetic way. All the French jokes, and in particular the distinctive word plays, are given a new English spin, often with very little link to the original. The names of major characters are regularly changed: the tone-deaf village bard Assurancetourix ('assurance tous risques', or 'comprehensive motor insurance') has become Cacofonix; the French dog Idéfix turns up in English as Dogmatix. Bell and Hockridge stick faithfully to the spirit rather than the letter of the humour. So, for example, on the *Raft of the*

Medusa, 'je suis medusé' is replaced by a suitably English hint at the point of the parody: 'we've been framed, by Jericho!'

The effect of the translators' intervention is almost always to produce a significantly different book. The classic case of this is *Astérix chez les Bretons*. In much the same spirit as *Astérix chez les Belges*, the French original pokes plenty of fun at the British, who are presented as every French cliché has always imagined. They stop for a hot-water break at five (Astérix has not yet shown them how to make tea), they drink warm beer, smother their food with mint sauce and speak a parodic and almost incomprehensible version of Anglo-French. 'Bonté gracieuse' ('goodness gracious') is a favourite phrase; 'plutôt' ('rather') follows up many a sentence; and adjectives are repeatedly inserted before their nouns ('magique potion' instead of 'potion magique'). In Bell and Hockridge's translation, however, waspish French chauvinism is transformed into characteristically English self-deprecation. There was hardly any need for the message from Goscinny and Uderzo included in the first editions of the British translation, assuring readers that the caricature was intended to be gentle and funny; Bell and Hockridge had already drawn its sting.

The basic storylines also reinforce the series' international appeal, at least in Europe. Intentionally or not, Goscinny and Uderzo exploited the legacy of the Roman Empire across most of the continent. For wherever Roman conquest reached, there are still tales of heroic resistance and glamorous native freedom-fighters. If, for the French, Astérix is inevitably keyed into the story of Vercingetorix, the English can read him as a version of Boudicca or Caratacus; the Germans as a version of their own Hermann (known in Latin literature as Arminius). As for the Italians themselves, they are usually happy to enjoy a joke about their Roman ancestors – particularly when they are presented, as Astérix's adversaries are, as rather amiable bad guys, held back from serious evil by sheer inefficiency.

The United States is the only country in the West where *Astérix* has remained a minority taste – despite one adventure that actually took the Gauls to the New World, in an effort presumably to drum up an American readership. This gap in the market has been endlessly and implausibly theorised. Cultural chauvinists in France have liked to believe that *Astérix* is simply too sophisticated for the Disney-fed masses of America; and they have pointed to the contrast between the relatively elegant, upmarket and very French Parc Astérix and the vulgarity of its neighbour, Euro Disney. Others have tried a political explanation, reading the cartoon conflicts between nice Gauls and nasty Romans as a thinly veiled attack on American imperialism and the dominance of the new superpower (hence, they suggest, the unexpected niche market for the series in China and the Middle East). But the bottom line is that *Astérix* is indomitably European. The legacy of the Roman Empire provides a context within popular culture for the different countries of Europe to talk with, and about, each other, and about their shared history and myths. It would be hard to penetrate that from the other side of the Atlantic.

Across Europe, the story of Astérix has also encouraged many people to think harder about the history and prehistory that it reflects and the myths it embodies. Archaeologists have not been slow to take advantage of the popularity of the series to introduce schoolchildren and parents to the pleasures of museums and site-visiting; a few years ago, for example, a British Museum 'education pack' on the Iron Age and Roman-British collections used Astérix as a slogan and frontman – 'Asterix at the BM'. Ironically, though, the interpretation of Roman history on which Goscinny and Uderzo's scenario of Gallic-Roman conflict is based has long faded out of academic fashion. Go back forty years or so and you will indeed find archaeologists reconstructing the history of the northern provinces of the Roman Empire largely in the style of *Astérix*. Roman imperialism was then generally seen in stark, clear-cut terms. It offered the natives of these conquered territories a simple choice: Romanisation or resistance; learn Latin, wear togas, build baths or (in the absence of a real-life magic potion) paint yourself with woad, take to the scythed chariots and massacre the nearest detachment of Roman infantry (Chapter 22). It is a choice hilariously dramatised in *Le Combat des chefs* (*Asterix and the Big Fight*), which contrasts Astérix's village with a neighbouring Gallic settlement. If Astérix and his friends have opted for resistance to Rome, the other village has equally enthusiastically embraced Romanisation. We see their native huts embellished with classical-style columns, their chief honoured with a Roman portrait in what must pass for the village's forum, and their children in school going through the 'grammar-grind'.

Approaches to Roman imperialism are now more realistic. As we have come to understand it, the Romans had neither the manpower nor the will to impose the kind of direct control and cultural uniformity that the *Astérix* model imagines. Their priorities were more

17. Was Roman Britain just an act? This cartoon is meant to
remind us that some aspects of Romanisation were wafer thin.

often money and a quiet life. Provided the natives paid their taxes,
did not openly rebel and, where necessary, made a few gestures to
Roman cultural norms, their lives could – if they wished – continue
much as before. This new version of Roman provincial life has not
yet been immortalised in a strip cartoon. But some years ago the
archaeologist Simon James drew a single comic vignette, which has
become famous among classicists for encapsulating the new approach
to the history of Roman imperialism in the northern provinces. It
shows a small native homestead, with a traditional round Iron Age
hut and an obviously native family. Next to it runs a Roman road,
and just disappearing on their march past the homestead is a party of
Roman legionaries (messily dropping behind them the kind of Roman
bric-a-brac that archaeologists will eagerly dig up in two thousand
years' time). Between the homestead and the road the canny natives
have constructed a huge cardboard cut-out of a classical facade with
pediment and columns, which they are gamely holding up to impress
the soldiers and temporarily disguise the native life blithely going on

behind. But they won't have to keep the pretence up much longer: 'It's all right, Covdob, they've gone!' shouts the native missus to her native husband, as the legionaries pass into the distance. It's a trick that has not yet entered the Astérix repertoire.

Review of Albert Uderzo, *Asterix and the Actress*, translated by Anthea Bell and Derek Hockridge (Orion, 2001)

Afterword

REVIEWING CLASSICS

The first chapter of this book explored the work of Arthur Evans at the prehistoric palace of Knossos, in particular his reconstruction of the architecture, the paintings and indeed the whole matriarchal and peace-loving civilisation of Minoan Crete. I mentioned only in passing one of his most important and intriguing discoveries there: that is, hundreds of inscribed tablets, written in scripts that – despite considerable effort – Evans himself failed to decipher. He did realise, however, that they fell into two distinct types: a few were written in what he called 'Class A' or 'Linear A'; the rest (the vast majority) were in what he called 'Linear B'. Neither, he thought, was any form of the Greek language, even a very primitive one.

Half a century later Michael Ventris, an architect and brilliant code-breaker, proved Evans at least half wrong. Although Linear A remains undeciphered, Ventris realised – with the support of John Chadwick in Cambridge – that Linear B was indeed a version of Greek. There was, in other words, a linguistic link between some of these prehistoric civilisations in the Mediterranean and the Greek world that we know much better, from Homer onwards. It was the most exciting decipherment of the twentieth century (even though, to the disappointment of some hopeful classicists, the tablets proved not to be early epic poetry but largely bureaucratic lists); and it gained, rather than lost, glamour when Ventris was killed in a car crash in 1956, at the age of just 34, before the full publication of his results.

But the cracking of Linear B had already been announced in 1952 – not in a scholarly publication at all, but in a talk on what was then the BBC Third Programme (now Radio 3). That was thanks to the enterprise of a young BBC radio producer, Prudence Smith, who much later reminisced about her scoop:

> Michael Ventris worked with my husband ... and we knew him and his wife well ... Michael was said to be working on the Cretan tablets – ha ha, a funny thing for an architect to do. But he was, he damn well was.
>
> One night (I shall never forget it) we went to dinner at his new house in Hampstead ... And Michael didn't appear; he was in another room ... His wife went on serving the sherry and niblets, but Michael did not appear and didn't appear. And we got a bit hungry. Finally he emerged, looking totally exhausted, saying 'I'm terribly sorry to have kept you waiting but I've done it, I've done it!' – as though he'd been putting up a wardrobe or something. 'I *know*' he said 'that the language is Greek'...
>
> The following week at the Third Programme Talks Meeting, I rather timidly said 'I know the man who has deciphered the tablets from Knossos'. 'What do you mean?' said someone, 'They're indecipherable'. 'Oh no,' I said, 'I do assure you, this is IT. We must put him on.' And they trusted me and it was put on; it was the first public announcement of the decipherment... It wasn't difficult to persuade [Ventris]. He thought [the radio] was the right place.

This is partly a story of serendipity, and partly one of good journalism. But it is also a happy reminder of how close 'front-line Classics', and big classical discoveries, have stayed to a wide audience in Britain. Ventris thought that 'the radio was the *right place*' to break the news of his decipherment. Many others too have found that the 'right place' to float radically new interpretations of Classics, and to continue debating the classical world, was outside the lecture room or academic journal. As we have already seen (Chapter 24), some of the most important re-readings of Greek tragedy have been devised on the stage not in the study; and probably the most influential version of Homer's *Iliad* for more than a 100 years, by Christopher Logue, also started life on the Third Programme. What is more – despite the sometimes savage cutbacks suffered by 'review sections', and literary journalism in general, over the last decade or so – you can still read careful and considered discussions of books on the ancient world in the average broadsheet newspaper or weekly magazine. One of my most influential predecessors in Classics at Cambridge – the American-born Moses Finley, brilliant and awkward by turns – published many more words in reviews and re-published radio talks in the late 1950s and through the 1960s than he ever did in academic journals.

In this context, I am very pleased to remind you that each of the chapters in this book originated in an essay or review in a non-specialist literary magazine. It is true that the 'reviewing business' has a decidedly mixed reputation. For a start there is the basic issue of partiality, if not corruption. The critical ones are often put down to some personal grudge, the favourable ones can look like thinly disguised back-scratching. But there is also the question of how much they matter, what impact they have, or even how carefully they are read at all. The irony is that, while publishers continue to harass literary editors to review their books, they also rightly reassure their anxious authors that what the reviewers say appears to have very limited effect on how many books get sold. To put it another way, the only person who can be absolutely guaranteed to read, and to re-read, a review with intense concentration is the author of the book concerned. (So, authors, however bruised you feel by what you think is a piece of unfair criticism, never write in to complain; the chances are that you will just draw attention to something that no one else has much noticed!)

But this is to miss the point of why book reviews are still so important – and why we need them more than ever. Of course, I am biased. For the last thirty years I have written dozens of reviews a year for papers and periodicals of all sorts, and for the last twenty years I have been the Classics editor of the *Times Literary Supplement*, choosing which books are to be reviewed, by which reviewers, and editing the pieces when they come in. Is this to be the centre of a little world of literary corruption? I think not. For what it's worth, my basic rule is never to send any book to any reviewer if I'm fairly sure I can predict what they will say about it. And if the reviewer knows the author (as in the relatively close-knit community of Classics is sometimes bound to be the case), I have to be confident that the reviewer would feel able to write either a positive or negative review, depending on what they found (I don't send books out to people who are only prepared to be nice about them). But the simple fact is that it's not all that difficult to be fair – indeed, it's probably a lot easier to be fair than to be successfully corrupt.

So what are reviews *for*? I am sure there are big differences here between fiction and non-fiction. But in my area, they have a vital job to do as a basic quality-control mechanism – not a perfect one, I admit, but about the best we've got. If the Latin is all wrong, or the mythology and dates all mixed up, then someone has got to say so (and not merely in a scholarly review appearing in an academic journal five years after the book has come out).

But even more important and engaging than that (for who would be bothered to read a series of glorified errata slips?), reviews are a crucial part of the ongoing debate that makes a book worth writing and publishing; and they are a way of opening up the conversation that it provokes to a much wider audience. For me, part of the fun of reviewing in literary magazines has been to reflect on some of the most specialist contributions to my subject, to try to get to the nub of their argument *and* to show why it might matter, be interesting or controversial, well beyond the walls of the library and lecture room (I think the author himself was a bit surprised to see his technical commentary on Thucydides discussed in the pages of the *New York Review of Books* (Chapter 3) – but I tried to show that it raised big issues about how we understand and misunderstand, quote and misquote, Thucydides even now.)

I hope that I have done this with all the fearlessness and frankness that it deserves. In taking on a book's arguments, I don't pull my punches. But I do have one golden rule: I never put something in a review that I would not be prepared to say to the author's face. 'If you couldn't say it, then don't write it', should (in my view) be the reviewer's unwavering maxim. In fact, looking back through the chapters of this book, I realise that sometimes I *have* said it to the authors themselves. After more than a decade, on and off, of debate and disagreement in seminars and conference bars, Peter Wiseman (Chapters 6 and 10) will not have been shocked to find me responding with a combination of admiration and dismay to his imaginative reconstructions of early Roman history and theatre.

Whether I am right or not is, of course, quite another matter. But, in editing and adapting the reviews for their new home in this book, I found that I had not often changed my mind very much (though I do think, in retrospect, that I was perhaps a bit over-enthusiastic about the various different 'mouths' of the Delphic priestess in Chapter 2). My hope is that they will find a new readership here, and will bring both old hands and new into the classical conversation. I hope – as Ventris put it, referring to a discovery much greater than I shall ever make – that this will prove the 'right place' for them.

FURTHER READING

In most cases, the obvious place to find out more, or to follow up the issues raised in my own discussions, is in the book under review. This section is not a systematic bibliography. It includes fuller references to some of the most important other works, or themes, that I have mentioned; and it offers a few pointers to (even) further reading – concentrating, I admit, on some personal favourites.

Introduction. Gary Wills's discussion of Christopher Logue's Homer can be found in the *NYRB* 23 April, 1992.

Section One

Chapter 1. The career of Duncan Mackenzie is the subject of Nicoletta Momigliano's *Duncan Mackenzie: A Cautious, Canny Highlander* (*Bulletin of the Institute of Classical Studies*, Supplement 63, 1995). The first two volumes (more have been promised) of Martin Bernal's *Black Athena: the Afroasiatic roots of classical civilization* were published in 1987 and 1991 (London and New Brunswick, NJ); Bernal stressed – not without controversy – the Egyptian, African and Semitic origins of classical Greek culture. One of the most stimulating recent treatments of the 'Knossos phenomenon' is C. Gere, *Knossos and the Prophets of Modernism* (Chicago, 2009).

Chapter 3. Important recent literary studies of Thucydides include: V. Hunter, *Thucydides: The Artful Reporter* (Toronto, 1973); T. Rood, *Thucydides: Narrative and Explanation* (Oxford, 1998); E. Greenwood, *Thucydides and the Shaping of History* (London, 2006).

Chapter 4. James Davidson's famous essay on Alexander appeared in the *LRB* 1 November, 2001. For those who would like some basic information on 'the duties of a satrap' and other aspects of ancient Persian society, T. Holland, *Persian Fire: The First World Empire and the Battle for the West* (London, 2005) or M. Brosius, *The Persians* (London, 2006) should fill in some of the gaps. Hadrian and Antinous are well discussed in C. Vout, *Power and Eroticism in Imperial Rome* (Cambridge, 2007).

Chapter 5. A selection of jokes in the *Philogelos* is translated in W. Hansen (ed.), *Anthology of Ancient Greek Popular Literature* (Indiana, 1998); a translation of the full text is provided by B. Baldwin, *The Philogelos or Laughter-Lover* (Amsterdam, 1983).

Section 2

Chapter 6. Arnaldo Momigliano's essay on Romulus and Aeneas ('How to Reconcile Greeks and Trojans') can most easily be found in his *On Pagans, Jews, and Christians* (Middletown. CT., 1987).

Chapter 8. A. Richlin, 'Cicero's head', in J. I. Porter (ed.), *Constructions of the Classical Body* (Ann Arbor, 1999) is an excellent exploration of Cicero's decapitation; to go with S. Butler, *Hand of Cicero* (London, 2002).

Chapter 9. Careful, technical studies of other themes in Cicero's attacks on Verres (showing just how tendentious some of Cicero's invective was) can be found in J. R. W. Prag (ed.), *Sicilia Nutrix Plebis Romanae: Rhetoric, Law, and Taxation in Cicero's Verrines* (*Bulletin of the Institute of Classical Studies*, Supplement 97, 2007).

Section 3

Chapter 11. J. P. Hallett, 'Perusinae glandes and the changing image of Augustus', *American Journal of Ancient History* 2 (1977), 151–71 is a detailed (and frank) study of the sling stones from Perugia.

Chapter 12. The papyrus recording Germanicus' speech is translated and discussed by Dominic Rathbone, in *World Archaeology* 36 (2009), available online at www.world-archaeology.com/features/oxyrnchus/. Adrian Goldsworthy's 'double biography' is *Anthony and Cleopatra* (London, 2010). Horace's 'demented queen' features in his *Odes* 1, 37 (though the rest of that poem suggests a rather more nuanced view of the queen).

Chapter 13. I discuss the political background to Carcopino's work in the introduction to a second edition of his *Daily Life in Ancient Rome* (New Haven and London, 2003).

Chapter 14. Philo's description of his embassy to Caligula is in his *On the Embassy to Gaius* (translated in Volume 10 of the Loeb Classical Library edition of the work of Philo, and available online at www.earlychristianwritings.com/yonge/book40.html (chapter XLIV and following). Walter Scheidel's discussion of the Roman Empire's bloody record in the transfer of power was part of a lecture given in Cambridge in 2011 (www.sms.cam.ac.uk/media/1174184). Pliny, *Letters* 4, 22 tells of the notorious dinner party with the emperor Nerva.

Chapter 15. The long-term history of the Colosseum plays a large part in K. Hopkins and M. Beard, *The Colosseum* (London, 2005).

Chapter 17. Roland Barthes's essay is conveniently reprinted in S. Sontag (ed.), *Barthes: Selected Writings* (London, 1982). Woodman's translation of the *Annals* was published in 2004 (Indianapolis); Grant's 'ever popular' Penguin translation was finally replaced in late 2012 by Cynthia Damon's new Penguin version. Seneca's joke is in his skit on the deification of the emperor Claudius, *Apocolocyntosis*, chapter 11. The complicated (and sometimes murky) history of the ancestral tomb of Piso is the subject of P. Kragelund, M. Moltesen and J. Stubbe Ostergaard, *The Licinian Tomb. Fact or Fiction* (Copenhagen, 2003); the sculptures also feature in a Royal Academy Exhibition catalogue, *Ancient Art to Post-Impressionism: Masterpieces from the Ny Carlsberg Glypotek* (London, 2004).

Chapter 18. The material culture of the reign of Hadrian is lavishly illustrated in T. Opper, *Hadrian. Empire and conflict* (London, 2008); and the erotic dimension is discussed in C. Vout, *Power and Eroticism in Imperial Rome* (Cambridge, 2007).

Section 4

Chapter 19. L. Hackworth Petersen, *The Freedman in Roman Art and Art History* (Cambridge, 2006) offers a sharp and well illustrated analysis of scholarly snobbery on the art of the ex-slave (quoting Howard Colvin on the 'egregious monument' of Eurysaces).

Chapter 20. A translation of *The Oracles of Astrampsychus* (and other selections of ancient popular literature) is included in W. Hansen (ed.), *Anthology of Ancient Greek Popular Literature* (Indiana, 1998).

Chapter 22. The Benjamin Britten score for Auden's lyrics is to be reprinted by Charlotte Higgins in *Under Another Sky: Journeys through Roman Britain* (London, 2013). The clearest introduction to the Vindolanda documents is A. Bowman, *Life and Letters on the Roman Frontier: Vindolanda and its People* (London, 1994).

Chapter 23. There is a magnificent new edition, with translation, of some of the bilingual dialogues by Eleanor Dickey, entitled (rather alarmingly) *The Colloquia of the Hermeneumata Pseudodositheana: Volume 1, Colloquia Monacensia-Einsidlensia, Leidense-Stephani, and Stephani* (Cambridge, 2012).

Section 5

Chapter 24. Christopher Morrissey discussed the re-use of the passage of Aeschylus at a Classical conference in Canada in 2002; his paper is summarised at http://morec.com/rfk.htm

Chapter 25. Hölscher's satirical article on Laocoon ('Laokoon und das Schicksal des Tiberius: Ein Akrostikon') was published in *Antike Welt* 31 (2000).

Chapter 26. The major account of the life of Leigh Fermor is now A. Cooper, *Patrick Leigh Fermor* (London, 2012).

Chapter 27. Dwyer has published a fuller account of the plaster casts in *Pompeii's Living Statues: Ancient Roman Lives Stolen from Death* (Ann Arbor, 2010); the recent history and reception of Pompeii is the subject of illustrated exhibition catalogue, V. C. Gardner Coates, K. Lapatin, J. L. Seydl (eds), *The Last Days of Pompeii: Decadence, Apocalypse, Resurrection* (Malibu, 2012).

Chapter 31. C. Goudineau, *Par Toutatis!: que reste-t-il de la Gaule?* (Paris, 2002) offers a spirited French debunking of the myths of French history represented by Astérix's plucky struggles against the Romans.

ACKNOWLEDGEMENTS

I have many people to thank in preparing these essays for their original publication and for this new book. John Sturrock first showed me what a good review was, and Ferdy Mount took the risk of trusting me with the Classics side at the *TLS*. Mary-Kay Wilmers and Bob Silvers have been my generous editors at the *London* and *New York Review of Books* (and it has been fun getting to know everyone involved with those papers, especially Rea Hederman). The *TLS* has been my second home for two decades now, and all the staff there (not least Maureen Allen) know how much they mean to me. I first met Peter Stothard when he started to edit the *TLS* in 2002. Since then he has been an indispensible friend, mentor and sparring partner – in projects classical and otherwise – and his influence lies behind many chapters in this book.

My family – Robin, Zoe and Raph – have lived through the writing and re-writing of these pieces, and have given me more ideas than they realise (while Robin has taken numerous photographs that I said I would never need, but did). Debbie Whittaker, as always, undertook an enormous amount of work in turning the raw material for this book into the finished product. At Profile, Susanne Hillen ably copy-edited the manuscript and Bohdan Buciak proofread with flair; and my friends Penny Daniel, Andrew Franklin, Ruth Killick and Valentina Zanca kept me on track and cheered me up from start to finish. Thank you one and all.

Confronting the Classics is dedicated to my very best of editors and one of my closest friends, Peter Carson (whose idea the book was). I've waited a long time to say this – but it was Peter who taught me that good writing and publishing depended not only on intelligence, expertise and hard work, but on tolerance, humour and compassion too. Those are lessons, and lunches, I shall never ever forget.

Sadly, Peter died before this book was published – but he had seen the proofs, approved the cover, wetted its head and saw its dedication. *In memoriam.*

SOURCES

Earlier versions of these essays appeared as follows:

Introduction: *New York Review of Books (NYRB)*, 12 January, 2012.

1. *London Review of Books (LRB)* 30 November, 2000; review of J. A. MacGillivray, *Minotaur: Sir Arthur Evans and the Archaeology of the Minoan Myth* (Jonathan Cape, 2000).

2. *LRB* 11 October, 1990; review of Jane McIntosh Snyder, *The Woman and the Lyre: Women Writers in Classical Greece and Rome* (Bristol Classical Press, 1989); J. J. Winkler *The Constraints of Desire: The Anthropology of Sex and Gender in Ancient Greece* (Routledge, 1990); Giulia Sissa *Greek Virginity*, translated by Arthur Goldhammer (Harvard, 1990).

3. *NYRB* 30 September, 2010; review of Donald Kagan, *Thucydides: The Reinvention of History* (Viking, 2009); Simon Hornblower, *A Commentary on Thucydides, Volume III, Books 5.25–8.109* (Oxford University Press, 2008).

4. *NYRB* 27 October, 2011; review of Philip Freeman, *Alexander the Great* (Simon and Schuster, 2011); James Romm (ed), translated from the Greek by Pamela Mensch, *The Landmark Arrian: The Campaigns of Alexander* (Pantheon, 2010); Pierre Briant, translated from French by Amélie Kuhrt, *Alexander the Great and his Empire: A Short Introduction* (Princeton University Press, 2010); Ian Worthington, *Philip II of Macedonia* (Yale University Press, 2008); James Romm, *Ghost on the*

Throne: The Death of Alexander the Great and the War for Crown and Empire (Knopf, 2011).

5. *Times Literary Supplement*, 18 February, 2009; review of Stephen Halliwell, *Greek Laughter: A study of cultural psychology from Homer to early Christianity* (Cambridge University Press, 2008).

6. *TLS*, 12 April, 1996; review of T. P. Wiseman, *Remus, A Roman Myth* (Cambridge University Press, 1995); Matthew Fox, *Roman Historical Myths: the regal period in Augustan literature* (Clarendon Press, 1996); Gary B. Miles, *Livy, Reconstructing early Rome* (Cornell University Press, 1995); Carole E. Newlands, *Playing with Time, Ovid and the Fasti* (Cornell University Press, 1995); T. J. Cornell, *The Beginnings of Rome, Italy and Rome from the Bronze Age to the Punic Wars, c 1000 – 264BC* (Routledge, 1995).

7. *TLS*, 11 May, 2011; review of Robert Garland, *Hannibal* (Bristol Classical Press, 2010); D. S. Levene, *Livy on the Hannibalic War* (Oxford University Press, 2010).

8. *LRB* 23 August, 2001; review of Anthony Everitt, *Cicero: A Turbulent Life* (John Murray, 2001).

9. *TLS* 30 September, 2009; review of Margaret M. Miles, *Art as Plunder: The ancient origins of debate about cultural property* (Cambridge University Press, 2008); Carole Paul, *The Borghese Collections and the Display of Art in the Age of the Grand Tour* (Ashgate, 2008).

10. *TLS* 13 May, 2009; review of T. P. Wiseman, *Remembering the Roman People: Essays on Late-Republican politics and literature* (Oxford University Press, 2009).

11 *NYRB* 8 November, 2007; review of Anthony Everitt, *Augustus: The Life of Rome's First Emperor* (Random House, 2006).

12. *NYRB* 13 January, 2011; review of Stacy Schiff, *Cleopatra: A Life* (Little, Brown, 2010).

13. *TLS* 13 September, 2002; review of Anthony A. Barrett, *Livia:*

First Lady of Imperial Rome (Yale University Press, 2002); Sandra R. Joshel, Margaret Malamud and Donald T. McGuire Jr (eds), *Imperial Projections: Ancient Rome in Modern Popular Culture* (Johns Hopkins University Press, 2001).

14. *LRB* 26 April, 2012; review of Aloys Winterling, *Caligula: A Biography*, translated by Deborah Lucas Schneider, Glenn Most and Paul Psoinos (University of California Press, 2011).

15 *LRB* 2 September, 2004; review of Edward Champlin, *Nero* (Harvard University Press, 2003).

16. *TLS* 24 June, 2005; review of Richard Hingley and Christina Unwin, *Boudica: Iron Age Warrior Queen* (Hambledon, 2005); Vanessa Collingridge, *Boudica* (Ebury Press, 2005); Manda Scott, *Boudica. Dreaming the Hound* (Bantam Press, 2004).

17. *LRB* 22 January, 2004; review of Cynthia Damon (ed.), *Tacitus: Histories I* (Cambridge University Press, 2002).

18. *LRB* 18 June, 1998; review of Anthony Birley, *Hadrian: The Restless Emperor* (Routledge, 1997).

19. *TLS* 29 February, 2012; review of Henrik Mouritsen, *The Freedman in the Roman World* (Cambridge University Press, 2011); Keith Bradley and Paul Cartledge (eds), *The Cambridge World History of Slavery, Volume One: The Ancient Mediterranean World* (Cambridge University Press, 2011).

20. *TLS* 17 March, 2010; review of Jerry Toner, *Popular Culture in Ancient Rome* (Polity Press, 2009); Estelle Lazer, *Resurrecting Pompeii* (Routledge, 2009).

21. *TLS* 31 January, 2007; review of Sheila Dillon and Katherine E. Welch (eds), *Representations of War in Ancient Rome* (Cambridge University Press, 2006).

22. *TLS* 4 October, 2006; review of David Mattingly, *An Imperial*

Possession: Britain in the Roman Empire, 54 BC – AD 409 (Allen Lane, 2006).

23. *TLS* 13 June, 2003; review of J. N. Adams, *Bilingualism and the Latin Language* (Cambridge University Press, 2003).

24. *TLS* 15 October, 2004; review of Edith Hall, Fiona Macintosh and Amanda Wrigley (eds), *Dionysus since 69: Greek tragedy at the dawn of the third millennium* (Oxford University Press, 2004).

25. *TLS* 2 February, 2001; review of *D'après l'Antique: Paris, musée du Louvre,16 octobre 2000–15 janvier 2001* (Réunion de musées nationaux, 2000); Richard Brilliant, *My Laocoön: Alternative claims in the interpretation of artworks* (University of California Press, 2000); Salvatore Settis, *Laocoonte, Fama e stile* (Donzelli, 1999).

26. *LRB* 18 August, 2005; review of Patrick Leigh Fermor, *Roumeli: Travels in Northern Greece* (John Murray, 2004); Patrick Leigh Fermor *Mani: Travels in the Southern Peloponnese* (John Murray, 2004); Patrick Leigh Fermor, edited by Artemis Cooper, *Words of Mercury* (John Murray, 2004).

27. *TLS* 6 September, 2007; review of Judith Harris, *Pompeii Awakened: A story of rediscovery* (I. B. Tauris, 2007); Victoria C. Gardner Coates and Jon L. Seydl (eds), *Antiquity Recovered:The legacy of Pompeii and Herculaneum* (Getty Publications, 2007).

28. *LRB* 26 July, 1990; review of Robert Fraser, *The Making of 'The Golden Bough': The Origin and Growth of an Argument* (Macmillan, 1990).

29. *LRB* 25 March, 2010; review of Fred Inglis, *History Man: The Life of R.G. Collingwood* (Princeton University Press, 2009).

30. *TLS* 15 April, 2005; review of Robert B. Todd (ed.), *Dictionary of British Classicists* (Continuum, 2004).

31. *LRB* 21 February, 2002; review of Albert Uderzo, *Asterix and the Actress*, translated by Anthea Bell and Derek Hockridge (Orion, 2001).

LIST OF FIGURES

While every effort has been made to contact copyright-holders of illustrations, the author and publishers would be grateful for information about any illustrations where they have been unable to trace them, and would be glad to make amendments in further editions.

INDEX